OLLE LUNDBERG

OLLE LUNDBERG

AN ARCHITECTURE OF CRAFT

Foreword by Andy Goldsworthy
Edited by Dung Ngo

PA PRESS

PRINCETON ARCHITECTURAL PRESS · NEW YORK

Published by
Princeton Architectural Press
A division of Chronicle Books LLC
70 West 36th Street
New York, NY 10018
papress.com

© 2025 Olle Lundberg
All rights reserved

Printed and bound in China

28 27 26 25 4 3 2 1 First edition

No part of this book may be used or reproduced in any manner without written permission from the publisher, except in the context of reviews.

Every reasonable attempt has been made to identify owners of copyright. Errors or omissions will be corrected in subsequent editions.

Editor: Jennifer Thompson
Designer: Paul Wagner

Library of Congress Cataloging-in-Publication Data
Names: Lundberg, Olle, 1954- author.
Title: Olle Lundberg : an architecture of craft / Olle Lundberg ; foreword by Andy Goldsworthy.
Description: First edition. | New York : Princeton Architectural Press, [2024] | Summary: "A monograph on the work of San Francisco architect Olle Lundberg and his studio's focus on handcrafted details and the use of recycled materials and objects" —Provided by publisher.
Identifiers: LCCN 2024056499 | ISBN 9781797236049 (hardcover) | ISBN 9781797236056 (ebook)
Subjects: LCSH: Lundberg, Olle, 1954- —Catalogues raisonnés. | Lundberg design (Firm)—Catalogs. | Lundberg design (Firm)—History. | Architectural design—United States—History—20th century—Catalogs. | Architectural design—United States—History—21st century—Catalogs.
Classification: LCC NA737.L854 A4 2024 | DDC 729.0973—dc23/eng/20250122
LC record available at https://lccn.loc.gov/2024056499

previous
Ninth Street Building, lobby stairs

CONTENTS

9 Foreword – Andy Goldsworthy

10 Preface

PART I. PERSONAL NARRATIVE

15 First Steps: 1971–86

23 Jumping Off: 1987–96

39 The Mattress Factory: 1996–Present

PART II. MATERIAL PALETTES

65 METAL

79 STONE

91 GLASS

103 WOOD

117 FOUND OBJECTS

PART III. FIVE PROJECTS

131 Rolling Wall Museum

151 Lava House

175 Curly's Cove

185 Dogleg House

215 The Cabin

247 Thoughts on Design

251 Afterword: Inside/Out – Dung Ngo

252 Viking Hot Sauce

254 Project Credits

255 Image Credits

256 Dedication

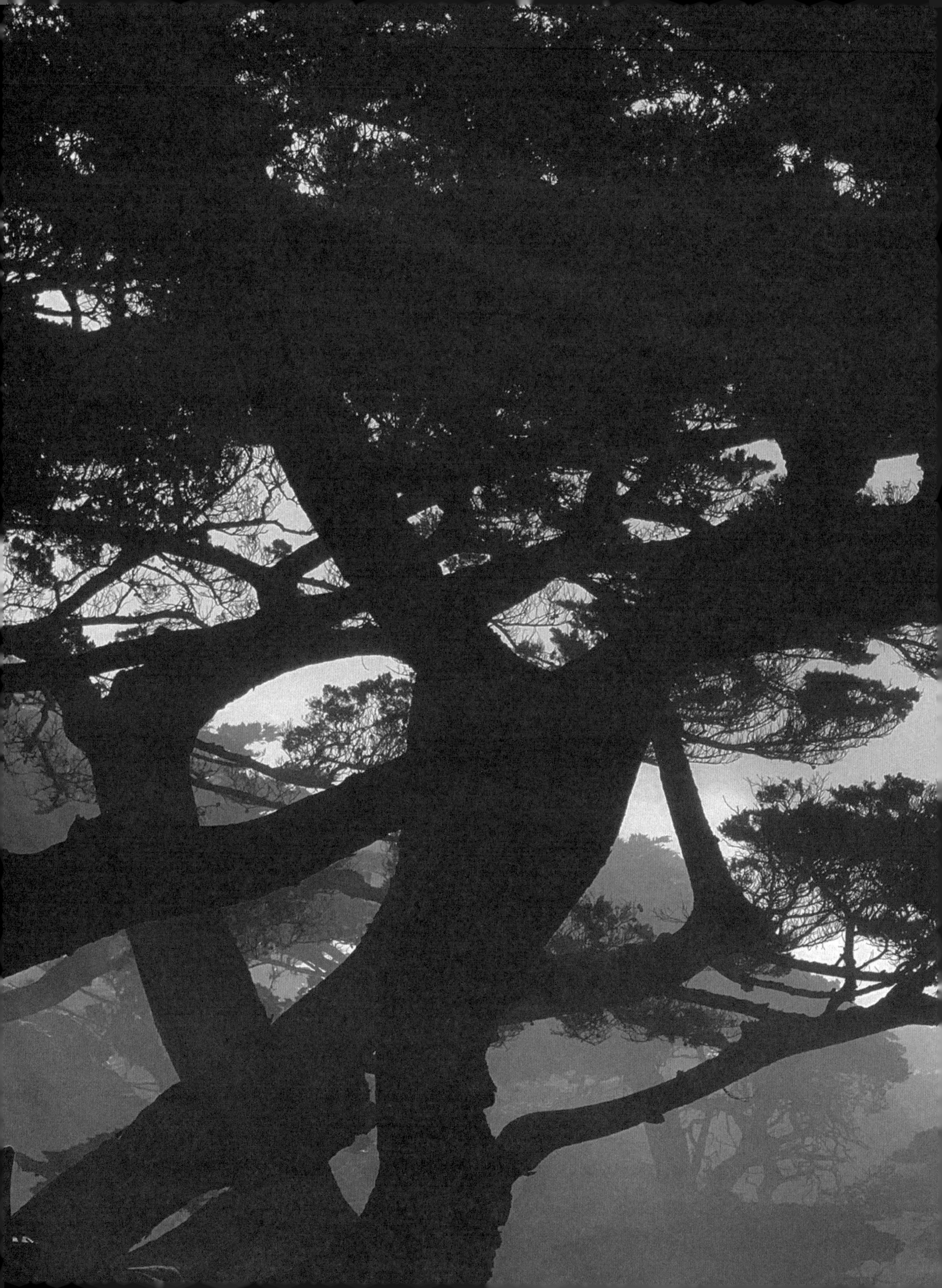

To my dear friend Charles Phan, who left us far too soon. Charles passed away unexpectedly in January 2025, just as this book was going to print. He was my hero in so many ways, and I am saddened by the fact that he will never get to read this.

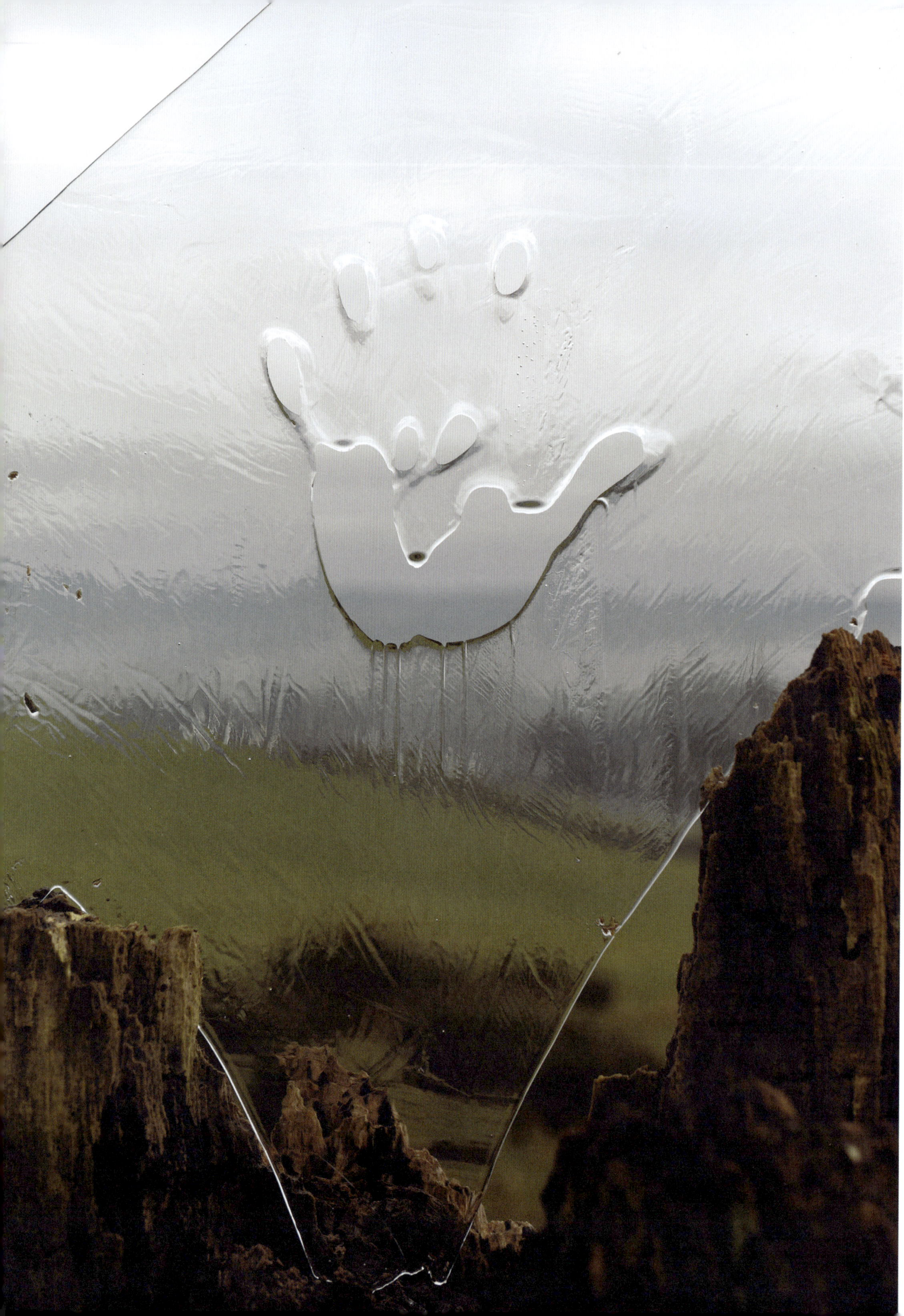

FOREWORD
ANDY GOLDSWORTHY

The hand is the cutting edge of the mind.
—JACOB BRONOWSKI

In 2004 I installed Scripps Cairn at the Scripps Research Institute, an institute for medical research in San Diego, California. Prior to making the work, I was given a tour of the facility. I visited one department dedicated to building models of viruses. I asked why there was a need to make a physical model when modeling could be done on a computer. The reply was that holding a model in the hand gives a better understanding of the virus. I don't know if this is still the case, but I would like to think so.

In an era when technology can create staggering feats of ingenious (and at times vacuous) architecture, Olle Lundberg speaks of the importance for an architect to also "hold" a building in their hands and mind—to know the place where it is to be made and understand the materials that will be used in its construction. For me, physical engagement with the world is likewise essential. Touch is an integral part of the creative process in which the hand feeds the mind. The feel, friction, resistance, shock, and unpredictable nature of touch provokes ideas. I make art directly in the land with my hands, but I also make large-scale construction projects that require technology, tools, equipment, machinery, and the help of many people. Works made with leaves, snow, ice, rain, stone, clay, wood, light, dark, or occasionally my own body feed my large-scale projects in a reciprocal exchange, creating a dialogue—a flow of ideas.

Olle describes the concern of his university professors that his knowledge of materials and making might restrict his imagination, and that ideas should be free from practical considerations. But for myself, and I believe also for Olle, practical considerations can be a powerful source of solutions and ideas. Lundberg Design is part architectural office and part workshop. The workshop—the engine that drives the practice—is where the hand and the mind are put to work. It is a source of energy, a library of possibilities, and a place where I felt at home during my collaboration with Olle during the making of Rolling Wall.

Rolling Wall (see pages 130–49) was an unprecedented and astonishing act of faith, openness, and generosity on Olle's part. Not many architects would willingly give over such a significant part of a building to an artist, and it was an even greater leap of faith for the clients. The wall had its origin in the many works that I have made from compacted snow, sand, earth, ferns, and branches, but the increase in scale and greater context took the making of this particular work out of my hands and passed it into the hands of others. Not once was it suggested that we build a fake wall (one that would be hollow inside but made to look as if it were solid earth). In the past, I have had ideas remain unrealized because an engineer wanted me to use "lick and stick" (adhered concrete masonry veneer) instead of stone. But what lies beneath is important.

Olle ensured the integrity of Rolling Wall by assembling a team of highly skilled, motivated, imaginative, talented people. I owe a great debt of gratitude to Olle, David Warner, and David Easton, who together with their respective crews figured out how the wall could be made and then carried out its construction. The result is a mass of compacted earth and human energy that continues to reverberate from the pounding of earth—the building's heartbeat. The wall was built ahead of the main building, and, as Olle recounts, it initially stood by itself. But this monolith needed the building to bring it to life, to transform it from something to be looked at into something to be lived with. For me, the conversation between building, wall, artist, and architect was inspirational. The building completes the work.

This book is about the conversations Olle has with his buildings, the places where they are built, and the people who occupy them. It has been a privilege to be part of that conversation, and of one of Olle's buildings.

opposite
Andy Goldsworthy handprint

PREFACE

Why am I writing this book? My work has now spanned thirty-five years, so there is a fair amount to show. This book is in great part about our fabrication shop—how it defines us as a firm, how it informs our work, and how it makes us different from most architectural firms. Craft in architecture is relevant, and my goal is to pass on lessons learned along the way and tell some of my favorite stories about the evolution of Lundberg Design.

In our world today we confront many issues that feel new, although perhaps they should not. As architects, we have a responsibility to try to make the physical world better, and in doing so, affect society in a positive way. Climate change is an overwhelming issue—net-zero buildings, sustainable design, and conservation of the world's resources are all fundamental to responsible architecture. We also need to be designing socially responsible buildings. As an architect, I cannot solve many of the world's problems, but my buildings should certainly encourage accessibility, diversity, and inclusion. We must always be mindful of our primary responsibility: to design buildings that function well, and are beautiful! However green a building is, however many LEED points it checks off, if people don't admire it, enjoy inhabiting it, and love looking at it, then it will quickly be replaced. We must design buildings that aspire to last for generations.

This is a difficult message to impart to students, because I do not believe that the ability to design beautiful buildings can be taught. But it can be learned. Education is part of it, but much of it is inherent in the desire to live an interesting life, to look at the world with a creative eye, to see things a little differently. I hope that this book will show how one architectural firm has tried to do just that, and I hope you will be inspired to embrace the adventure of living such a life.

Olle Lundberg
Lundberg Design
San Francisco, 2025

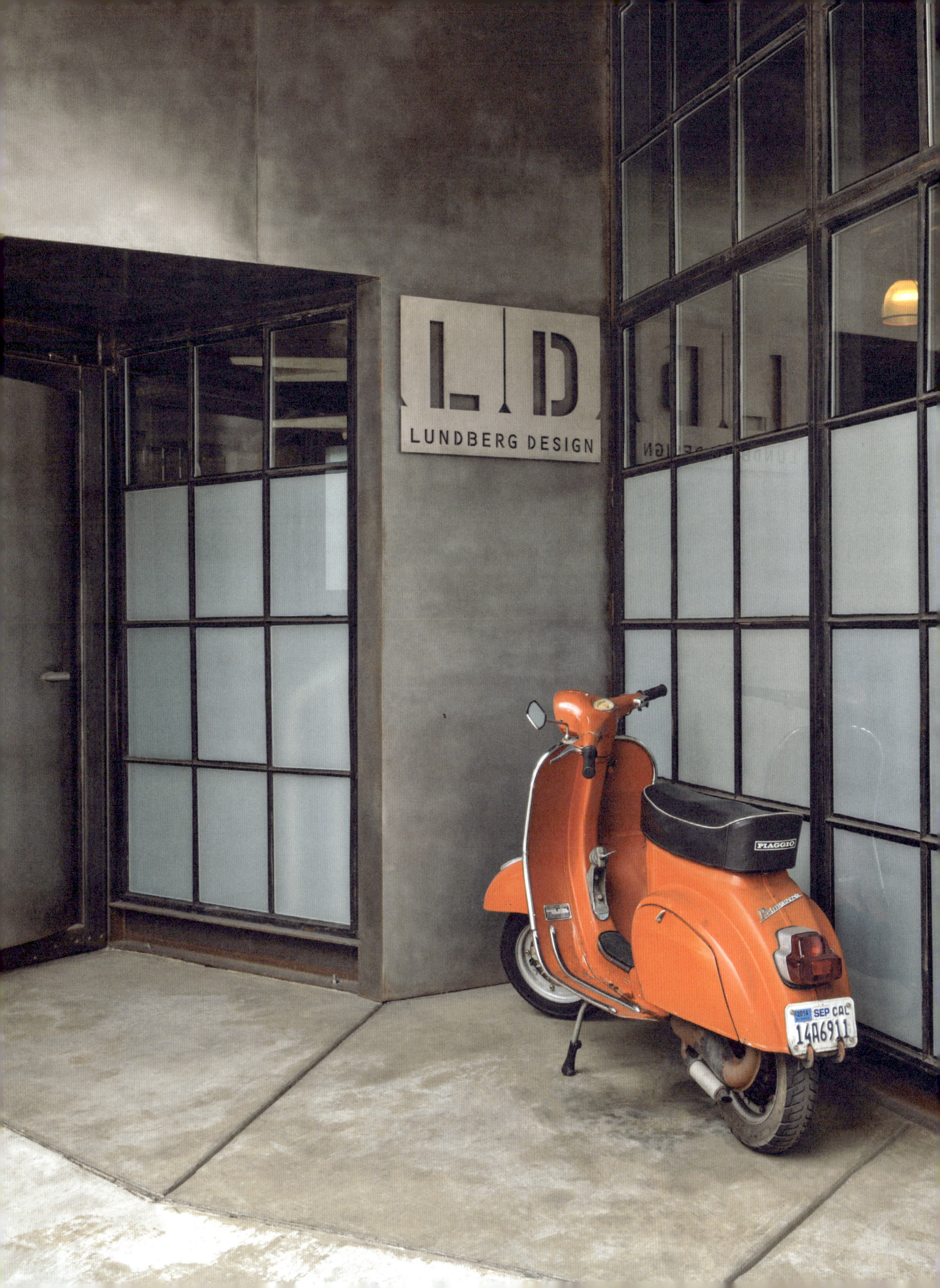
LD
LUNDBERG DESIGN
PIAGGIO
SEP CAL
1446911

> *"After such knowledge, what forgiveness?"*
> —T. S. Eliot, "Gerontion"

PART I.
──
PERSONAL NARRATIVE

FIRST STEPS: 1971–86

JUMPING OFF: 1987–96

MATTRESS FACTORY: 1996–PRESENT

above
Puff and Olle, 1973

right
The church, Lexington, Virginia

14   PART I.   PERSONAL NARRATIVE

First Steps
1971–86

I've got plenty of common sense, I just choose to ignore it.
—BILL WATTERSON as Calvin, *Calvin & Hobbes*, October 15, 1986

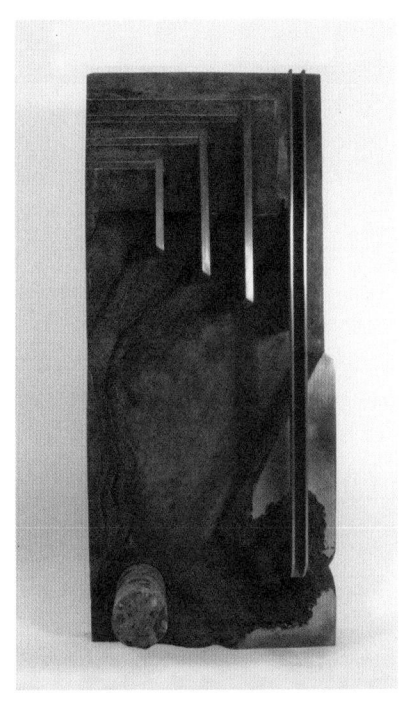

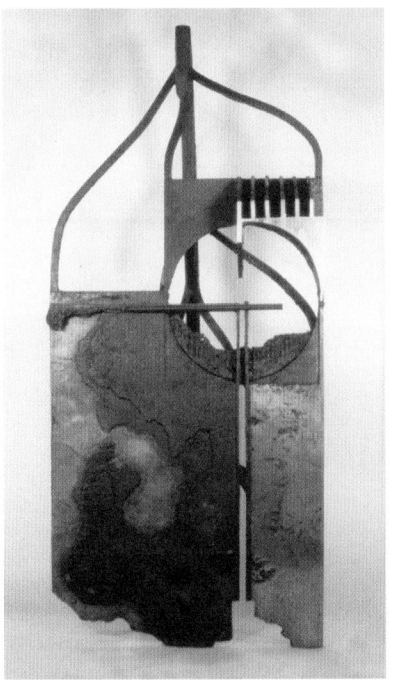

In the summer of 1972, when I was eighteen, I convinced my father to let me buy an abandoned chapel outside of Lexington, Virginia. I had just completed my first year at Washington and Lee University, and I needed to find housing off campus (Washington and Lee had dorms only for freshmen). My good friend Bill Smith and I worked as parking lot attendants at Natural Bridge State Park during the day, and on weekends and evenings we converted the chapel into a five-bedroom house. We were certainly out of our depth, but it wasn't much money (the purchase price had been $10,000), and Bill and I learned a lot about construction, and partnership, that summer. Upon completion, we rented the other rooms out to three friends, and for the next three years we lived fairly close to rent free. I suppose if I'd really paid attention to the economic lesson, I would have become a real estate developer. (Bill did end up becoming a real estate attorney.) But it was the act of building, and in particular the act of building something different than I'd seen before, that excited me. It would take me a while to absorb the lesson, but that was the summer I started my path toward becoming an architect.

I was an English major, with a focus on the Southern novel. I had no real career plan (what English major does?), but I hoped I would get a good liberal arts education and find a passion, or at least something I was good at, along the way. I finished my major midway through my junior year, and, needing more credits to graduate, I decided to explore sculpture. A young assistant professor, Joe Blouin, profoundly inspired me. He was a master of making. I learned how to weld, cast bronze and aluminum, blow and cast glass, solder silver, and polish stone and metal, plus all kinds of studio tricks. He taught me to believe I could build anything, that no process was beyond learning, and he turned me into a builder, a person who could create with his hands. In those eighteen months, I learned to love and understand tools; I learned to pay attention to the materials at hand; and I began to understand the freedom of imagination that comes with technical competence.

I also knew that I wasn't a sculptor. My pieces were at best unusual, and they lacked focus. I had no idea what I was trying to say with my work, and while I loved the act of making, I never felt that it was my gift. My brother, Peter, is a sculptor, and he makes extraordinary pieces that have been refined by more than forty years of dogged effort. Peter always believed he was a sculptor; for him there was no single defining moment. Beyond talent, I believe that determination, stubborn focus, is what you need to succeed

Bronze pieces, 1974

Clearview, 2016

Carbon Arc, 2002

Untitled, Peter Lundberg, 2014

in a creative life. It is difficult to find that confidence, and without support and mentors, one never gets there. I have been fortunate in that I have found my voice, but I owe many for that gift.

In my senior year I had to figure out my career path—something I felt profoundly unprepared for. I took all the standardized tests, and according to the results, my best bet was business school. So I applied to Harvard (denied), Stanford (waitlisted), and Wharton (admitted), but on a whim of sorts I also applied to the University of Virginia's architecture school. I really wanted to go to Stanford, mostly because I liked the idea of California, so I went out to meet with the dean and see if I could charm my way past the waitlist. That didn't work, but the dean said that if I did something interesting, they would let me in the following year. I suggested that maybe a year of architecture school could be somewhat unique, and she agreed.

So my plan was to go to UVA for a year, then transfer to Stanford. Amazingly, UVA had accepted me based on my sculpture and my work on the church, but because I had no real architecture training, it was to be a three-and-a-half year program, and it started a week after graduation. But the move to UVA was easy. Charlottesville was only an hour away from Lexington. I was already a Virginia resident, so I could afford school solely on the profit Bill and I made on the church's sale. I figured I would learn about architecture for a year, then go to Stanford and become an enlightened real estate developer. For the first time in my life, I had what felt like a real plan. But like most of my early plans, it went awry.

UVA is a design school. They teach you how to design *architecture*, not *buildings*. The program was intellectually challenging; we studied a lot of architectural theory. But how do you teach design? You start by copying. Postmodernism was in its heyday, so Michael Graves was big. Le Corbusier was the modernist of choice. Frank Lloyd Wright was regarded as too flamboyant, too instinctual, and lacking in intellectual rigor. Perhaps because I knew so little about any of these (or any other) architects, I didn't fall in love with any of their styles. I took it all in, but I never found someone I wanted to emulate. But I loved the school, the intense all-nighters, the dedication I saw in my classmates, and the lure of perhaps finding a voice, some creative vision, that I hoped I had inside me. After a year, the plan was evolving, and I wasn't sure I wanted to go to business school any more.

My father needed help with his business, so I decided to take a year off and work for him, helping him out until he could get back on his feet. My father, the original Olle, was a chemical engineer by training, but he'd gone into management relatively quickly. He had been recruited by Procter & Gamble, so he and my mother, Jane, emigrated from Sweden in December 1953, and I was born in Cincinnati on January 7, 1954. He ended up eventually managing paper mills across the Midwest, and we lived in places like Green

PART I.   PERSONAL NARRATIVE

Olle Sr. and Olle, 1990

Bay and Cheboygan and Niles, Michigan. I never went to the same school two years in a row, which eventually spurred my parents to send me to boarding school, namely, Westminster in Simsbury, Connecticut.

Eventually Dad left Procter & Gamble and worked for American Can for a while, but he had some bad luck and made some bad career moves, so when I entered UVA, he was out of work. Desperate, he bought a dry-cleaning business, but then shortly after that he was offered a job in Sweden setting up a program that was to eventually shift to the United States. That was when I took the year off, so I could run the dry-cleaning business; the idea was that he could accept this job offer, and meanwhile he'd build a full year of financials on this other business and then be able to sell it. It wasn't exactly fulfilling work. My mother, sister, and I were all involved (Peter was lucky, he was too young), but we persevered and eventually sold the business. It was a critical moment, because it gave me time to reflect on what I'd learned. That perspective enabled me to return to UVA (not Stanford) with a new focus, a realization that I wanted to be an architect, and a confidence that comes only with time for reflection.

In that year off I read a lot, and discovered the Finnish architect Alvar Aalto. Finally, an architect with whom I felt a kinship. I suppose the Scandinavian connection helped, but it was his affection for materials, especially wood and brick, that resonated

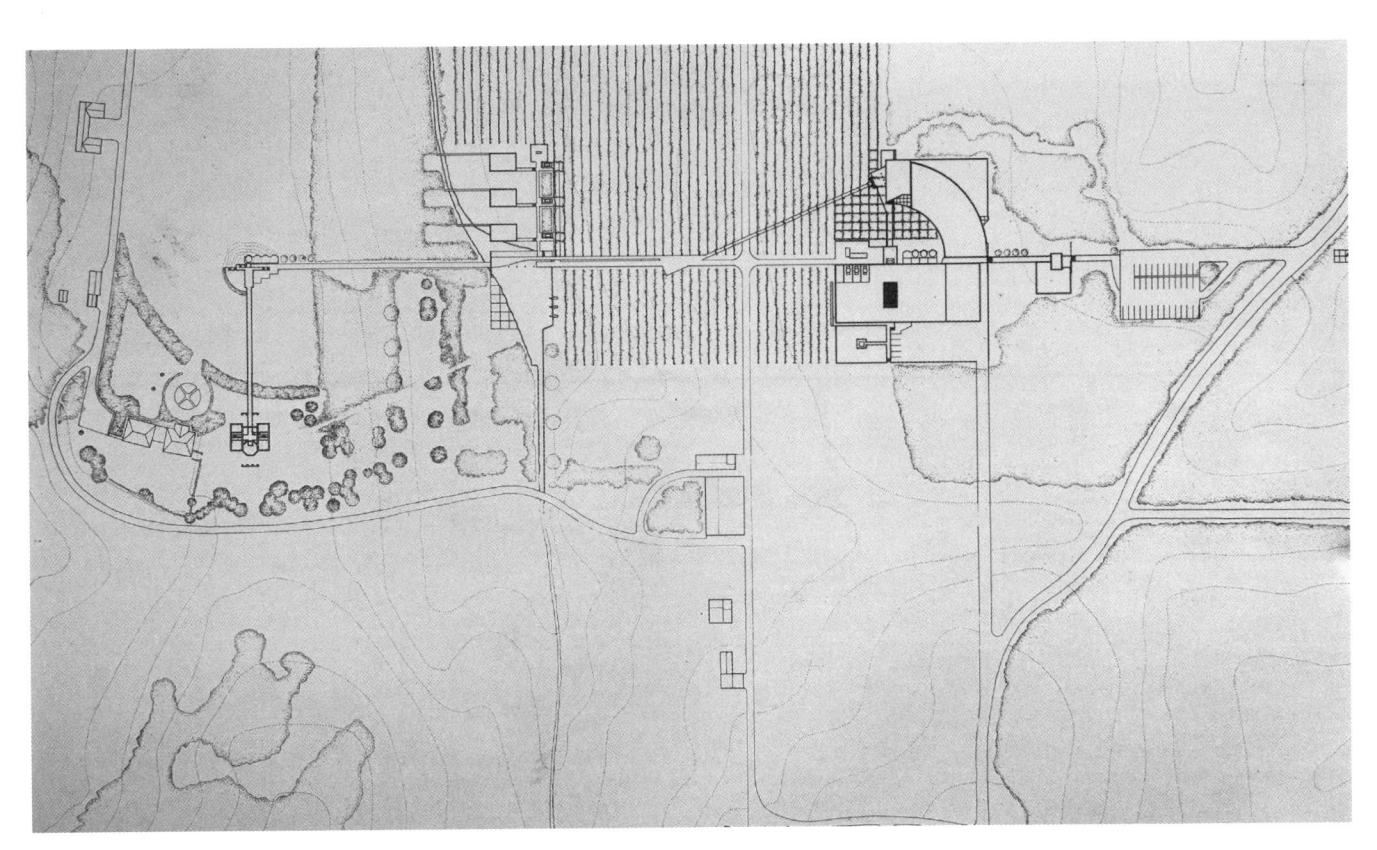

Barboursville Winery site plan, 1979

FIRST STEPS: 1971–86   17

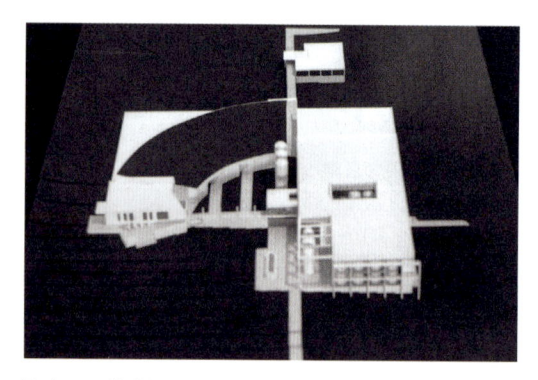

Barboursville Winery model, 1979

Castelvecchio, Carlo Scarpa, 1977

with my desire to express how buildings were put together. I also saw in his work an appealing contrast between the organic and the human-made. How the combination of the two emphasized both, and how a strict geometry, when violated, added emphasis. I returned to architecture school with a point of view, and a conviction that I could trust my aesthetic instinct to tell me when something was good. To be an architect or an artist, you must have that confidence, and then always question it. Questioning doesn't mean you don't believe the voice; you just always look to improve it, hone it, let it evolve. You see that in the evolution of our work at Lundberg Design.

During my last year at UVA I worked as a model builder at the Vickery Partnership, a firm founded by a professor of mine, Robert Vickery. I'd met Bob when I was a graduate student in the Vicenza Program, a summer-abroad semester that introduced me to Italy. Mario di Valmarana—or Count Valmarana, as he was known in Italy—was a professor at UVA and ran the program. Mario also happened to own the Villa La Rotonda in Vicenza, which was not a bad place to entertain a bunch of architecture students. Bob was the rotating professor in 1977, the year I was there, and we became friends. My parents had instilled in me a love of all foods, and what better place to discover a passion for cuisine than the Veneto? Bob and I shared great meals, wine, grappa, and the work of Carlo Scarpa. Scarpa's design for the Museo Civico di Castelvecchio is without doubt the most influential building project I have ever experienced. It changed my life. Here was a ruin lovingly left intact, with this stunning modern insertion slipped delicately inside it. The craftsmanship, which so spoke to the history of Italian artisans; the materials, which were both common and precious; and the composition, which demonstrated an eye that looked at every moment as a jewel—I had never seen anything so beautifully built, and I wondered how I might capture that spirit in my own work. Eventually it was the answer to that question that led me to make a fabrication shop part of my architectural practice.

Two classmates of mine, Bob Moje and David Oakland, were already working at the Vickery Partnership, and after I graduated, Bob offered me a full-time job. The firm did mostly schools. In a very conservative arena, they did (and still do) very accomplished modern buildings, albeit at times with the necessary red brick and white columns that the institutional clients demand. It was a great place to work, full of passion and joy, and I owe them much. They let me be a project architect at a time when I clearly did not have the experience to be one. But I also realized that Virginia was never going to be the environment I wanted to work in. It was just too enmeshed in the colonial Jeffersonian aesthetic. So, after two years, I started to make plans to move out to San Francisco. The Bay Area still spoke to me, even if Stanford was no longer the destination. When I told Bob Vickery of my plans, he suggested that I take that

Vickery Cabin, Blue Ridge Mountains, 1980

Marquis Associates softball cartoon, 1989

summer to build a cabin for him on a piece of wilderness he owned in the Blue Ridge Mountains. I had run the woodshop at UVA while I was there, and I was an excellent model builder, so he knew I had the skills for the task he had in mind. It was a 12-foot-square floor plan with a 12-foot-square deck outside, next to a large boulder on a wooded hillside overlooking a stream. It had a single sliding glass door, two awning windows, a wood stove for heat and cooking, and a simple shed roof. There was a small one-bed loft accessed by a ladder, and the outside was clad in clear-grain redwood. The challenge was that all the materials had to be carried in by hand, across the stream and up about 500 feet. That sliding glass door was not fun, but we managed it somehow. I camped on-site and got it built in three months, and with that money I moved to San Francisco with my girlfriend, Kristin Hawkins. But what I really learned from that summer was the power of the simple poetic gesture, executed perfectly (or as perfectly as I was able), on a great site. As I look back, I realize how many of our best projects honor that statement.

Just before that summer of 1980 I'd met Bob Marquis, who was the acting Thomas Jefferson Professor at UVA that semester. Bob had a thirty-person architectural firm in San Francisco called Marquis Associates, and when he heard I was planning on moving out, he offered me a job. Bob and his wife, Ellen, were so gracious, they let Kristin and me stay with them while we looked for an apartment. They took us out to fantastic restaurants, and just exhibited a joy for a life together that was so infectious. They introduced me to iconic eateries like Vanessi's, Yuet Lee, and Chez Panisse. I've never had better dinner companions.

I was at Marquis for three and half years and got to work on all kinds of projects. I did their residential work (no one else had much experience doing houses), but I also worked on a terminal at San Francisco International Airport; the Aaron Copland School of Music in Queens, New York; the Highlands Inn in Carmel; some affordable housing; and the primate center at the San Francisco Zoo. Some of the projects I managed, but mostly I worked on

FIRST STEPS: 1971–86   19

Kimball House, Washington, Connecticut, 1986

detailing. I was the one who put things together; I celebrated the connection, the meeting, of materials. We had good budgets and good clients, and it was a talented group of people. We also had a good softball team, and I drew (modified, really) cartoons for the games. The firm was run like a family business, and we enjoyed the work and the play—a model I have tried to carry on at Lundberg Design.

In 1984 I designed a house for my sister, Anne, in Washington, Connecticut. She and her husband, Eben, who was a farrier, had a 13-acre lot that was pretty much a field surrounded by forest, with a nice view of a classic New England valley. Anne asked me to design her a saltbox—a simple colonial typology—but that was of course way too traditional for me. I designed a sort of New England–inspired structure that was too big and too complicated, and it came in at double her budget. She said I'd have to redesign it, but I suggested that instead I just come out and build it myself. If she housed and fed me, I was confident I could get it done with the money she had.

I'm her older brother, so she of course believed me, and thus in April 1984 I drove back to Connecticut with all my belongings in a Chevy Blazer and started building her house. Kristin had gone back to graduate school at Yale, so there was the double benefit of being closer to her. I designed a 3,000-square-foot house with a 2,000-square-foot basement. Anne's budget was $125,000, and I'd obviously been crazy; I think she ended up spending $175,000. Poor Eben had to shoe a lot of horses to keep up with the cost overruns. I'm not sure every architect should learn how to put on a cedar shingle roof in the middle of the New England winter or help a stonemason wrestle five-hundred-pound stones into position for a fireplace mantel, but I know it was important for me. I either personally built or helped build every part of that house. But of course, it was a team effort, and I learned so much from everyone involved.

All the tradespeople were patient with this young California architect (who at least wore a tool belt), and I enjoyed watching them all at their respective crafts. Seeing a mason shape a stone, a plumber sweat a copper fitting, a framer swing a 22-ounce hammer, or a finish carpenter perfectly hang a door are lessons I will never forget. If you want that level of quality, that level of care, then one must be able to speak the person's language. To inspire their best, they have to know that you respect their craft. Too much of their working lives are spent toiling on projects where their work is taken for granted, where the only thing keeping them performing is their own pride. When you can change that, when you can inspire them by acknowledging their skill, then often you get their best efforts.

The best thing about the house was that it was flexible; the plan allowed Anne to adapt the house to her evolving life. Maybe it wasn't so bad that I designed it too large. She ended up raising two

Kimball House living room, 1986

Bob Marquis at bat, 1983

sons (they weren't planning to have kids when we started), and she gave up the root cellar, greenhouse, and screened-in porch, but all those spaces evolved into new functions for her family. The landscape grew up around the house, and now it fits quietly into the landscape. She still lives there, thirty-five years later. Eben has passed and the boys are grown, but it is still the center of her life. Today if she asked me to design a saltbox house, that is exactly what I would do, albeit with an end wall completely out of glass, or some such gesture. Perhaps someday the old house will be too big for her, and I'll get to do that saltbox, but I suspect not. The house is too much a part of her, and too big a gift for both of us.

My relationship with Kristin did not survive graduate school, but she was a great partner in this and many other adventures. She can wrestle a concrete block with the best of them. In April 1986, with nothing keeping me in Connecticut, I rejoined Marquis Associates, this time as a principal. But I quickly learned that in the two years I'd spent working on my own, I'd gotten accustomed to being my own boss, and as much as I loved Bob, I didn't want to work for him any longer. He gave me one unexpected parting gift: he introduced me to Mary Breuer, whom he had hired as a marketing consultant. Mary is one of the smartest people I've ever met, and while she is more risk averse than I (most smart people are), she is generally up for an adventure. Five years later, we got married.

Bob was very kind when I told him that I was quitting; he said that's what he'd done at my age and that he perfectly understood. We remained dining friends until he died. One of the last things he said to Ellen was "We should have eaten out more," a great last line and so very Bob. I still miss him. In April 1987 I started Lundberg Design.

FIRST STEPS: 1971–86

22   PART I.   PERSONAL NARRATIVE

Jumping Off
1987–96

The enemy of art is the absence of limitations.
—ORSON WELLES

Starting an architecture firm, or probably any business, is a leap of faith—a belief in one's own abilities and in the good humor of the gods. Looking back, it all strikes me as absurdly optimistic. I had few contacts, very little money, and one kitchen-remodel client. In hindsight I wonder what I was thinking, but sometimes fortune smiles. As much as I believe in myself and my creative instincts, I know that without a very large measure of luck, I would not have enjoyed the career I've had.

There have been, to date, three transformational projects that changed the course of my career. The first came in my first year of practice, the Chase House in Napa. I was recommended by a friend who was a general contractor, Tim McDonald. Tim recommended three architects: myself, Stephen MacCracken (his brother), and a third whose name I do not remember. At the time I was working out of my apartment, but when I learned of the interview, I asked Bob Marquis if I could rent desk space at his office, and he generously agreed. So now I had a conference room in which I could meet the Chases. But I knew from Tim that they were looking for a modern, western-style home, part barn and part Santa Fe. At this point I'd done a modern New England interpretation and some Sea Ranch–style remodels, and I was pretty sure the Chases weren't looking for any of that. So I went to William Stout Architectural Books and proceeded to buy everything I could find on barns and modern desert homes. I dove in and flagged all the images I liked.

opposite
Oracle Lobby, 1990

below left
Olle and Chutney at 483 Tehama Street studio. Chutney spent most of her life glued to my hip.

below right
Diesel at the cabin

JUMPING OFF: 1987–96   23

When we met, I started the interview talking about my training and the two years I'd spent building my sister's house, but then I deliberately shifted from my qualifications to ask them about their property and what their hopes for the house were. Once I got them talking about the various aspects of the desired design, I summarized those thoughts into a few categories: courtyards, indoor-outdoor relationships, materials, quality of light. I then pulled out my stock of books and proceeded to show them images that I loved and that I hoped would reflect an understanding of their design aspirations. And it worked! They knew the pictures I was showing them were not of my work, but I demonstrated that I'd tried to anticipate their aspirations and that I was not going to enter the design discussion with a pile of preconceived notions. At the end of the meeting, they told me they weren't going to interview any other architects. I was their choice.

I felt pretty clever—my little sleight of hand had worked—but the fact is that the real luck happened before I ever met the Chases. Steve MacCracken was to have been interviewed first, but he had an unexpected conflict and had to change his interview to follow mine—an interview he then never got. Who knows what would have happened had he kept that appointment? Steve has always been gracious about the gift he gave me that day. The truth is, the opportunity he missed was the start of Lundberg Design; it was my first ground-up building, and it moved me out of the remodel arena.

Chase Main House model, St. Helena, 1990

above left
Chase Main House south facade, 1991

above right
Chase Main House entry, 1991

right
Chase Caretaker's House, 1989

JUMPING OFF: 1987–96   25

Beam Table, 1988

While I was still renting desk space at Marquis, I was also renting the basement of a friend, Jon-Mark Chappellet, as my shop/studio. I didn't have a lot of equipment—a secondhand arc welder, an oxyacetylene cutting torch, a small band saw, and some grinders and such. Most of my fabrication work was for friends, or clients of friends. I did a dining table for a project by Peter Duxbury, a high school friend who had a practice in Los Gatos. The client, Wayne Rosing, had an art consultant, Glenda Martin, and both she and Wayne loved the table.

One day, Glenda mentioned that she was working on the new Oracle headquarters in Redwood City, being designed by Gensler. She was working directly with Larry Ellison, Oracle's cofounder and CEO, and he wanted an outside designer to do the main lobby. His first choice would have been Isamu Noguchi, but since he was no longer alive, she was tasked with finding a second option. Would I be interested? It all sounded interesting. And although I had no idea what Oracle was or who Larry Ellison might be, I said that of course I'd be happy to make a presentation. About two hours later I started thinking, "Oh, sure, competing against Noguchi's ghost, this should go well!"

Glenda had arranged for an initial presentation to Laura Seccombe, Larry's interior designer. If I convinced her, she would clear the way for me to present to Larry. They were of course thinking that I would show a portfolio of work and then discuss with them some design concepts for the lobby. Given that I didn't really have a portfolio of work, and certainly nothing that in any way resembled a lobby for a giant tech company, that was obviously not going to happen. But I'd learned from the Chase House interview: if you can get a client to talk about their project, about their ideas, then they may give you a pass for what you haven't done, and the focus will shift to what you *could* do. But I wasn't going to have much time here. I figured I'd have ten minutes or so to impress, and the very first impression was probably going to make or break the interview. I needed a design.

I got the base building drawings, as the construction was only at the foundation stage, and in a week I came up with a design, drew rendered plans, put together a material board, and built a full model of the lobby. None of this would have worked if the design wasn't any good, but it was bold and presented well, and Laura was excited by the concept. She made a few suggestions, which I incorporated (now she had ownership too!), and then she introduced me to Larry.

My design caught him off guard—it surprised him—and I don't think that happens often. In my subsequent years of working with him, that has always been the key: do the unexpected. Larry loves originality and is quickly bored by things he's seen before. I got lucky at our first meeting, but I read him accurately, and that kicked off our design relationship.

top
Oracle Lobby seating, sketch, 1989

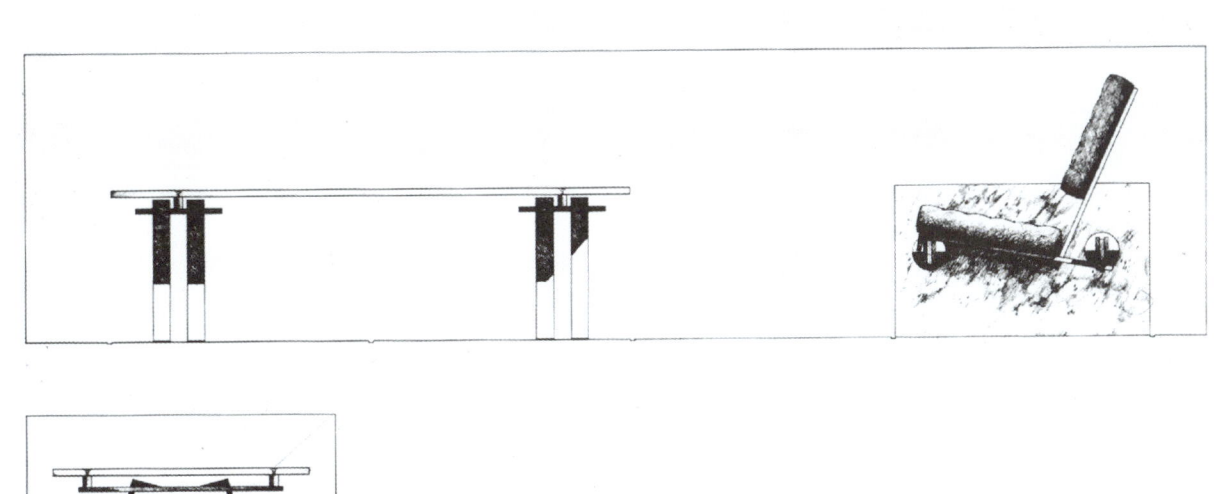

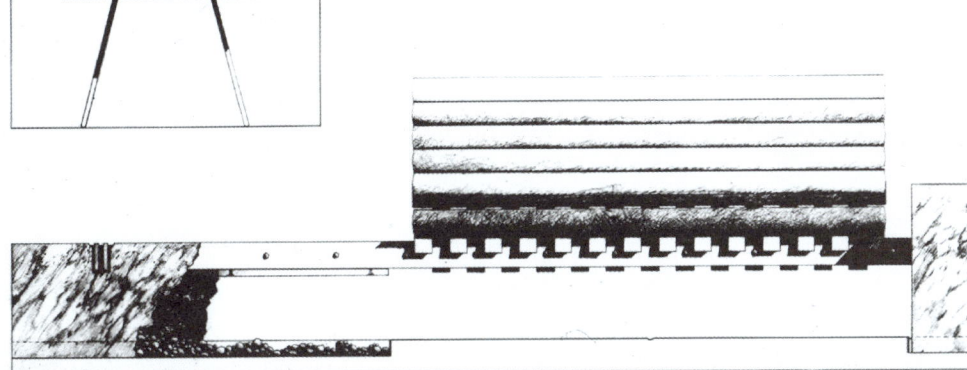

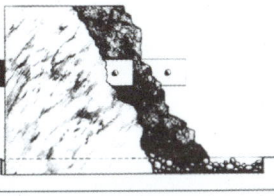

middle left and right
Oracle Lobby models

right
Oracle Lobby seating finished installation

JUMPING OFF: 1987–96 **27**

LD Studio, Twelfth Street, 1992

LD Studio, Tehama Street, 1989

When we won the commission, it gave me the confidence (and the funds) to rent my own building, so the design studio and fabrication studio could occupy the same space. We were going to build this lobby, and we needed a better shop to do the work. It was complicated—we had Brazilian marble blocks, steel beams and molten lead, cast glass slabs from the artist John Lewis, and a lot of polished stainless steel. We pushed our fabrication skills, but I'd never had a budget like this before, and I needed to make it perfect. It went well. We were almost finished with the most complicated parts of the fabrication (the seating armatures and the reception desk) when the Loma Prieta earthquake hit. Our building was hit hard and condemned. We were fortunate to get out unharmed; we had to go out the back, as the front doors all jammed. As we sat on the sidewalk that evening, the fire marshal passed by and told us that if we went back into the building, he'd have us arrested. My whole life was in that building. I told my staff I couldn't ask them to help, but that I was going to return after midnight and try to unload what I could. They all returned as well, and we managed to empty the place—all the tools, all the fabricated pieces and raw materials, the computers, the drawings. It was astonishing. My staff saved Lundberg Design that day, at their own physical peril. The studio has always felt like my family, but that was probably the day it truly hit home.

I sublet some industrial space, and we quickly set up shop in order to complete the fabrication. On Christmas Day, someone broke in through the roll-up door, backed in a truck, and used the gantry crane to abscond with all of our tools. Merry Christmas! Fortunately, they didn't take the fabricated pieces, which to us were far more valuable. I had replacement insurance, so we replaced all our old tools with brand-new ones. We got a much better welder, and in the end nicely upgraded the shop's equipment. Sometimes even bad luck works out (good insurance helps).

We finished the lobby installation, working nights and weekends to try and catch up to the earthquake-caused delays. The marble blocks had to be fractured, but the quarry couldn't understand what we wanted, so I had them ship fully polished cubes, which I then broke with a sledgehammer out in Oracle's parking lot. That got a little dicey—someone thought I was vandalizing something and security was called. I was arrested. It took a while to straighten out. John Lewis cast the wonderful glass tops that still look molten for the reception desk. One evening Larry left a note: "What do we do when the ice melts?" I took that as a good sign. It wasn't Noguchi, but maybe it was more emblematic of what Oracle was trying to become. Most importantly, Larry was happy with it.

As we approached the end of the lobby project, Larry asked if I'd be interested in working on a house in San Francisco. He'd bought a William Wurster house—known as the Coleman House—on Broadway, in Pacific Heights, and he wanted to remodel it.

Coleman House, William Wurster, architect

Of course I wanted to do it. The A/V system alone was going to cost more than any other building I'd ever designed! But there was a hidden challenge: Wurster is a historically important Bay Area architect (he was dean of architecture at UC Berkeley), and his legacy is fanatically protected by the historic planners in the city's building department (as most of it should be). But honestly, this was not a very good example of Wurster's work. Mrs. Coleman was a pretty willful eccentric, and at some point, it was pretty clear to me that Wurster had given up. The giveaway was the 2-foot-deep front balconies that were inaccessible from the interior, given that their level was a few feet below the interior floor. They were just decoration, and I'm sorry, but even for Wurster that is not okay.

So we went for it—a dramatic redo of the building that added no square footage (making it a remodel according to the planning code of the day), but replacing the entire floor plan and every finish, inside and out. Laura Seccombe did the interiors, and between the two of us, we turned it into a very special project. I think it is the only time I've entered one of our houses in an award competition (I find the ritual of architects giving each other awards a bit absurd), but the AIA indeed gave it an award, and it was published in *The New York Times Magazine*. San Francisco eventually changed the planning code so that the "serial permitting" approach we used can no longer be employed as a strategy. Ah well, at least we leveraged it to make something beautiful. One change to the firm certainly happened afterward—since that project, I'm pretty sure no one has asked for references.

So, our two Ellison Projects—the Oracle lobby and 2850 Broadway—all happened because of a dining table I built. Years of effort went into realizing the projects, but the door was opened because I had a fabrication shop. And having the ability to build the Oracle Lobby was critical to the selling of that idea. Not only could we offer a design, but we could provide a schedule and a budget, at a cost far lower than the general contractor (which was an enormous firm) could ever have. To this day I am amazed that we landed those two commissions; they changed the firm and my career. I am forever grateful to Larry for trusting his instinct enough to hire a young architect with a very small portfolio, and for enabling me to do some of my best design work. He was an interesting, incisive client, with a good site and a great budget. It is not often that you get all three.

The Ellison residence also marked a turning point in my design work. My early houses were inspired by their rural sites. Kimball and Hansen (rural Connecticut) and Chase (rural Napa) had in common landscapes with a history of agricultural barns, from which I took my inspiration for those houses. While I was happy with the floor plans, I was dissatisfied with their massing. The forms were too additive; they lacked the simplicity of great barn structures. Barns are pure expressions of program. They

Ellison Residence, San Francisco,
central courtyard, 1997

top left
Front entrance

top right
Upper-level hallway

bottom left
Courtyard, stepped garden

bottom right
Living room

JUMPING OFF: 1987–96

Charles Phan and Olle playing golf in Vegas

generally don't have windows, and the quality of the light streaming through the cracks in the siding is so arresting. The hay dust paints the light beams. My houses captured none of that. In my attempt to fit into the local context, I was designing houses that were forced, and lacking the elegance of simplicity. They were polite, they worked well, and they had some beautiful interior spaces, but the overall composition was without strength of conviction.

Ellison gave me the opportunity to change that. It was my first urban house, in a neighborhood (Pacific Heights) that had almost every kind of design expression, except perhaps a good example of abstract modernism. Here was my chance to complete the collection. And with that opportunity, my eye shifted. The forms became simpler, I paid more attention to composition and proportion, and I began to focus on how planes defined space. From that moment on, the work of Lundberg Design changed. One architectural critic likened the Ellison residence to a "Krups coffeemaker." I can live with that.

The third game-changing project was our first restaurant—the Slanted Door, in San Francisco's Ferry Building. Charles Phan, the chef and owner, is now one of my best friends. We have done numerous restaurants for him, and we are currently designing more. At times, the Slanted Door has been the highest-grossing restaurant in California. Charles has won James Beard Awards for best chef and best restaurant in the country, and he has introduced fine Vietnamese cooking to countless Americans. But when I first met him, he had only the one restaurant. He had opened the original Slanted Door in the Mission District, which he designed himself. Charles went to Berkeley for architecture, and although he completed only three years of the program, he has a great background in design. He then got busted for an illegal mezzanine (by an architect who couldn't get a reservation, *not me*) and temporarily moved to a location on the Embarcadero while he corrected the mezzanine code violation (he owned the building). But that work took time and money, and after two years he realized that in moving from the Mission, his clientele had changed. President Bill Clinton and his daughter, Chelsea, had eaten there twice, but many San Franciscans were apparently hesitant to venture into the Mission. On the Embarcadero, his client base had expanded, and he worried that if he moved back to the Mission, he might lose that. He worked out a verbal agreement with the landlord to extend his lease, but at the last minute the landlord reneged and stated that he wanted different terms—possibly one of the greatest greed-driven mistakes in the history of leasing. Charles walked out of the meeting and over to the Ferry Building, which at the time was being renovated into a food hall. There were two adjacent spaces left, and Charles took them both, combining them into one 8,000-square-foot restaurant.

The Slanted Door, San Francisco, Ferry Building, 2004

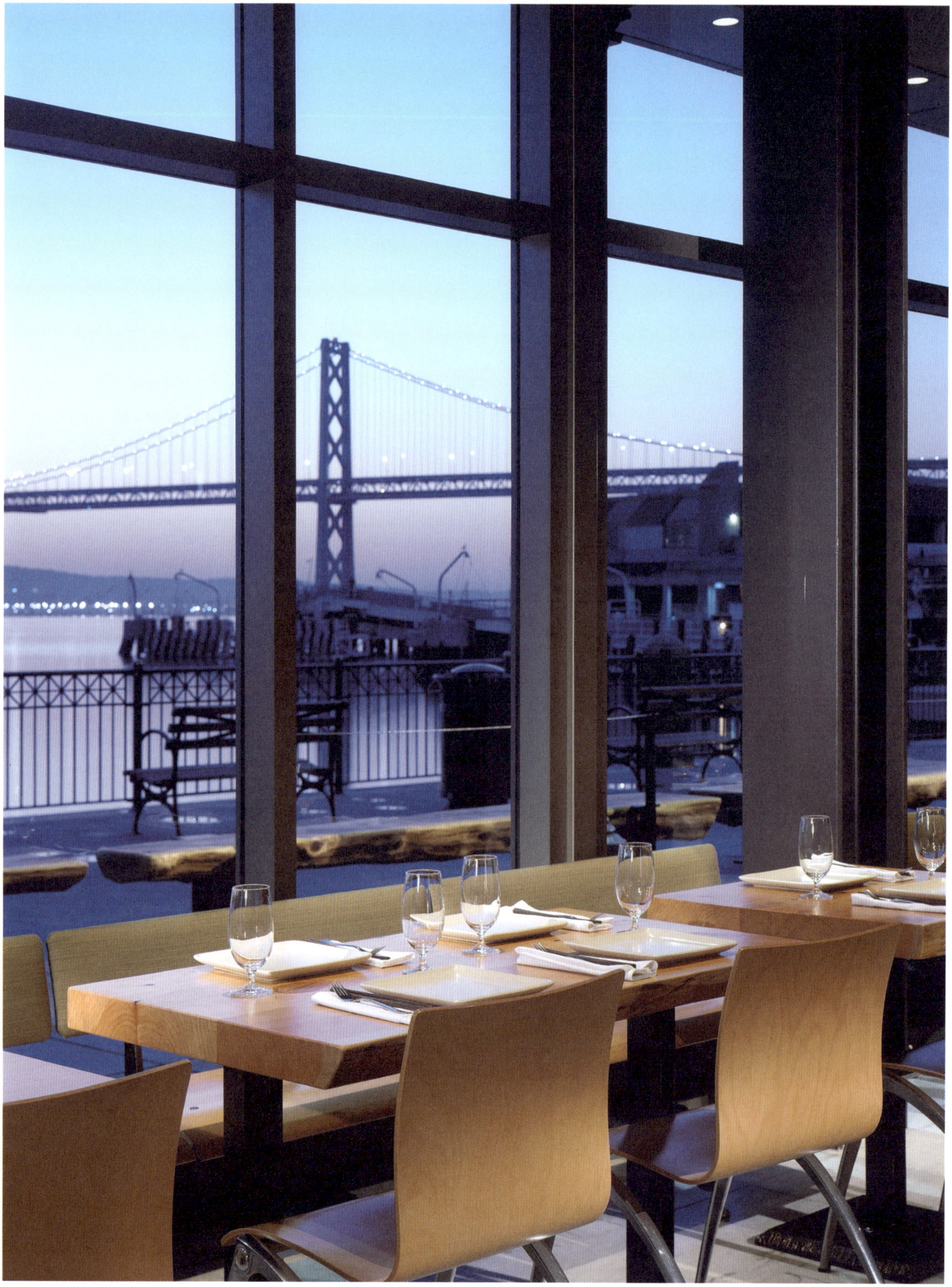

opposite
Slanted Door, view of the Bay Bridge

above left
Olle laying out the waterside benches

above right
Redwood log benches

The next day, on his way to the dump, he decided to stop in at Lundberg Design. I was not in the office, but Debra Sassenrath, our office manager, greeted him. Although his trash-day attire caused her some concern, she eventually ascertained that he was, in fact, in the right place. He left a card and asked to have me call him. The next day we met. He brought over the Ferry Building floor plan, and at our conference table, with a roll of tracing paper, he and I designed the new Slanted Door. He started the meeting by point-blank asking me how I'd design his restaurant. Now, I'd only eaten at the Slanted Door twice—it was nearly impossible to get a reservation—but I loved the food, and I had a stab at an answer. I told him that he was doing, in my opinion, something similar to what was being done at Chez Panisse (how could he not like that comparison?), where Alice Waters was using hyper-local ingredients in Mediterranean-style cooking. Charles was using great ingredients, mostly local, to create food that was *based* on Vietnamese cooking, but really a new California cuisine. I wanted to approach the design of his restaurant the same way—to use beautiful natural materials, locally sourced, in a modern expression, to redefine how his food would be perceived. Materials like bamboo, red lacquer, and rice paper, in my opinion, had nothing to do with his food, and they lacked the creative expression that the innovative approach he was taking deserved.

JUMPING OFF: 1987–96

36   PART I.   PERSONAL NARRATIVE

top left
Hardwater Bar, Pier 3, San Francisco, 2013

top right
Hardwater whiskey shelving, detail

middle left
Slanted Door, San Ramon, interior

middle right
Slanted Door, San Ramon, dining room detail

bottom left
Rice and Bones, Wurster Hall, Berkeley, interior, 2017

bottom right
Rice and Bones entrance

I don't think Charles had ever heard that before. He told me he'd had architects sending him pictures of Buddha (especially odd, since he's not a Buddhist), and how insulting he found it to see Buddha used as an element of interior design. My approach, however, resonated with him. He also loved the shop; Charles, like most chefs I've come to know, is a hands-on type who loves to make things. Seeing the fabrication shop gave him a lot of confidence that he and I shared, at the very least, a love of tools.

All the other shops in the Ferry Building are oriented toward the central hallway, but since our space was at a corner at the north end, with two walls of glass looking out over the Bay, I felt that we should place the front door facing the water so that we could emphasize a relationship to the San Francisco Bay. We located the kitchen in the center of the plan, ringing it with dining tables and enabling easy access to the kitchen from three sides. And with very little modification, that was the plan we ended up constructing. At the end of that meeting Charles stood up, shook my hand, and said, "I don't know if I can afford you, but I'd love to work together." I remember smiling and telling him that for me, this was a dream job and that we'd make it work. Ten months later, the Slanted Door opened, and ten restaurants and one house later, we are still making it work.

I don't know if Charles realized I'd never designed a restaurant before; we never discussed it. We so quickly became immersed in the project that it was irrelevant. Again: good clients care far less about what you've done than what your ideas for them are. Trust your initial instinct, and be ready to talk about a big idea. Listen carefully and find out what's important, and then incorporate that into an approach that addresses those needs but also surprises and delights. Don't be afraid of an unusual concept, because the unexpected is often what the client is hoping for. If you aspire to do good work, be bold and trust your initial reaction to a design problem. Over the years, that approach has served me well, but no example has been more important than the day I met Charles.

Four projects and four clients—John and Barbara Chase, Larry Ellison, and Charles Phan—changed my life and my career. The Chase House got me out of remodels and into custom single-family residences. Oracle's lobby opened the door to super-custom commercial work. Larry's residence qualified me for the high-end residential market. And Charles gave me my introduction to restaurants. Now, of course, at LD we claim to be experts in all of those typologies, but I know that some of my best work has come on projects where we are designing that project type for the very first time. I am eternally grateful for the generosity of the clients who gave me those opportunities.

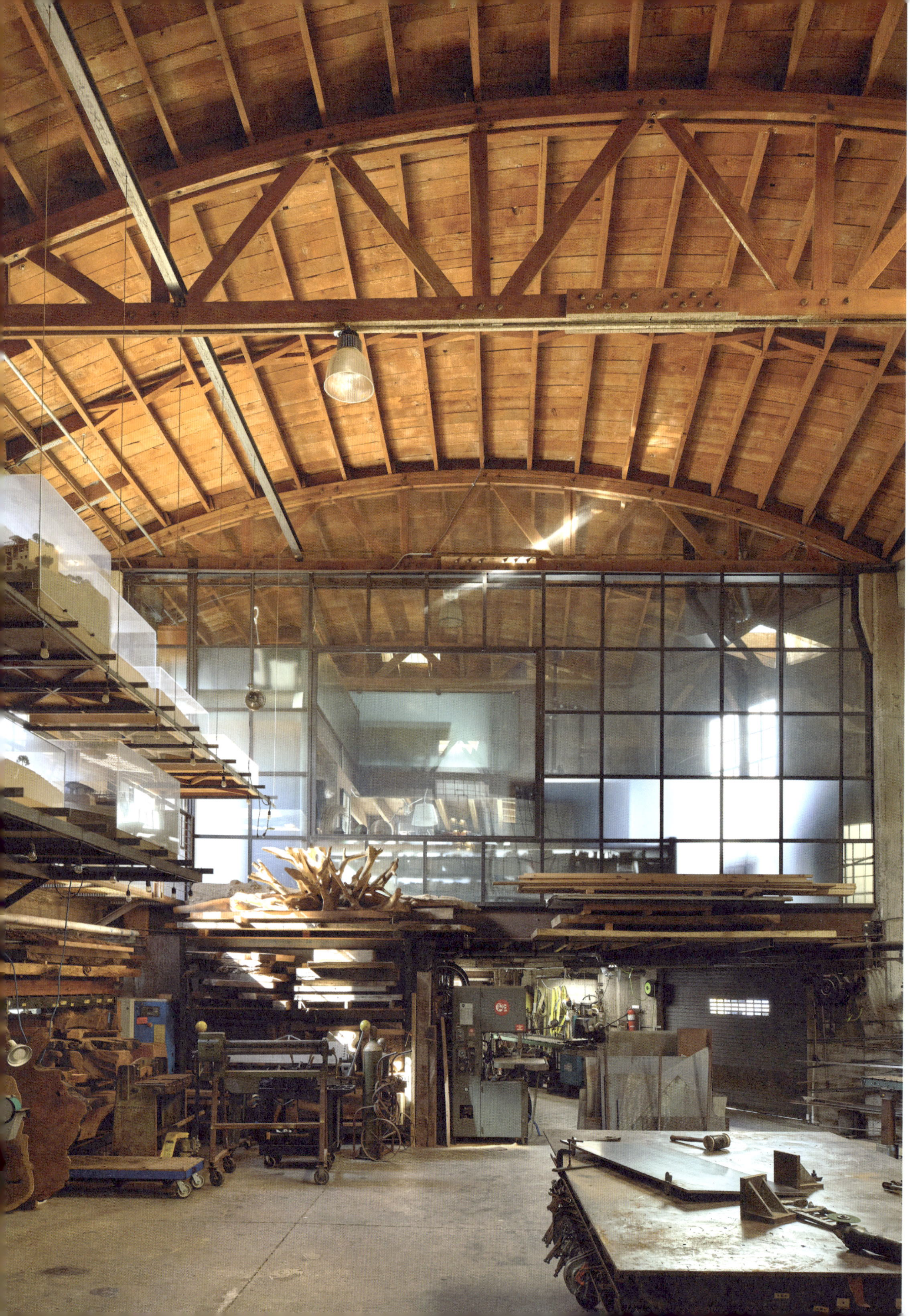

The Mattress Factory

1996–present

Some materials promise far more than others but only the workman can bring out what they promise.
—DAVID PYE, *The Nature and Art of Workmanship*, 1968

I have always loved building things. But my father was the least mechanically inclined person I've ever met. He could break anything. Lawnmowers, chain saws, cars—you name it, he broke it. Part of why I became so hands-on was because I had to fix the things Dad left in his wake. As for his attempts at carpentry, they were truly comical. I remember him once deciding to panel our basement. He bought some sort of cheap pressboard paneling, the kind with just a photograph of wood on the surface. The studs were on an 8-foot layout, the same height as the paneling sheets, so he just nailed them into the studs. They were a little tight, but he managed to squeeze them in. The next morning, we came downstairs to walls that had swelled due to humidity and looked like the surface of an angry sea. Half the nails had popped out. My brother and I looked at the instructions printed on the back of the sheets, and sure enough, in bold letters, it said to be sure and leave a quarter-inch gap around each panel, but Dad was never much on reading directions. Anyway, he just walked away in disgust, and eventually Peter and I fixed it. So I credit Dad with giving me my initial training in the building arts.

When I was in architecture school at UVA, my work-study job was managing the woodshop in the evenings. The dean, Joe Bosserman, kindly gave me the job for all three of my years there, but I did know my way around those tools. No one ever got hurt on my watch. I quickly learned the difference between students who didn't know a tool but had aptitude, and those who would never warm to the process. Often it was just easier to do the work for those in the second category. If the shop was quiet, I'd work on building my models or some furniture; it was a great way to learn the difference between a builder and a craftsperson. I didn't always devise the best designs in my studio, but I built some very nice models!

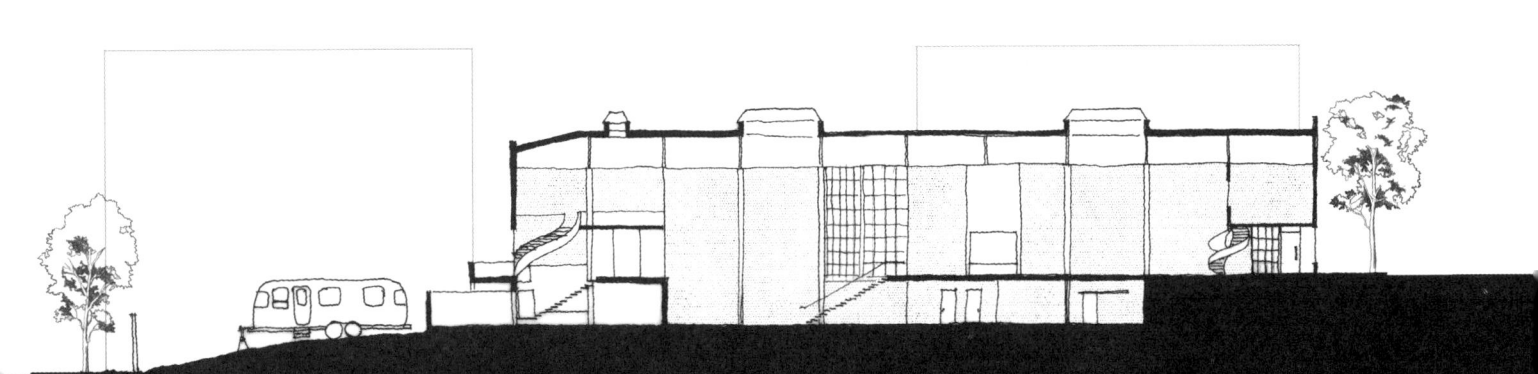

opposite
2620 Third Street, San Francisco, Lundberg Design, workshop with apartment beyond, 2025

below
2620 Third Street site section

left
2620 Third Street historic photo, (pre–Lundberg Design)

below left
2620 Third Street site plan

below right
Workshop with conference room beyond

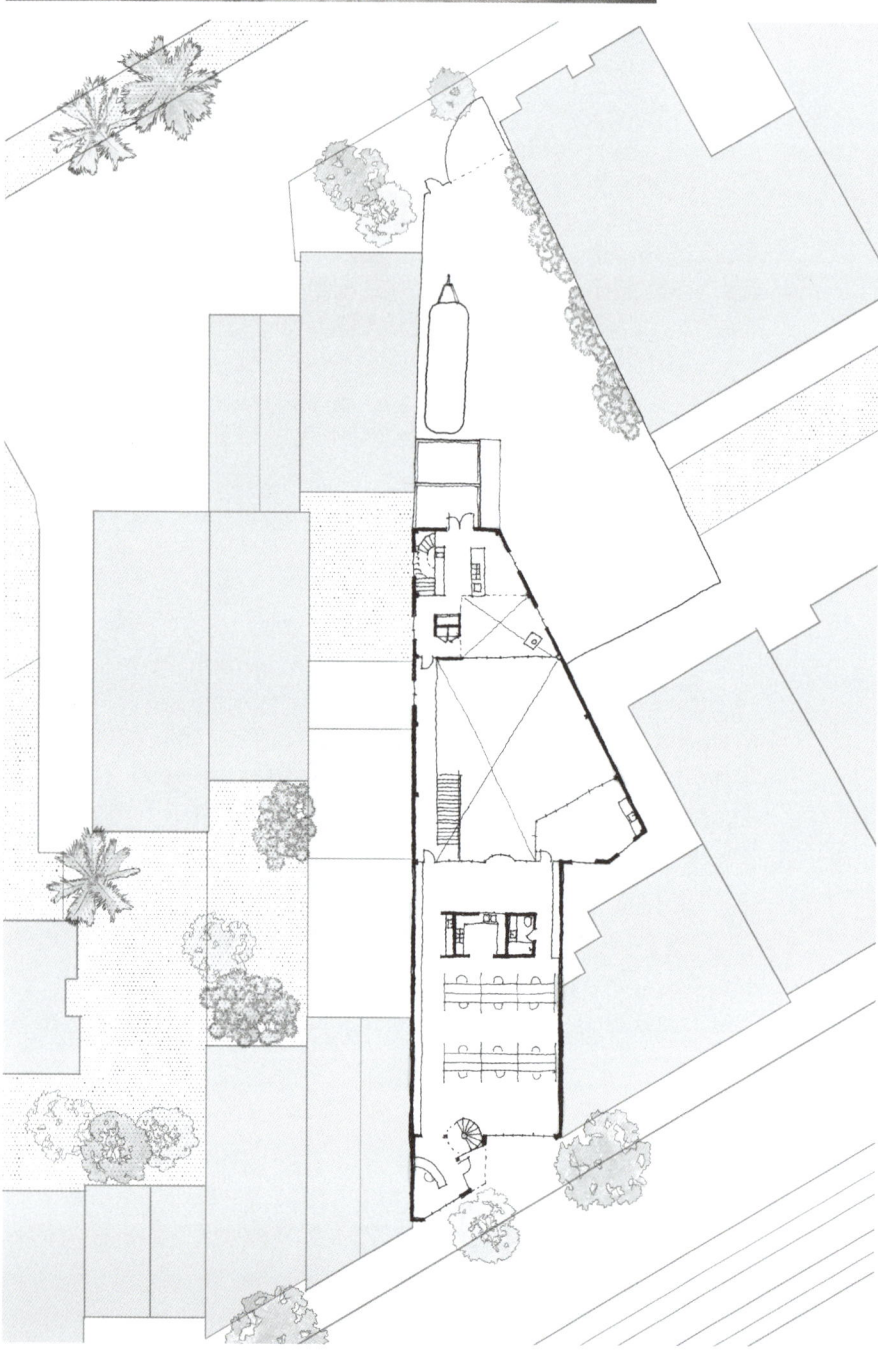

40   PART I.   PERSONAL NARRATIVE

In grad school, I recall many of my professors expressing concern that my knowledge of building practices might limit my imagination; rather than thinking of form in a theoretical way, they worried, I would focus too much on whether something was buildable. I understand that argument, and I am grateful to have been introduced to that line of thinking, because that can happen. But the actual practice of architecture does not count until it is built. Until you occupy a building, until you see it in the environment, until you witness the play of light and the engagement of the occupants, you never know if it is a successful work of architecture.

THE MATTRESS FACTORY: 1996–PRESENT

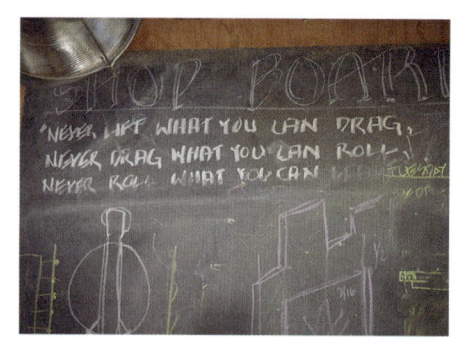

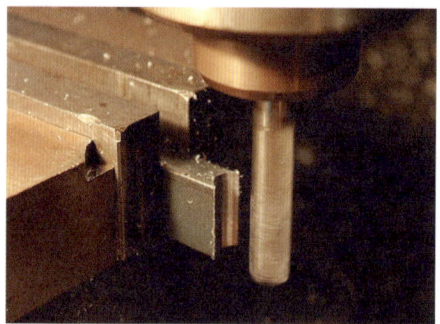

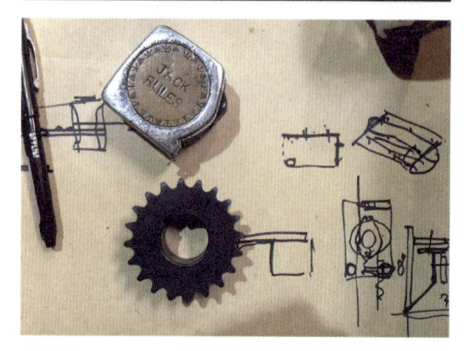

Workshop vignettes

And understanding building technology has helped immensely in seeing my designs get realized. Often, understanding a building process will open your imagination to what can be done—the form will emerge from the possibilities inherent in the particular building techniques being used. Look at the brickwork or woodwork in some of Alvar Aalto's buildings. He clearly understood the traditional methods associated with those materials, but then he pushed the boundaries of both. As I mentioned earlier, in Vicenza, my professors Mario di Valmarana and Robert Vickery introduced me to the work of Carlo Scarpa, and I think that was the moment I first came to deeply appreciate the beauty of a well-executed detail. To this day, Castelvecchio in Verona is one of my favorite buildings in the world. It is a fifteenth-century fortified castle that Scarpa converted into a modern art museum. He used stone, concrete, steel, and glass to "float" the new program in the old masonry walls. Every corner, every step, every change in material is carefully thought out and crafted. The stark yet sympathetic contrast between old and new was like nothing I'd ever seen. Here, old and new not only coexisted but were mutually celebratory. So often in the United States we see imitations of "traditional" architecture, which always feel like parodies to me. But here was a way to embrace the legacy of what came before while expressing new architecture of today. Finally, I understood what Ludwig Mies van der Rohe meant when he said "God is in the details." In fairness, I hadn't experienced much of his work yet, but I finally truly grasped the potential of that statement. I knew that I wanted my work to have that same care in the detailing, although at the time I had no idea how expensive that kind of attention could be.

To produce such work takes craftspeople—people who know their materials and then lavish skill and care far beyond the ordinary. It is the hand of the craftsperson that makes the end result so special, and so unusual in our age. I loved the uniqueness of the work of architects like Aalto and Louis Kahn, and I searched for a way to emulate that expression of care, that connection to the personal. And so, I came up with the idea that having a fabrication shop, a facility that could build unusual things, might be a way to accomplish that.

When I started Lundberg Design in April 1987, I had a space where I did mostly metalwork. In 1991 we rented a building on Tehama Street in San Francisco, where the equipment expanded to include woodworking tools. Then in 1996 we bought our current location—2620 Third Street, in the Dogpatch neighborhood—where the shop became what it is today, namely, a place where we can work in many mediums and at a large scale. Most importantly, we have a big yard, which is indispensable not only for certain kinds of work but also for housing the various found objects that I'm sure I'll use someday.

above
Olle and Curly

right, top to bottom
Conner trimming the Mourad root ball
Michael on the table saw
Jack TIG welding

We live in a world of extraordinary design. The computer age has brought with it a democracy of great design, to which we all have access. A great example is Apple's iPhone, an extraordinary piece of design both functionally and aesthetically. How you use and program it does, in part, define you as an individual, but the object itself does not. It is so ubiquitous (I don't think I know anyone who does not have one) that it says far more about you if you do *not* own one. So what makes an object personal? For me, it is the work of a craftsperson, something that is unique and possessed only by you. What I call "signature pieces." To make something like this, for instance, a table (we have made many over the years), and then sell it to one of my clients often feels more like a gift than a transaction. And the way we work on those pieces is usually quite different from how we work on our building designs. We can be sculptors, where instead of drawing something up and then turning it over to a builder, we can use the making process to inform, and sometimes modify, the design. As architects, we so often turn over our designs to others to execute, which can be wonderful, but then we lose the ability to take advantage of those people's knowledge. They are to build-what-we-draw, that is their job. But they may have experience and knowledge that we then fail to tap into. Having a shop, and craftspeople who work in it, lets us, at least at many important moments, use that knowledge of making and materials to find expert expression. When that works, it is a magical moment—personal to us as the makers, and personal to the client, who now has something beautiful made just for them.

Having the shop also encourages a more collaborative relationship between our firm and the general contractors we work with. They know and respect that we know how to build things, but at times we can help them as well. Especially our experience and facility with all kinds of metalwork can assist them with certain problems, and in doing so, we develop a camaraderie that becomes

THE MATTRESS FACTORY: 1996–PRESENT

Casting pewter in teak door

invaluable in the execution of the project. The kind of work we do, highly custom design, demands a collaborative relationship between the architect and the general contractor. If it is adversarial, the end product will never be as good as it could have been. For that reason, we have never agreed to do work where the client wants the project competitively bid. Certain kinds of architectural work, such as institutional projects, are by law required to be carried out that way. It is an attempt to protect the taxpayer from "sweetheart" deals where the work is funneled to a friend and then potentially leads to corruption. So, in competitive bidding, the low price wins.

But one of the ways to win this kind of work is to exploit errors and omissions in the construction documents. Such projects may consist of hundreds of pages of documents, and anything of that scale is bound to contain mistakes; architects, like other humans, are not perfect. So, from the very beginning, we find it invaluable to have the contractor provide input on materials, techniques, and of course the budget. Ideally, when the permits are issued, all of the questions—about how we are building, what it will cost, and how long it will take—have already been answered. The client, the architect, and the contractor all must be on one team with clearly defined roles and a common interest in producing a great project. I strongly believe that this does not cost my clients more money. The kind of custom work we do can be expensive, but sometimes we have smaller budgets, and we treat those projects the same way. Of course I want us and the contractor to be properly compensated for our work, but that arrangement should be spelled out at the beginning of design. Our approach facilitates efficiency of thought and labor, which is in turn economical, no matter what the budget may be.

Another way the shop influences the way we practice design is that it can act as a laboratory for design and construction ideas. We all learn from what we build. The architects push the shop crew, and they in turn open us up to new materials and techniques. We can build models of details, showing how the materials might go together. We can make full-scale mock-ups of a building moment to make sure we like it, and we can discover, in that process, better ways to execute the end result. The crew might make a suggestion—like using molten lead to seal a hole in an old teak board—that elevates a piece into the realm of jewelry.

And we can build models, which I love. We have fully embraced the computer, and we are very good at producing fantastic photorealistic renderings (design review boards love these), but I prefer a wood model for several reasons. First, a wood model is an abstraction, which focuses your attention on the form as opposed to the finish materials. Renderings can be a sort of architectural pornography, full of children with balloons and unrealistic shadows and coloring to help sell the project.

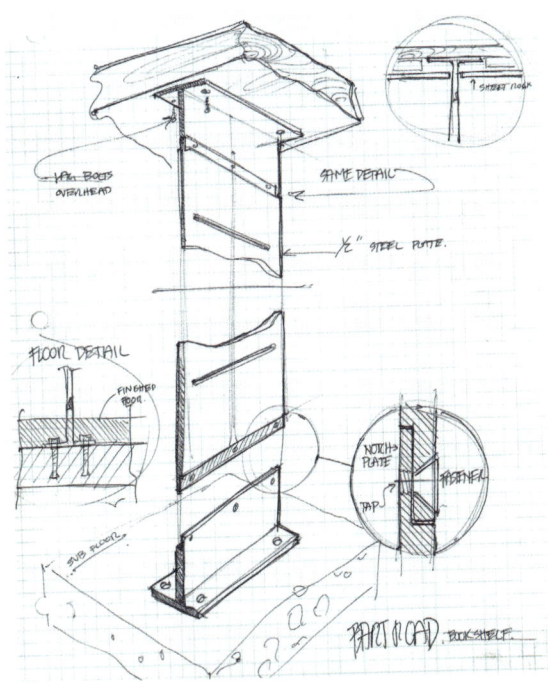

top left
Steel bookshelf and steel/wood pivot door

top right
Shop sketch

middle
Basswood models in the studio

bottom row
Vice Versa winery model

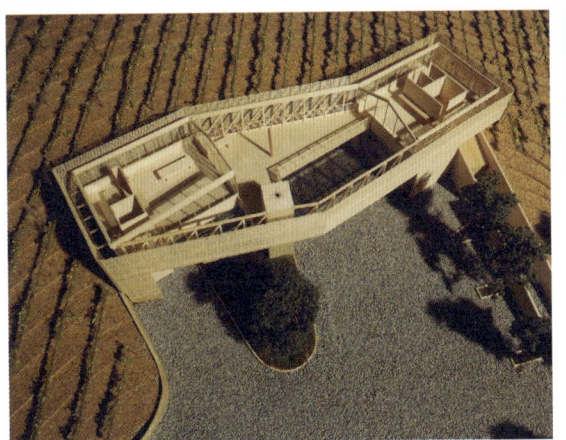

THE MATTRESS FACTORY: 1996–PRESENT   **45**

46　　PART I.　　PERSONAL NARRATIVE

opposite
Maritol in dry dock

above
Maritol at Pier 54, San Francisco

right column
Water-blasting the hull

Unless you do a rendered walk-through (and very few projects currently have the drawing budget for this), the rendering is a frozen image, likely taken from the architect's favorite angle, meant to show the building in its best light. A model forces you, the viewer, to engage your imagination—to peer into a miniature world and try to understand how everything will look and feel. You control the view, you determine your path, and as a result, I believe that you understand the building far better. I do know that I have never built a model where I have not in the end changed some aspect of the design, because a model will never let you ignore the problem moments.

At certain points in my life I have owned buildings that have helped define me and my work. The first was the church in Lexington. Then came the cabin (more on that later). Then Mary and I purchased an Icelandic car ferry (she really does embrace an adventure), which was big enough that I count it as a floating building. Since we could not afford waterfront property in San Francisco, I thought I'd be clever and create some. But let me be clear: this next part of the story is a cautionary tale!

Once the useful life of a ship is over—and this can have little to do with the condition of the ship—it has very little value, for ships are usually very expensive to reconfigure. I figured, if we could find one with a relatively open plan (a car ferry or freight vessel), built for

THE MATTRESS FACTORY: 1996–PRESENT   47

a cold climate (enclosed), I could have a floating version of an industrial loft. We traveled to Orlando, Seattle, Malta, and beyond looking at potential vessels, until finally in Iceland we found our ship—the *Maritol*. She was a 135-foot-long roll-on/roll-off (doors at both ends) car ferry that had been used to transport vehicles and goods from Reykjavík to the other side of the island. New roads and tunnels had made her obsolete, but she had been maintained and was still operating up until three months before we visited.

She was perfect—my largest found-object project! The main car deck was enclosed but with no partitions, a classic loft space 135 feet long by 20 feet wide and 17 feet tall. The bottom level was the old dining/kitchen with crew cabins, and the top deck had the captain's quarters and wheelhouse. She had been built for the North Atlantic, so she was ice class, and she ran. We had her outfitted in Reykjavík, cutting a hole in the car-deck floor to bring light into the lower level, repainting the entire exterior, and updating the various systems to prepare her for the journey to San Francisco. We located her original crew and captain and hired them to deliver the vessel. Amazingly, that all worked.

We lived on the *Maritol* for ten years—five at Pier 54, then five at Pier 50, both large commercial piers in Mission Bay (the new basketball arena, the Chase Center, now sits adjacent to those piers). Liveaboards are not allowed on San Francisco's commercial piers, but our primary residence was at the cabin, so we qualified, and Mary had her office on the ship. Over time, we remodeled the *Maritol*, and she was the site of some legendary parties. We loved living on the water. The birds, the seals, the constant subtle motion, and the reflected light off the Bay made life there profoundly inspiring.

But buying a ship is just the entry fee. Maintaining a steel vessel in salt water is a challenge, a ton of work and money. Insurance is based upon how much fuel you can carry (thank you, *Exxon Valdez*), and you need to pay a part-time ship's engineer to keep her happy. Let's just say it might be smarter to put your money in an appreciable asset—like, say, Bay Area real estate—than in something that always wants to sink. But if you want an adventure...

top
Maritol back deck, Pier 54

above
Back deck viewed from the interior

opposite, clockwise from top
Dining level
Car deck converted to the living level
Car deck with hatch above, dining below

48   PART I.   PERSONAL NARRATIVE

THE MATTRESS FACTORY: 1996–PRESENT 49

below
2620 Third Street

opposite
Studio, railing shadow

But as cool as the *Maritol* was, no building has had as profound an effect on me as 2620 Third Street in San Francisco. It is the perfect building for our needs. Originally constructed in 1933 as a mattress factory, and located in the Dogpatch neighborhood, the construction is heavy industrial—cast-in-place concrete walls and arched timber trusses, which I had sandblasted with my last $7,500 of credit in December 1996. The building is 10,000 square feet, which at the time I bought it seemed luxuriously large. But over the years we've managed to fill it up. We have the aforementioned yard off a one-way alley, volume, natural light, and square footage—all typically expensive features and hard to find in San Francisco these days. We live in the building, our dogs come to work with me (all 40 feet of my commute), and Mary has her office there as well. To have found this building when I did is one of the great moments of good fortune that have befallen me over the course of my career. It makes the kind of practice I've wanted to have possible. If the shop was somewhere else, if it was not part of my architectural practice, it would all be different, and not as good. I am living proof that a man can fall in love with a building.

THE MATTRESS FACTORY: 1996–PRESENT

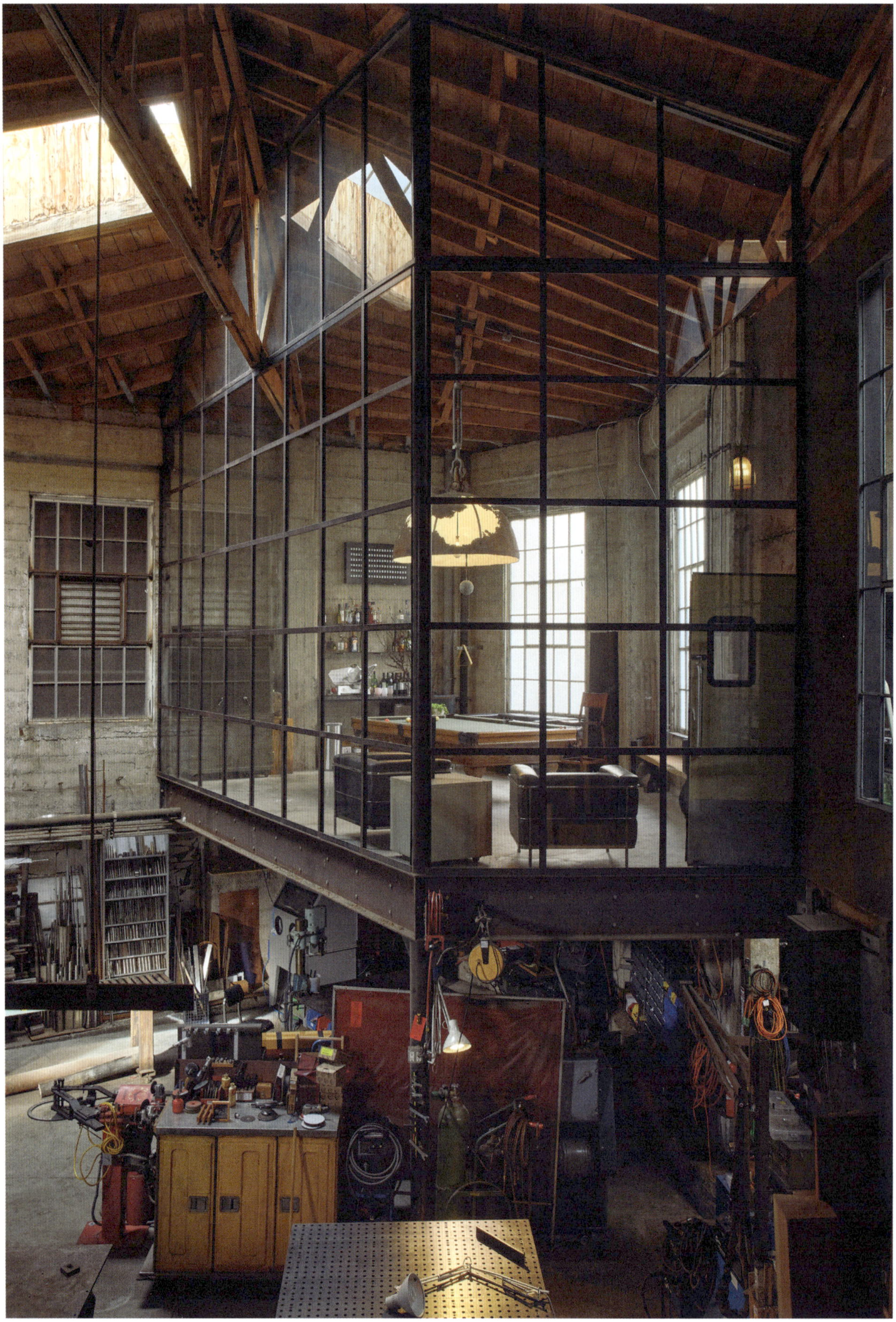

opposite
Lounge with "Death Star" buoy light

below
Lounge overlooking workshop

From the entrance on Third Street the structure seems quite modest, but as you enter and move back, it keeps getting bigger. The property runs through the block, from Third Street to Tennessee Street. In the front part is the architectural studio, the center of the building is occupied by the shop, and the rear portion is our apartment. The volume opens both up and out, with the shop at the widest point—it is both the actual and symbolic center of Lundberg Design. The studio, a conference room, Mary's office, and the apartment all overlook the shop, such that the energy embodied in the physical act of building permeates those other spaces. We do not look like other architectural offices because what we are trying to do is in fact different. We could certainly locate the shop somewhere else, in less expensive real estate, but then we would lose the impact that the making of things has on our practice.

The shop is in part a laboratory—a place for us to experiment with materials and the physical properties of our ideas. It is in part a collection, a repository for found objects within which I sense some potential. But most of all it is a place of craft, where we try

THE MATTRESS FACTORY: 1996–PRESENT

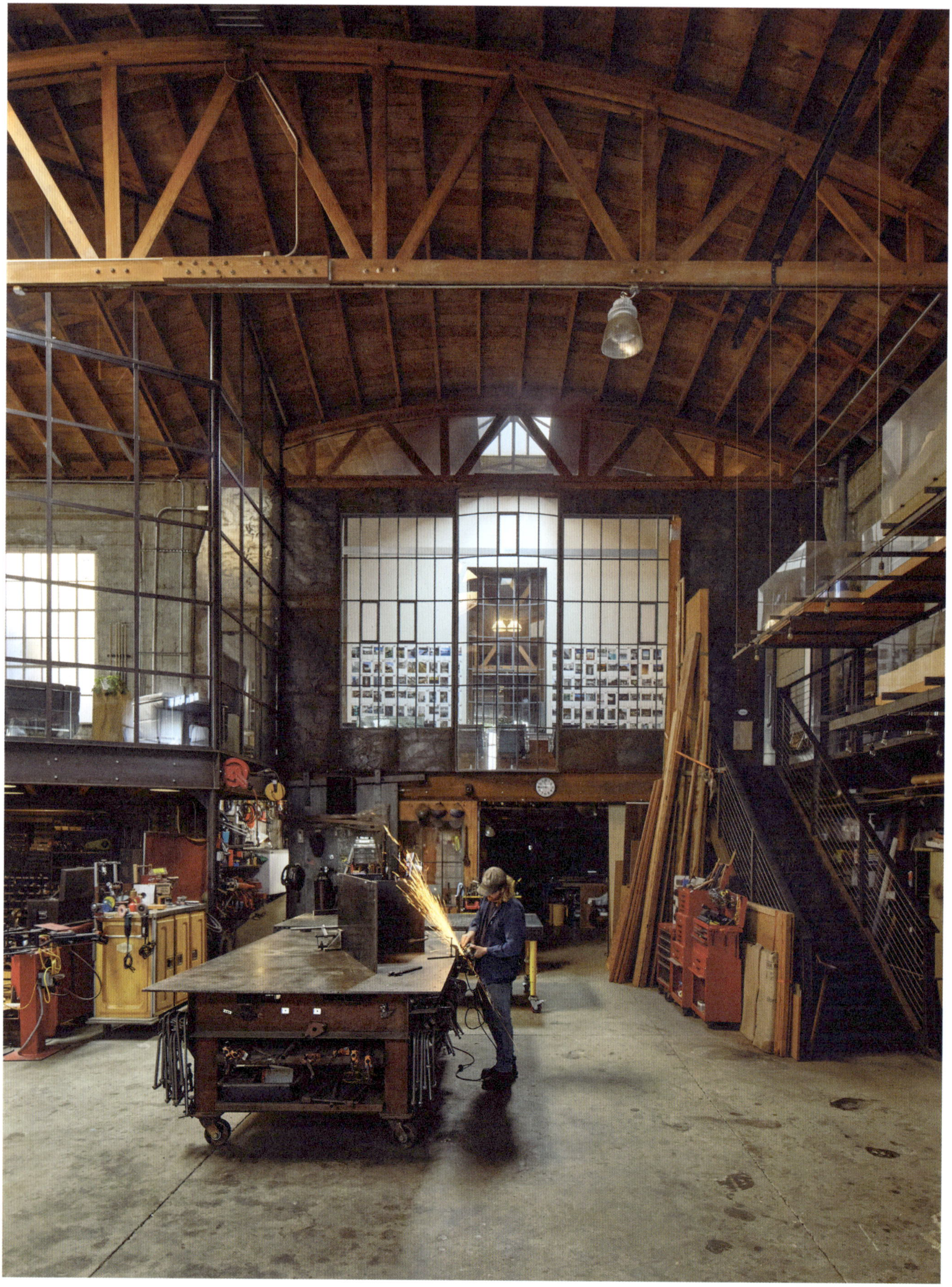

opposite
Workshop with conference room beyond

below, left to right
Lundberg Design workshop: Bridgeport mill, scrap rod, ironworker

overleaf
Apartment entrance (page 56)
Catwalk to apartment (page 57)

to build perfect objects, pieces of meaning that are intensely personal to both us and our clients. Many of the tools are generations old—the Bridgeport vertical mill and the Cincinnati lathe are both older than I am. They are heavy, hulking machines that operate with incredible precision. The DoALL vertical band saw is the largest machine in the shop and can crosscut 24-inch I beams perfectly square. We have a Hitachi forklift that gets used more than any tool, for it lets us handle materials that exceed human strength. We have every kind of welder, hydraulic presses, saws, drills, and hand tools beyond counting. Because we are so well equipped, the act of building is made easier. Our access to all kinds of building technology expands our ability to invent. Just walking through the shop, seeing the tools and materials and craftspeople at work, I can't help but be inspired. That personal proximity to tools and materials of making has always been a great creative spark for me; it is why details have found such expression in our architecture.

I firmly believe that the shop defines us as a design firm. It makes us who we are, and our work what it is. From the way we approach design to the beautiful objects and details we build, it is our signature.

THE MATTRESS FACTORY: 1996–PRESENT

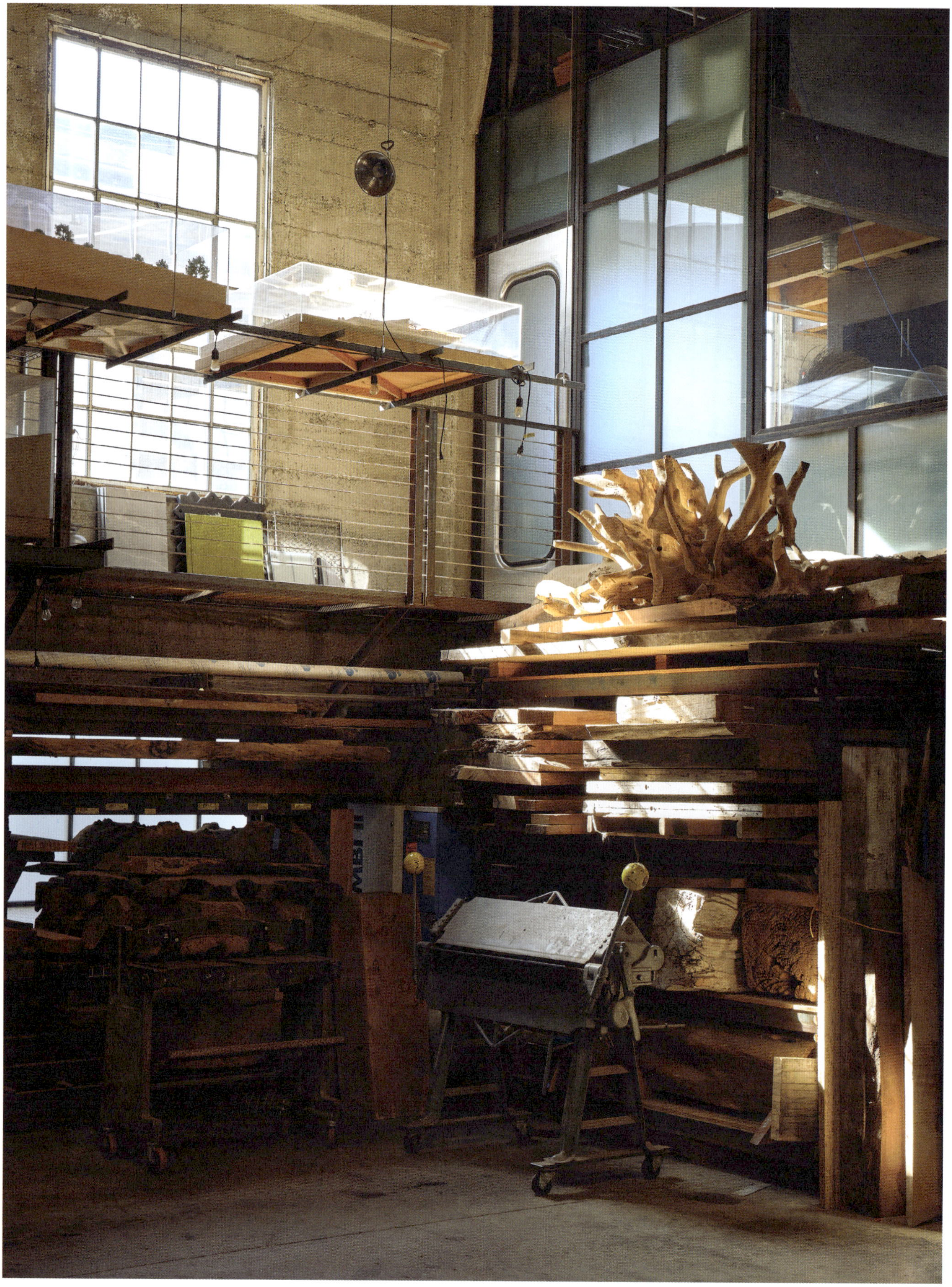

THE MATTRESS FACTORY: 1996–PRESENT

top and opposite
Apartment living room

left
Office staff installing glass in window wall

right
Stair to bedroom loft

58   PART I.   PERSONAL NARRATIVE

THE MATTRESS FACTORY: 1996–PRESENT

PART I.   PERSONAL NARRATIVE

opposite top
Studio, 2025

opposite bottom
Studio, with Olle's office upper right

above
Studio from front door

THE MATTRESS FACTORY: 1996–PRESENT 61

"*Life is too short for boring food.*"
—Unknown, but probably Calvin Trillin

PART II.

MATERIAL PALETTES

METAL

STONE

GLASS

WOOD

FOUND OBJECTS

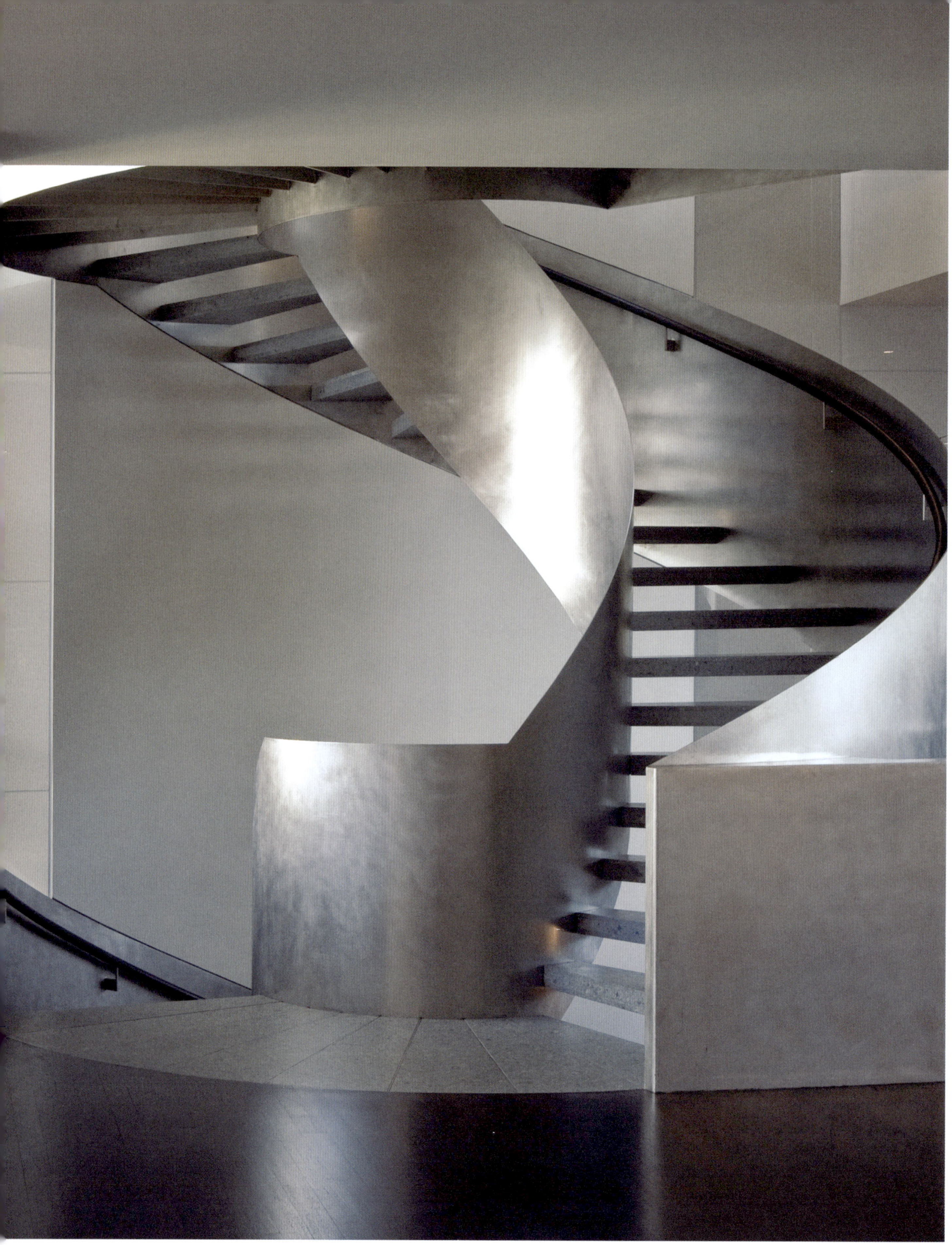

METAL

As a child, I remember having a fascination with all things metal. When I was around five, we lived in a house in suburban Cincinnati that backed up against a forest of giant beech trees containing all sorts of animals. We had a black wrought iron railing on the back outside stair, and a very friendly black snake would wind his way around the handrail to warm himself. While he startled a lot of people, he was my friend and I remember petting him as he languished in the sunlight. I recall thinking that he must have liked our railing because the vertical members were twisted in a way that mimicked his contortions as he wrapped himself around the horizontal rail.

Like many boys, I had a fascination with the bulldozers and other heavy machinery of the type that excavated our foundation. The giant paper mill machines that were such a part of my father's life were infinitely interesting. And from a very young age, I loved knives. I started out with pocketknives, but as I got more interested in cooking, I fell in love with chef's knives—the variety of styles, the different types of steel used, the precision required in the making and maintenance of them. I now own far too many, and I still love a good kitchen knife, especially a vintage carbon steel one, and the simple act of sharpening one on a whetstone is one of my favorite meditative pleasures.

Looking back, I realize that my first impulse to make a fabrication shop part of my work was based on a desire to incorporate steel detailing into my architecture. My building experience had all been focused on wood—standard wood framing, wood furniture, cabinetwork. But I had always been drawn to steel as a building material, and once I learned to weld, I began to explore its structural and finish potential.

The fabrication facility at Lundberg Design is at its heart a metal shop. We work primarily in steel—stainless, mild, and Corten alloy. But bronze, copper, titanium, lead, and aluminum have also appeared in our work, although mostly on a secondary detail level. Steel has some very appealing properties, foremost its strength-to-size ratio. While it is very heavy, it can also be visually very light, with a small cross section providing remarkable strength. At the Ellison residence, we designed a fountain with a suspended granite boulder weighing six thousand pounds—three tons!—with all that weight suspended by a half-inch-diameter woven stainless steel cable. The visual contrast between the mass of the stone and the delicacy of the cable is the heart of the work; you sense the boulder floating. While the fountain may appear at first glance to be about the rock, it is in fact about the steel cable.

Steel is quite forgiving. Carbon steel is made by melting iron ore and carbon at about 2,600 degrees Fahrenheit. Born from fire, it can also be manipulated through the application of heat. It can be heat treated to add hardness; it can be heated and then easily bent; but most importantly, it can be welded. You can take two pieces of steel

opposite
Pacific Heights Residence staircase, a stainless steel ribbon

top
Knife rack at the cabin

above
Ellison fountain boulder suspended by a ½-inch stainless steel cable

PART II. MATERIAL PALETTES

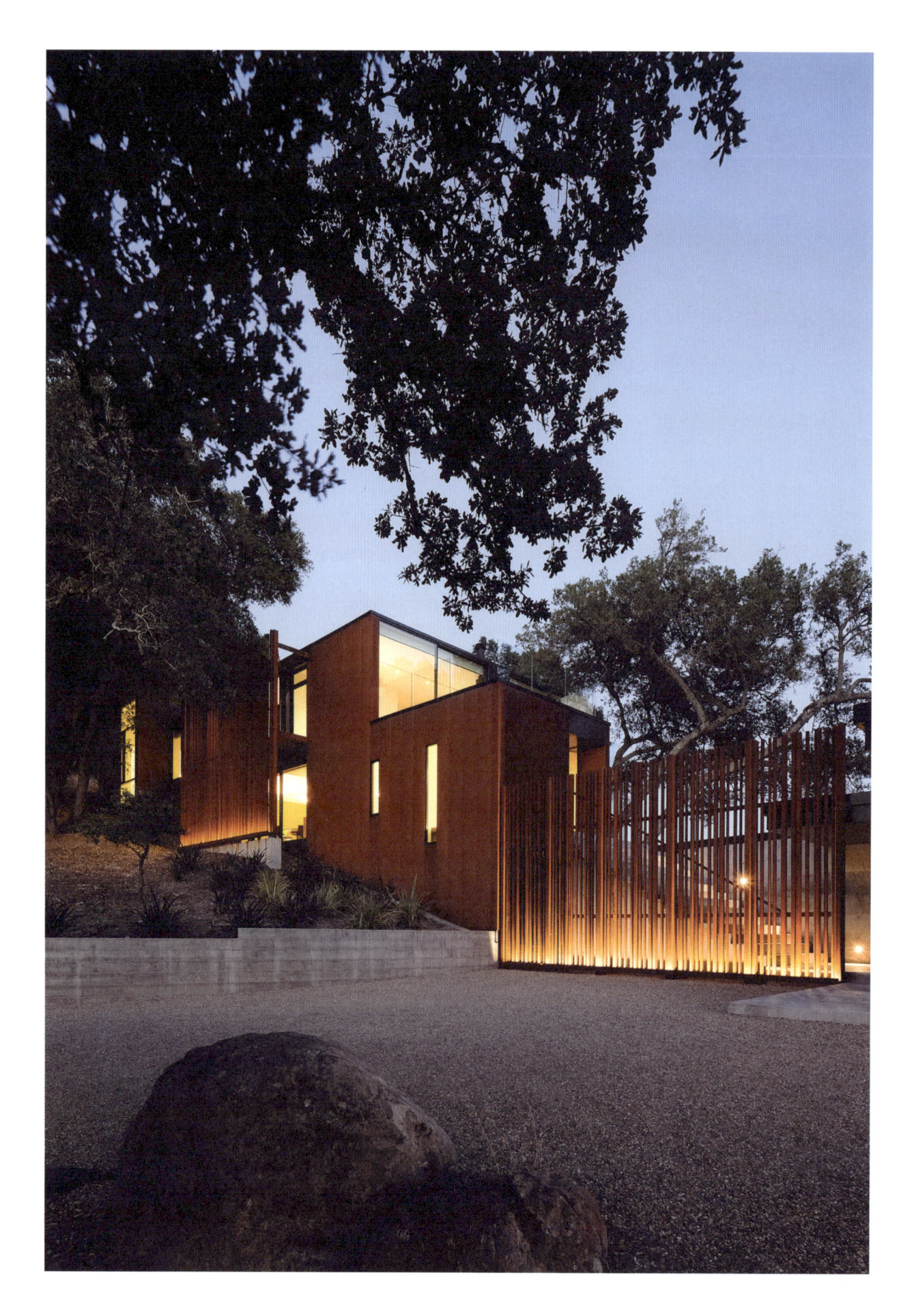

opposite
Sonoma Residence, Corten steel siding and fence

left
Perforated Corten detail

below
Fence, Corten tube and flat bar

METAL 67

Fabrication of stair at Mare Island Shipyard

below
Sunnyvale staircase

opposite
Sunnyvale staircase, Corten steel detail

and turn them into one, and when done expertly, the welded joint is as strong as the constitutive parts. For me, welding is the magic; it makes steel unlike any other material. In addition to all those characteristics, steel is also relatively inexpensive. The primary component is iron ore, which is the Earth's fourth most common element and makes up 5 percent of its crust. It is easy to separate (magnets) and a hundred percent recyclable; it can always be re-melted and re-formed. It is in fact a very green material, in spite of the energy it takes to produce it. Steel scrap is collected worldwide. It is too valuable and too easy to re-melt to waste, but even if it is left in a landfill, where the addition of water and oxygen start the rusting process, it just turns back into iron ore.

Sometimes rust can be controlled, and if you use a Corten alloy, that rusting actually seals the surface, preventing further degradation. The rust is iron oxide, its color evoking the earth, and the raw character of the metal. When a piece of steel starts to rust, you know that it is returning to the earth—the iron begins to flake off and melt back into the ground. As an artist, you can decide to control that evolution—you can stop it (well, just delay it, really), interrupt it at a certain moment, or allow it to proceed.

With the right tools, steel is also very simple to manipulate—it can be welded, cut, machined, ground, and polished. If you make a mistake and cut too much off, you can weld a piece back on and start over, so it is very forgiving. Because of its hardness and density, each process typically leaves a mark, so a beautifully executed weld speaks to the craftsmanship of the piece, but you can also grind that weld so that it is completely flush with the base metal, and to the naked eye invisible.

PART II.   MATERIAL PALETTES

METAL 69

above and opposite
Pacific Heights Residence, four staircase details

70 PART II. MATERIAL PALETTES

Cold-rolled steel is another readily available ferrous metal option. This is hot-rolled steel that is then further processed at room temperature under very high pressure. This removes the mill scale (an uneven iron oxide coating that manifests during the forming process) and creates a denser surface and a "bluer" color. It also makes the edges and corners very precise. Hot-rolled steel shapes tend to have rounded corners, while cold-rolled tend to have very crisp right angles. Generally, carbon steel products—sheet, plate, structural shapes, and pipe—are formed through multiple passes through rollers and/or dies that deform the red-hot ingot into the desired shape. On mild (carbon) steel, this leaves mill scale, which needs to be cleaned off before welding to prevent degradation of the weld, but is otherwise often left on the piece. Any sanding, grinding, or other machining will remove the mill scale and expose the base metal, which will then look different. This is just a characteristic that needs to be accounted for in the end result.

Early in my career I discovered gun bluing, a chemical process developed to darken and provide corrosion resistance for rifle barrels. It is a beautiful finish, deep and mysterious. It can be technically challenging, and requires hyper-clean surface preparation, but the end result makes mild steel a precious material. It will not hold up in corrosive or exterior environments, but for most interior applications, it works quite nicely. It has become one of our signature steel finishes.

Four details: gun-blued mild steel contrasted with polished stainless steel

Stainless steel, while chemically very similar to mild steel, is a completely different thing. The various alloys—involving chromium, nickel, silicon, manganese, and nitrogen—behave differently, but for the most part, stainless steel is bright and shiny, similar to silver or chrome but with more visual depth. Alloy 304 (common) and alloy 316 (marine grade) are the two most available, but 316 is much more expensive than 304. That said, 304 will oxidize (rust), particularly at the welds, where the molten metal allows impurities to float to the surface. This oxidation is not harmful to the base metal, as it is primarily just a surface condition, but it is usually aesthetically

72   PART II.   MATERIAL PALETTES

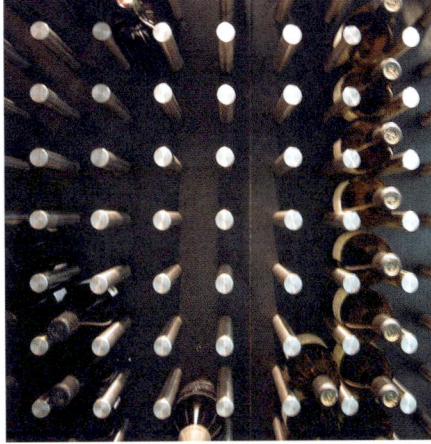

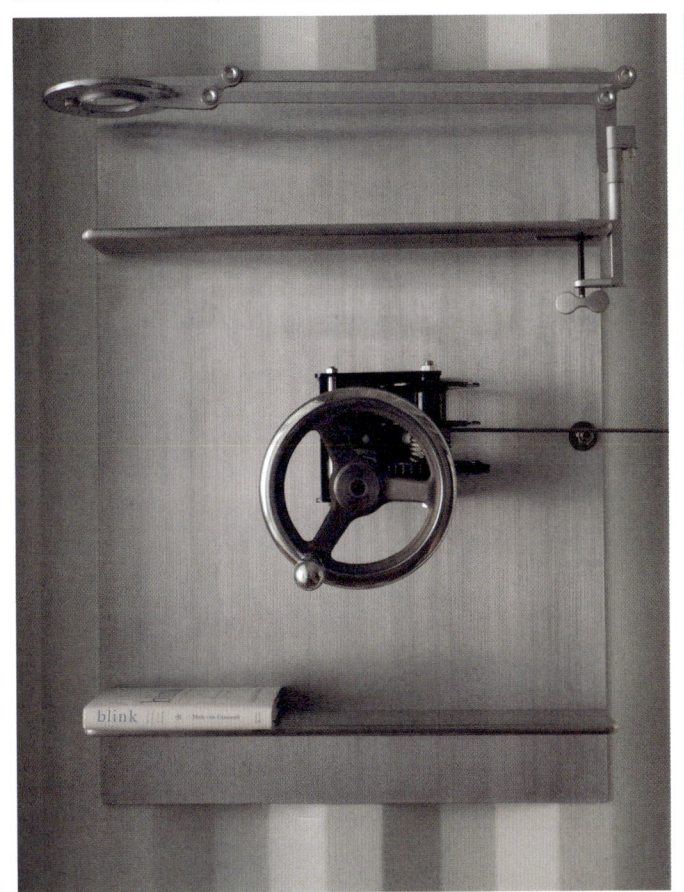

top row
Stainless steel details

bottom row
Stainless steel details: grained, polished, and blued

METAL 73

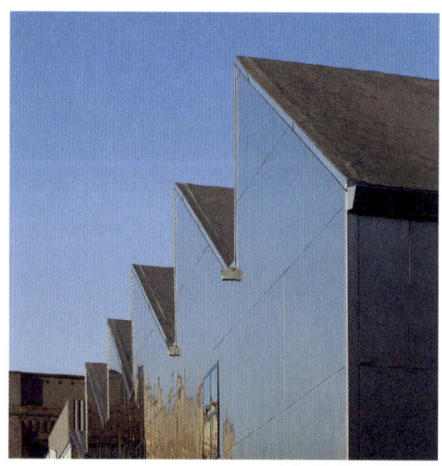

undesirable. Water and oxygen will initiate the process, but salt (marine fog or spray) will greatly exaggerate it. Stainless steel can be polished to a mirror finish, sanded with different grits and patterns to provide a variety of effects, and even sand or grit blasted to provide a very matte, almost gray finish. Because it is "stainless," meaning highly corrosion resistant, these effects do not change dramatically over time. Stainless steel finishes beautifully. It can be grained, random-orbit finished, or polished. There are other specialty finishes, but these are the ones we tend to lean on. I am particularly fond of the random-orbit finish, which is easily repaired by anyone with the right tool.

Then there are other metals, all with their own specific properties. One thing they all have in common: they are all considerably more expensive than steel. Copper and the various bronze alloys (which are primarily composed of copper) are beautiful metals to work with. In a corrosive environment (salt fog) they will develop a blue-green patina that shields the base metal. In a noncoastal environment the metal will turn a dark red-brown that blends beautifully in a forest. In most cases, the metal's useful life will exceed that of the architect. It can be welded, although copper is quite easy to solder. It is much softer and weaker than steel, but that softness allows it to be formed easily, even by hand. And

74   PART II.   MATERIAL PALETTES

opposite
Stainless steel details and facade

below
Copper mesh and plate details, verdigris patina

since bronze melts at a lower temperature than steel (1,700 versus 2,400 degrees Fahrenheit), it is also much easier to cast. Other casting metals that we often incorporate are aluminum (1,250 degrees Fahrenheit) and lead (700 degrees Fahrenheit).

In our work we often try to celebrate the original form of the material. For me, "original" in this context means the form in which I received or discovered that material. Steel comes in myriad shapes and sizes, but I am particularly fond of hot-rolled shapes such as channels, tees, and I beams. I love the crispness of their geometries, and how precisely they can be machined. Often, we will combine metals with more organic materials, such as wood, to contrast the perfection of the former with the flamboyant, organic character of the latter. In those contrasts, one begins to see the inherent character of the materials at play.

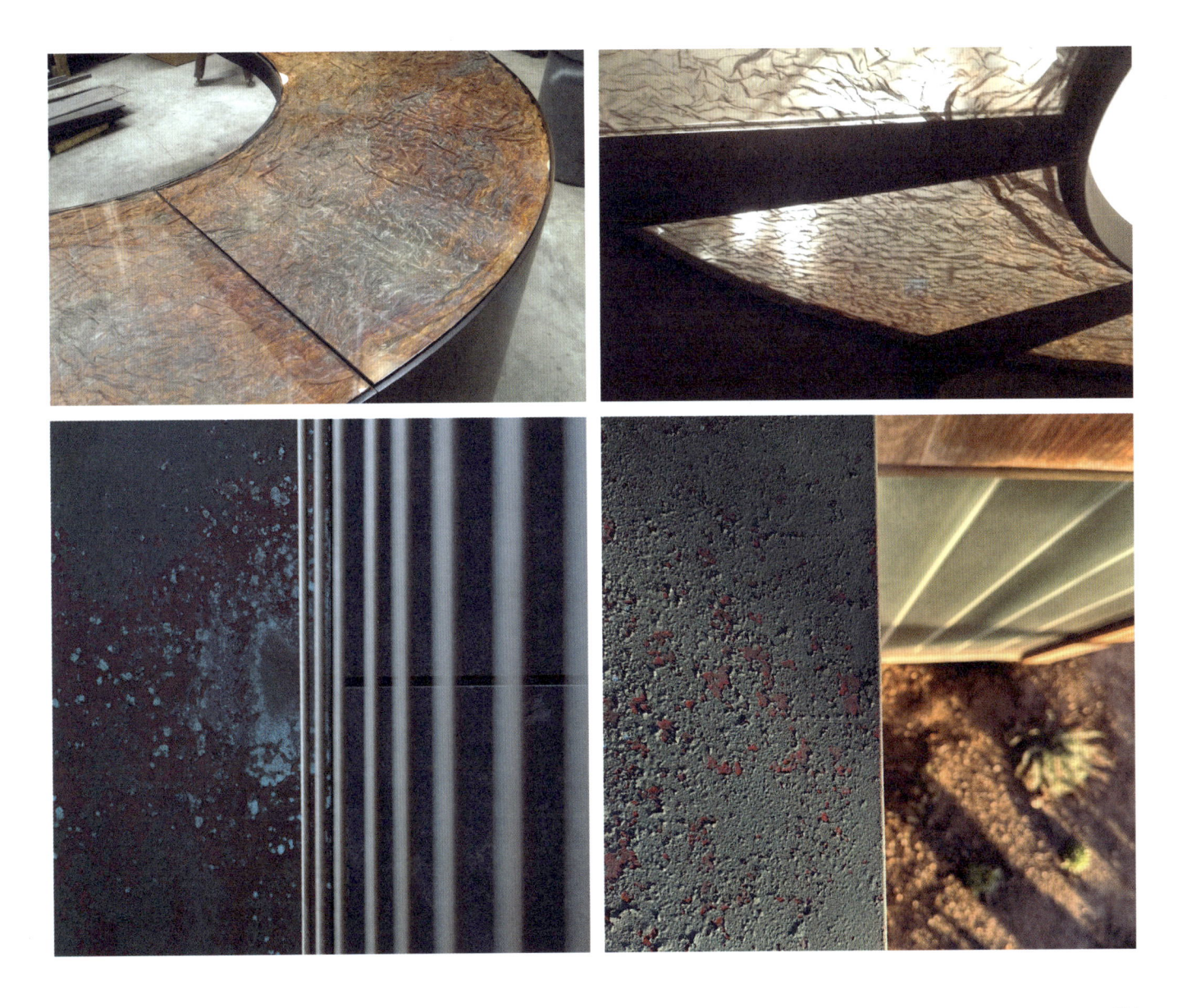

METAL 75

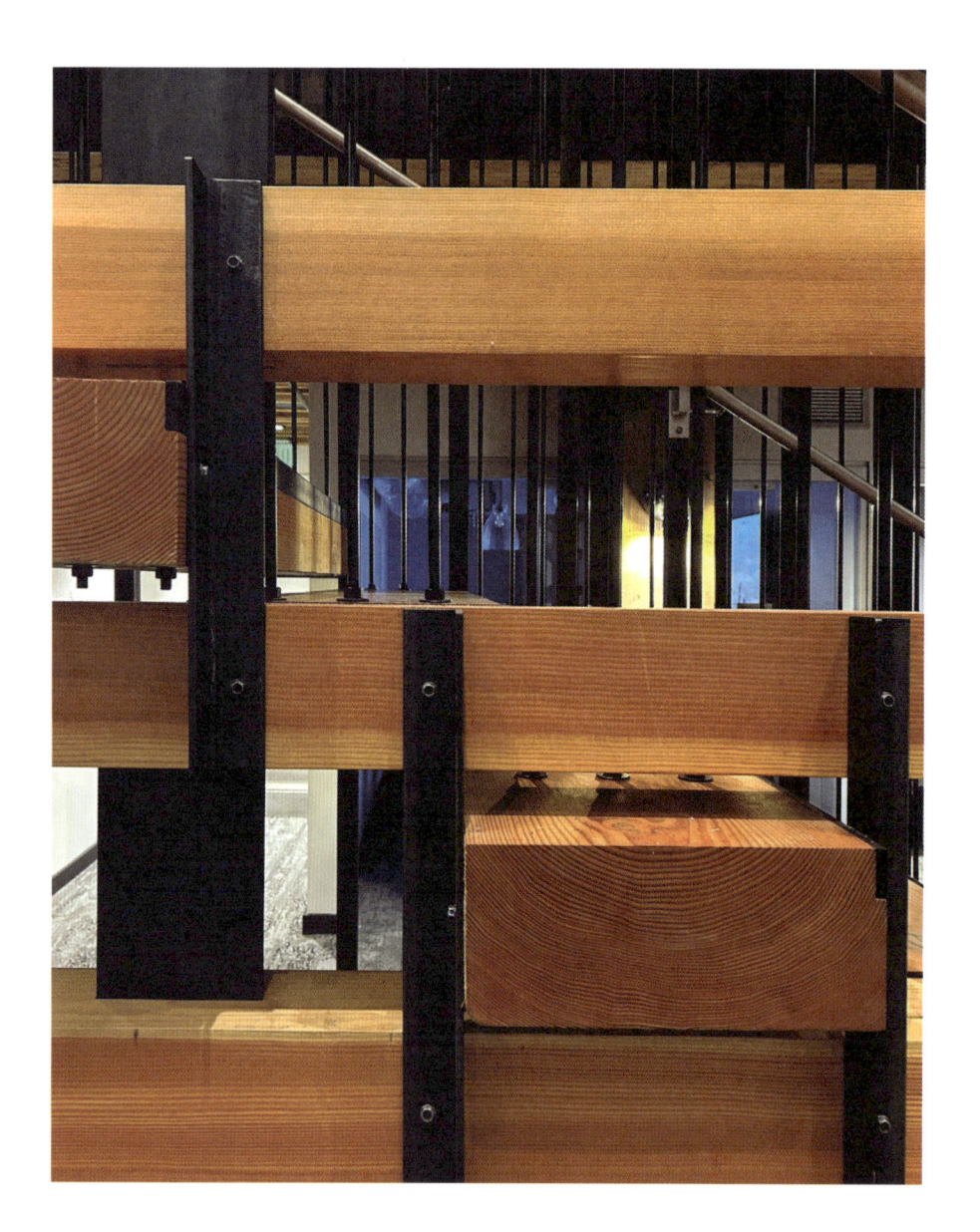

left
1000 Sansome, wood and steel stair detail

below
Steel combined with other materials

opposite
Hardwater, copper die wall and naturally corroded steel buoy light

76 PART II. MATERIAL PALETTES

METAL 77

78   PART II.   MATERIAL PALETTES

STONE

Stone and iron are both sourced from the molten center of the Earth (at least poetically), but as architectural materials they couldn't be more different. Whereas iron ore is processed into steel, and is thus always a human-made thing, stone is completely natural, at least in the beginning. It starts as the mountain, the crust of the planet. And there is no civilization on Earth that does not have access to stone; it is the most universal of building materials.

There are historic examples of buildings being constructed from the mountain—prehistoric cave dwellings, cliff dwellings, and more recently the Temppeliaukio Church in Finland. Those are special sites, and we haven't yet had one of those come along (an abandoned quarry would be a fantastic building site). Perhaps one day. The closest we've come are the wine caves we designed, where the concrete walls reinforce the fractured stone of the mountain. In cave tunneling, often the end of the bore will be solid stone, so whenever conditions allow, we try to expose that, the mother. Outside, if there are grapevines growing in that soil, that stone is what gives them their particular terroir. Exposing the end bore reminds you that you are in the ground, not inside some concrete warehouse.

opposite
Lava four ways: natural surface, cut, fractured, and honed

below
Hourglass cave, stone end-bore

STONE

right
Hourglass cave, ribbed texture

below left
Cave and bore,
Vice Versa cave boring

below right
Entrance to Rudd Estate cave

80   PART II.   MATERIAL PALETTES

above
Granite scraps with drill marks, signage for the Moss Room

below
Moss Room, interior sign

A stone block is a piece of the mountain that has been split or cut off the face. Usually cuboid or rectangular (to make handling and processing easier), blocks are most frequently sliced into slabs for use as building veneers or countertops. But sometimes we can leave the block intact. By leaving intact a natural surface of the rock, be it a weathered face or a fractured surface, we honor the source, the natural state. I find the expression to be quite powerful when an organic natural surface is juxtaposed with a precise, machined face where the stone has been cut and polished. The visual and tactile contrasts engage both sight and touch; I have always found that a good detail beckons the hand.

The boulder comes next. As the surface of the mountain begins to erode, it sheds rocks, large and small. They can be irregular in shape or perfectly round, polished by water and erosion, or jagged and sharp. In the past, these boulders were often broken into rectilinear rocks of various sizes to be used in masonry construction—Machu Picchu, the Egyptian pyramids, and Stonehenge are among the most dramatic examples. But modern building technology has rendered this type of stacked-masonry construction generally obsolete. Stone is a poor insulator (although it has great thermal mass, meaning the ability to store heat), it is heavy and difficult

STONE   81

PART II. MATERIAL PALETTES

to join together, and it performs poorly when subjected to lateral loads (such as happens in an earthquake). But I love a good rock, and incorporating one into our architecture always provides an opportunity for unexpected moments of visual and tactile emphasis.

Stone slabs don't interest me much. When they are used to clad buildings as a veneer, essentially stone wallpaper, the building is pretending to be stone but is just a typical framed structure that could have been clad with anything. The three-dimensional character of the material is lost, and with it the association back to the mountain. But sometimes, as I mentioned, we find ways, even with slabs, to leverage the inherent contrast between the cut surface and the split edge. One face is refined and precise, the other organic and random. The top is smooth, the edge is rough. Sometimes we build walls by stacking cut strips of slabs, an effect that ends up referencing sedimentary stone. Sometimes the cut face of the stone is so beautiful that we are compelled to use it on surfaces, almost as a painting. And sometimes we manipulate the surface of the stone to reveal its composition. Traditional methods such as carving, or techniques such as high-temperature flaming, cause the surface crystals to pop off as they expand. Occasionally we have used slabs cut off the drilled faces of quarried blocks, where the exposed drill marks create a visual effect very similar to actually being in a quarry. What I like about all these techniques is that they reveal the natural structure of the stone, and in doing so, remind us of the natural state of the material.

Concrete is an unusual material; it starts as a liquid and then turns solid. It can be placed in forms and cast, so it is unlike most stone material we use, but given its solid end product, I tend to think of it as a version of stone. It does not have the birthright of the mountain—it is a chemical composite—but in many ways, it behaves as stone. It is remarkably strong, and it can be cut, polished, carved, and textured. Once hardened, it can be treated exactly like stone, but because it can be cast, it has the potential to encase reinforcing

opposite top row
Oracle Lobby, marble blocks fractured

opposite middle row
Cast stone fractured with stainless embeds

opposite bottom row
Entry stones: Slanted Door, left; Robin, right

above
Ellison fountain, Academy Black granite boulder

STONE   83

PART II.   MATERIAL PALETTES

opposite
Slanted Door reception desk,
granite boulder slice

top
Robin entry stone,
natural cleft basalt

bottom
Seaglass service counter, Sierra
white granite with drill marks

STONE 85

86 PART II.   MATERIAL PALETTES

opposite top
Lava natural surface (left) and diamond cut (right)

opposite middle
Limestone: water-blasted

opposite bottom
Concrete chiseled (left) and stone block with quarry drill marks (right)

right top
Pacific Heights stair

right bottom
Stone steps/landing: Virginia slate, black honed

rods, which makes it structurally much stronger, as it then has tensile as well as compressive strength. One can add powdered pigments to modify the color, although I will admit to a fondness for concrete's natural gray coloration, which comes from the cement component.

A relatively inexpensive way to alter the appearance of concrete is through manipulation of the formwork. Rough-sawn wood boards will transfer their grain pattern to the concrete surface. It is subtle, indenting no more than one-thirty-second of an inch, but the effect easily lasts for decades. Carlo Scarpa was a master of complex geometries within his formwork, creating levels of detail that would be almost impossible using any other material. Tadao Ando uses such highly polished formwork that the end result is a reflective surface similar to polished stone. We at times carve the concrete, contrasting the chisel marks and broken surfaces with the smoothness of the overall piece. It is a material that welcomes explorations of texture.

PART II.   MATERIAL PALETTES

opposite
Concrete wall with fractured fins

above
Sonoma Residence, concrete wall cast with polished formwork

STONE

PART II.   MATERIAL PALETTES

GLASS

opposite
Sunlight striking edge bevel

below
Strips of plate glass, laminated together

The property of glass that I find most intriguing is that it captures light. We often think of glass as just something that allows light to pass through it—a clear pane—and in buildings we use it as such. But then it is almost an absence of material, an illusion of openness, and there is nothing unique about that usage. As our work has evolved, the composition of the exterior surfaces has become more of a study in planes—large expanses of solid and void—rather than isolated openings within a larger solid field.

above left
Glazing detail, Carmel

above right
Corner glazing detail, Mary's office, Sonoma

right
Casting glass, John Lewis studio, Oakland

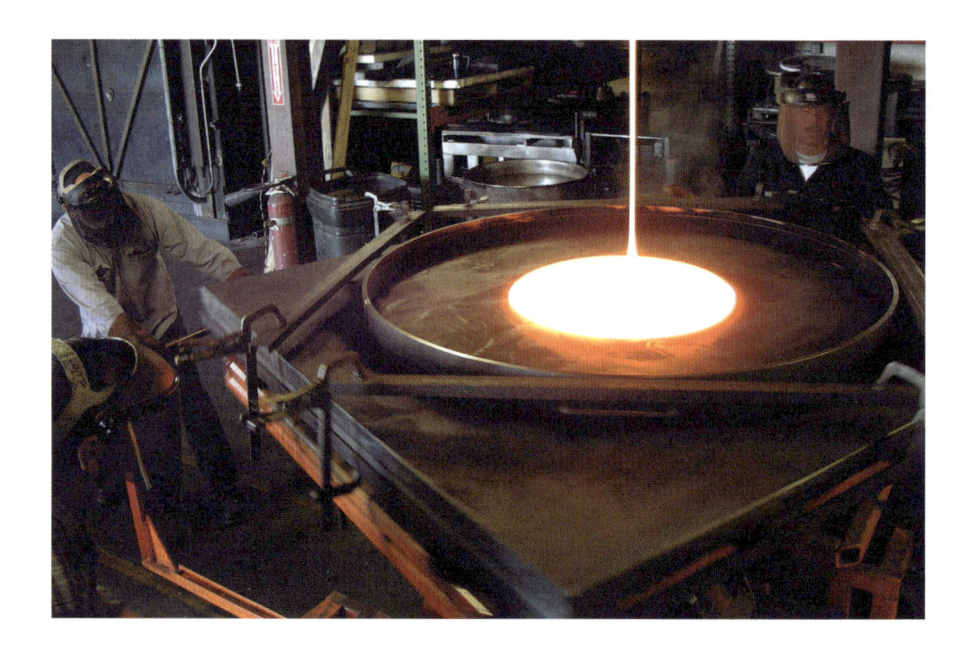

above left
Cast lead in concrete pier block

above right
Cast glass ashtray

right
Cast glass slab detail

Recently we have been exploring the ability of glass, when it has color or texture, to hold and then change light. Casting glass, where you start with a very hot liquid and pour it into a mold, is a fantastic process. John Lewis Glass in Oakland, which has the largest kiln in the country outside of Owens Corning, is an extraordinary facility. They make glass from scratch, melting silica (sand) and adding pigment. It is a process that is simultaneously simple and incredibly complex. The temperature is very high (2,600 degrees Fahrenheit), and that heat is fundamental to understanding the nature of glass. It is a liquid, and it comes out of the furnace bright red. It is viscous and moves slowly, like lava. It shrinks as it cools, so it must be cooled slowly in annealing ovens or the surface will shrink before the core, creating internal stresses that will cause the piece to explode. Because cast glass is imperfect, it sometimes retains bubbles and ripples that recall its molten state. It often reminds me of blocks of ice, particularly glacial ice, which holds the color of the sky within. It is interesting that three of my favorite materials—glass, stone, and metal—all share this same molten birth. On occasion we have been able to express that.

GLASS 93

above
Ribbed cast glass details

below, clockwise from top left
Stacking plate-glass strips for Slanted Door
Slanted Door, finished installation
Laminated plate-glass canopy
Laminated plate-glass strips

I love plate glass. Standard plate glass, when viewed on edge, appears green. This color is in the glass; when we look at the edge, we are just seeing a much thicker cross-section. And the thicker the glass, the greener the tint will appear. We have often stacked pieces of plate glass to create a sedimentary, layered effect. It reminds me of water, or perhaps layers of ice. It has a liquid quality that I find appealing, as though one were peering into a glacier. If the edges of the glass are just "snapped," as opposed to polished flat, then the optics are distorted, and each layer is quite different. Each band of light has its own quality. If one polishes the edge, then each layer still reads, but now the effect is more transparent—now you are below the surface of the water.

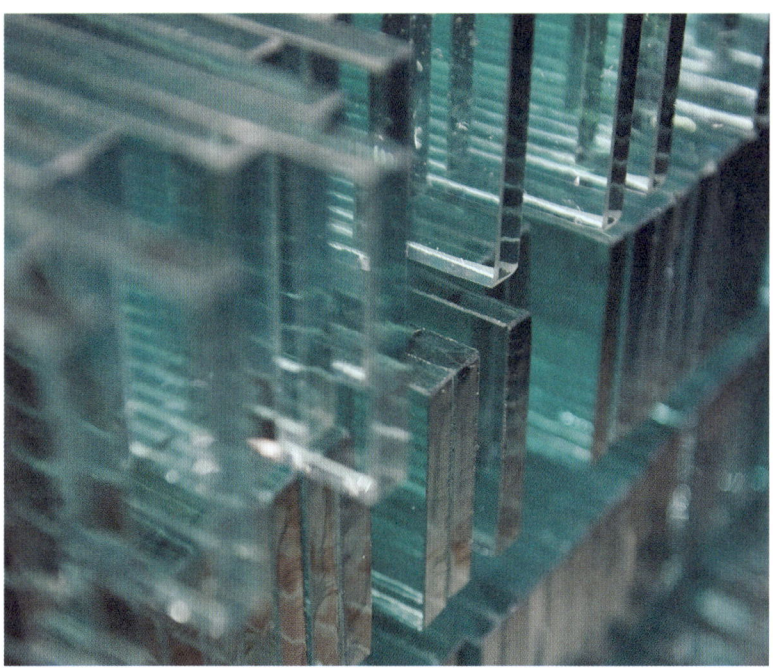

GLASS   95

96 PART II. MATERIAL PALETTES

opposite
Seaglass Restaurant sushi counter, stacked-glass details

below
Hawai'i Residence, laminated "wall jewels"

A right-angle corner of glass is very fragile, so when an edge is polished, that corner is often "eased"—a small 45-degree bevel is ground off. Typically this is also polished on thicker plate. Something we discovered quite by accident is that if the light is directed in a linear fashion, by blocking the light source from the sides, these bevels become prisms. Each beveled face "fractures" the light. It is an interesting effect—a narrow beam of light turning into a splay of light beams and colors. The thickness of the glass band and the size of the bevel are the two major factors that influence the effect, but there are other variables that we continue to explore. Varying the layer thicknesses and contrasting ground versus polished surfaces, and even different colors and types of glass, are just some of the possibilities. We will see where they lead, but I think our expression wants to stay simple. A beam of light etched upon a dark plane is a wonderfully poetic gesture, and I keep returning to it.

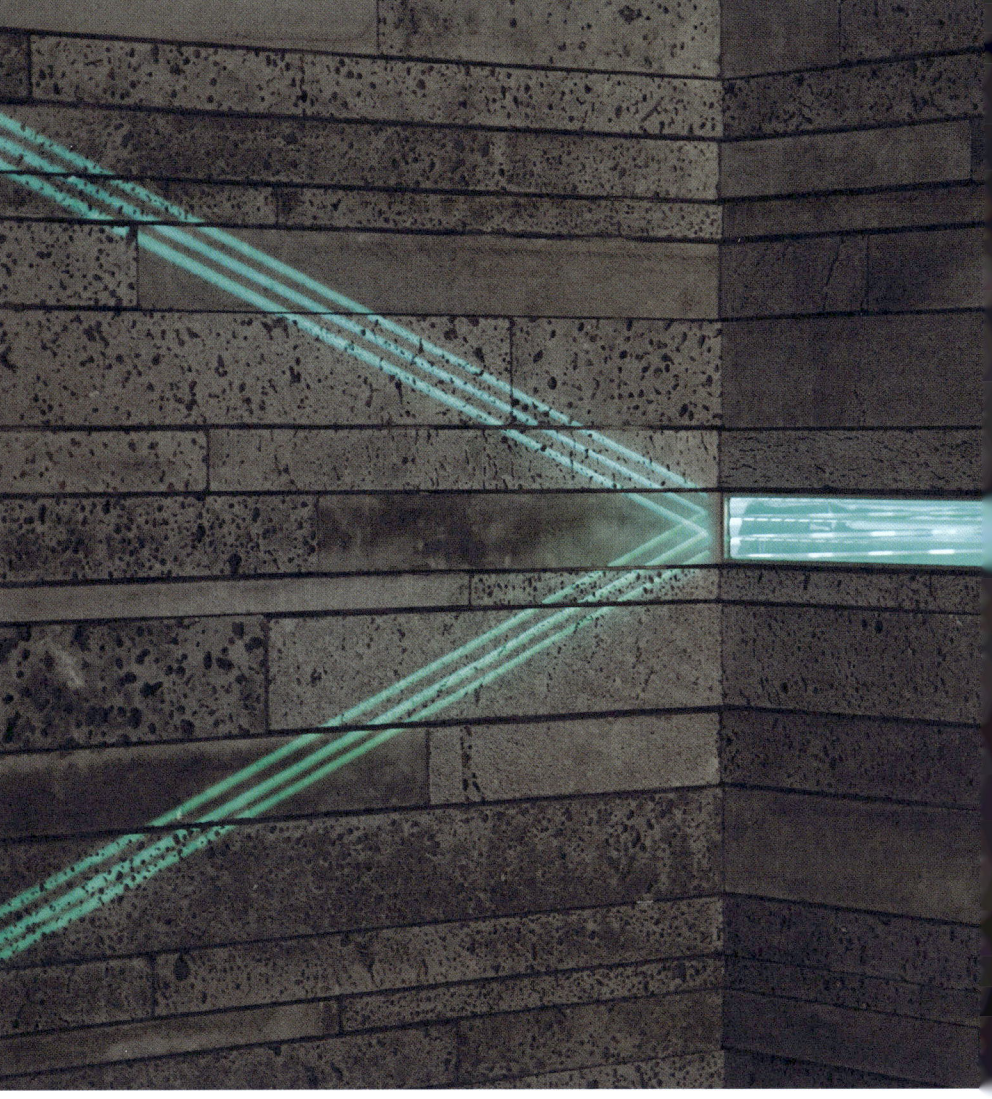

GLASS

PART II. MATERIAL PALETTES

opposite
Sunlight refraction

below
Channel glass viewed from inside and out

Recently we have used a product called channel glass, which is tempered glass in a flat-edged C shape about 10 inches wide, 2 inches deep, and up to 16 feet long. Because the shape is self-supporting, it requires no additional structure or frame. And because of the heat-forming process required to create the shape, the glass is optically distorted, so it usually comes with a texture that ends up making it semi-opaque. The end result is a plane of glass with a vertical pattern, not dissimilar to vertical board siding, but translucent. As a stand-alone plane, the partition has a different pattern on each side, with the vertical ribs being dominant on the one side, and the 10-inch faces forming a fairly flat surface on the other. But we have also used in it spaces where there is limited natural light, backlighting it as a perimeter wall and creating the illusion of sunlight hitting the surface.

GLASS   99

below
Channel glass detail

opposite
Channel glass lobby walls

Most of the channel glass we have used is made by Pilkington in the UK, and it is a wonderful product, but very expensive. However, a few years ago there was a parking garage in San Francisco that had channel glass on the exterior and the pieces started to break (parking structures flex a lot, especially when everyone leaves at the same time). The owner elected to replace all the glass with a kind of aluminum laser-cut screen (sadly, not as nice a design) and donate the remaining channel glass to a building materials recycling yard called Building Resources. We know them well, having donated and purchased a lot of materials from them over the years, so they called me and suggested that rather than the parking lot people taking all of these pieces to their yard, I should just buy it all and the parking lot people would bring it to us—free delivery! So of course we did buy it, at about ten cents on the dollar, making Lundberg Design undoubtedly the largest owner of used channel glass in the world! Now we can use this wonderful product in projects that don't have big budgets. The only challenge is that we can't cut it, so we have to use it as is, in 8- or 10-foot lengths. But we've come up with a slot detail that allows the top to slip up into the ceiling framing, so that adds some flexibility. To be able to use this beautiful but expensive product in limited-budget projects like Wurster Hall café (at UC Berkeley) or Curly's Cove (more on this soon) makes us very happy. Sometimes that junkyard-dog mentality ends up enabling us to create elegant, detailed work in places that normally would have to settle for ordinary.

PART II. MATERIAL PALETTES

GLASS 101

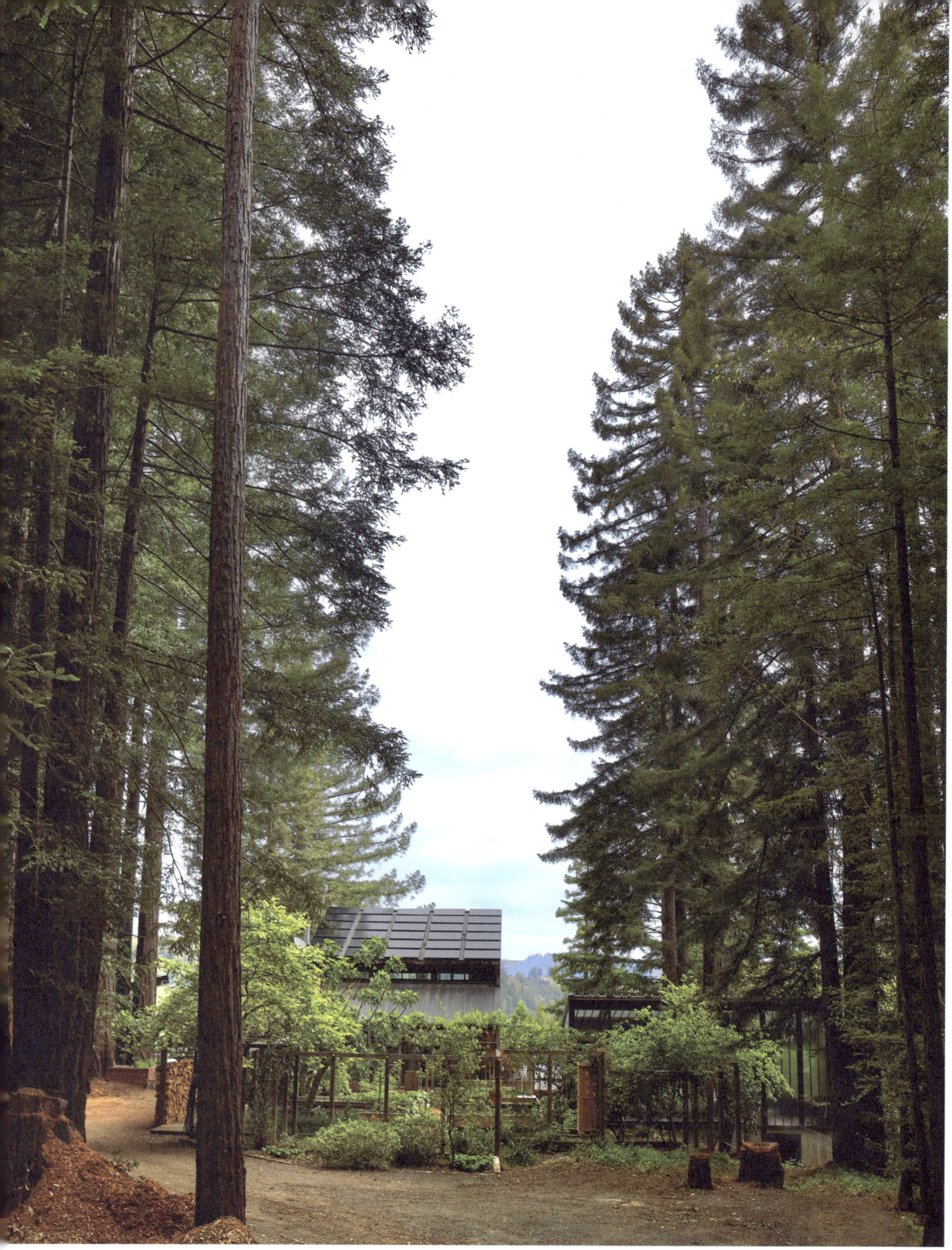

WOOD

There is nothing more beautiful, or more useful, than a tree. Trees nourish the planet, replenish our atmosphere, and provide habitat for so much of the wild/nonhuman world. To me, they are the embodiment of nature, and even when they are cut into lumber, they remind us of our connection to that world, the world of the forest. I have lived in and around forests all my life; they are where I feel most at peace. So for me, the use of wood in our work is always an attempt to connect to the forest, to nature, and to the infinite beauty it always reveals.

The larger a piece of wood is, the more I tend to like it. Blocks, slabs, trunks, and root balls are, to me, very close to the actual tree because they haven't been processed much. A product such as veneer, while still evocative of the tree, has been so manipulated that it is difficult to sense the tree it came from. Also it is too perfect, too even. So much of wood's beauty comes from the imperfections—a knot, a check, a live edge. For that reason, we almost never use veneers and instead lean toward slabs and boards that reveal thickness, that recall the trunk of the tree.

opposite
Redwood forest, Sonoma

below
Breuer/Lundberg cabin and office

I admit to a particular affinity for root balls. Each one is an extraordinary organic sculpture. It is difficult to get them out of the ground, but when it's possible, the gift they offer to a piece can be stunning. If still attached to the trunk, then the root ball begins to reference the entire tree; it honors the whole.

104   PART II.   MATERIAL PALETTES

opposite top
Redwood root-ball table

opposite bottom row
Redwood table construction, base, and installation

right
Teak root ball, Mourad Restaurant

WOOD 105

106   PART II.   MATERIAL PALETTES

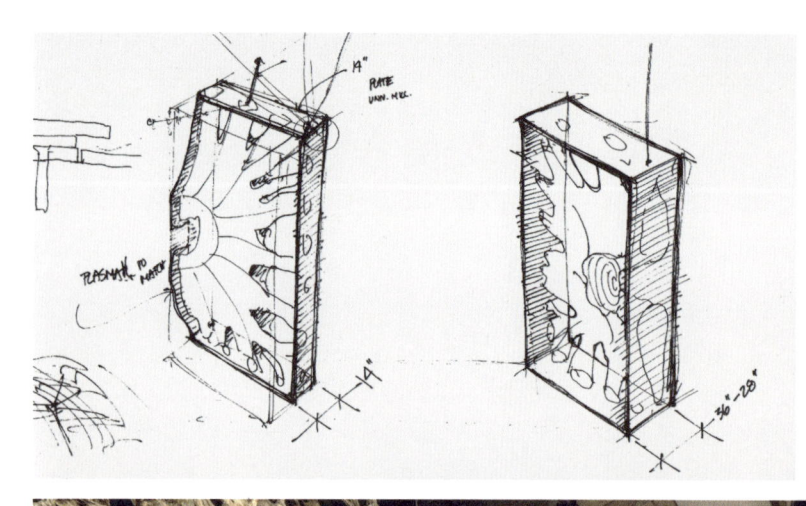

opposite
Root balls, process and finished installation

top left
VMware, end-cut, claro walnut log bench

top right
Redwood log transaction counter

middle left
Bookmatched walnut slabs with birch dovetails

middle right
Finger joint (reclaimed bowling lane), reception desk, Twitter

bottom left
Pine board with walnut dovetail

bottom right
Bookmatched black walnut slabs (electronics raceway)

WOOD

As architects, we tend to want to control the materials we use, and wood can be particularly challenging in this regard, for it is not at all inert. It takes on moisture, it shrinks and moves (and checks) as it dries, and in the presence of moisture it eventually decays. This is quite different from, say, stainless steel, but it is a design opportunity. A butterfly inlay to control a check calls attention to that act, emphasizing the imperfection and celebrating it. Charring wood renders the surface more impervious to decay. A finger-joined corner allows the wood to move without compromising the structure, or the appearance of the corner. Wood is full of imperfections, and in those imperfections lies the potential for expression in detail.

opposite
Black walnut conference table

above
"Uncle Burt" black walnut room divider

WOOD

PART II.   MATERIAL PALETTES

opposite
Maum Restaurant, Douglas fir tabletop, screens, and shelves, all milled from one tree

right
Flour + Water, walnut screens

WOOD 111

We have a redwood slab stored in the shop that I bought twenty-three years ago at an estate sale up in Mendocino. It is 3 inches thick, 17 feet tall, and 6 feet wide, with no sapwood (the sides were cut square). It was probably milled a hundred and fifty years ago. I have it strapped to the side of our stairs, which originally was just an efficient way to store it, but now, vertically is the only way I can see this piece. Only by standing next to it do you realize the scale of the tree, and the forest it came from. Upright it is still heroic; horizontal, it would be a fallen giant. I have never used this piece because I have never had a project worthy of it, but now I am designing a chapel where it will be the perfect backdrop for the altar. If you ask me if I believe in the divine, this wood slab will be my answer.

Don't forget the log. When we cut down a tree, we divide it into the branches, the log, and the root ball. As builders, the log is the most useful piece, and because it is so straight and so easy to subdivide, we tend to do just that. But sometimes the log deserves to be left alone; sometimes the branches and roots do too.

top
Root ball / slab inventory

above
Six-foot-wide redwood slab

right
Claro walnut log bench, detail

112   PART II.   MATERIAL PALETTES

top left
Twitter reception desk, Douglas fir
(reclaimed bowling lane), detail

top right
Twitter twig light, madrone

bottom left
Walnut slab room divider, detail

bottom right
Twitter dining room, reclaimed
Montana log cabin

WOOD   113

114   PART II.   MATERIAL PALETTES

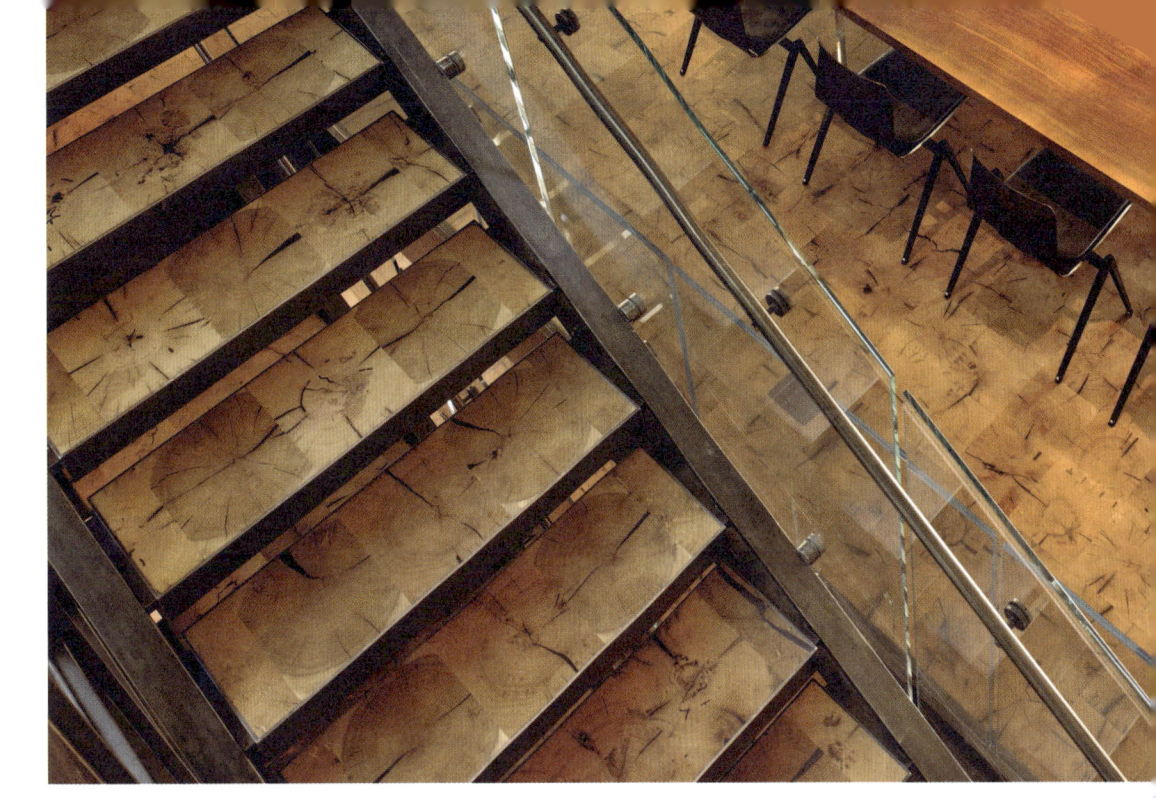

opposite
Oak tile floor, sliced from split firewood, Sonoma

right
Oak tile floor, sliced from reclaimed beams, San Francisco

PART II. MATERIAL PALETTES

FOUND OBJECTS

There is a history, and potentially an energy, that comes with a found object. The patina of age, the remnants of a past story, and the inherent uniqueness of a survivor are all latent when you find something to repurpose. The challenge lies in knowing how much to alter it. How do you make it into something new without destroying its acquired patina, its soul?

We make a fixture called the Buoy Light, a pendant light that utilizes old ship buoys. These are steel spheres that sat in salt water, where they have been struck by ships, encrusted with various forms of marine life, shat on by seagulls, and often repainted several times. What I like about the Buoy Light is that it started out its life perfect—sheets of steel exactly formed and welded into a watertight sphere. Then it was placed in that magical zone where land meets the sea, the literal source of life, to react to the elements. There is so much life in saltwater surf, and its caress transforms all it touches, especially steel. Often there are stray electrical currents present near the shoreline, and these, combined with the salt water and a sacrificial metal, create the ideal environment for a battery, which leads to accelerated corrosion. The moment the buoy hits the water, it starts to rust. Any microscopic flaw in the paint, any scratch, initiates the process of decay. But it is that decay—the colors of it, the textures, its accidental nature—that I find so beautiful. Like an autumn maple leaf held in your hand, you cannot replicate it. All you can do is celebrate the finding.

opposite
The *Maritol* docked at Pier 54, San Francisco

right
Oyster shell embedded in steel buoy

overleaf left
Various buoys being converted to light fixtures

118 PART II.   MATERIAL PALETTES

FOUND OBJECTS 119

previous right
"Death Star" buoy light with salmon counterweight

below
Installing and fabricating buoy lights

opposite
Buoy light at Hardwater

We start by cutting the buoy in half, making it into a dome. Then we sand and paint the interior a bright white, an intentionally stark contrast to the mottled patina of the exterior. In doing so, we abstract the form. It is, to most, no longer immediately recognizable as a buoy. Is this important? Yes and no—the object is what it is, crafted by humans and time. Its previous life, its history, is not relevant to one's appreciation of the form. But there is something endearing about discovering its story. It makes the piece unique and gives it a personality. Most of its history has disappeared, yet enough remains—a dent where a ship struck square, paint layers that somehow survived the corrosion cycle, a particularly stubborn oyster—to make each piece singular.

I think the history, often only possible to guess at, is what makes reclaimed objects so appealing. Each has a unique story, and the craftsperson and the client become part of that story. The key is in the altering, the adaptation, of the object into something new. Otherwise it is just an artifact, a remnant. Those can be very beautiful on their own, as antiques, but that is not what we are trying to find. I am looking for things that I can see differently, that I can change with my hand. I want to respect the history of the thing while adding to it. I want to give it new life. At our best, those pieces become art.

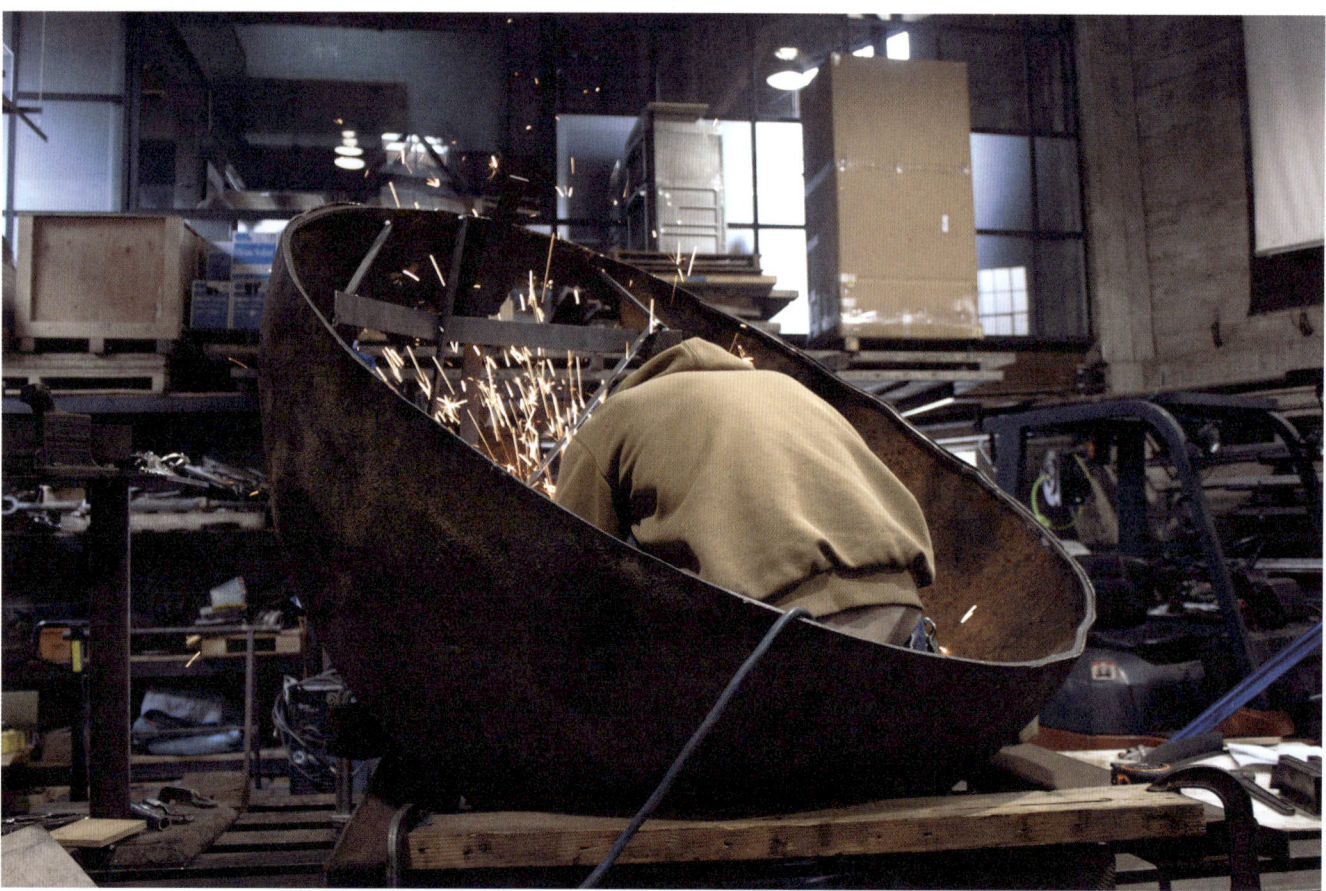

FOUND OBJECTS

Working with reclaimed materials requires hands-on attention and is very different from fabricating something from scratch. It is a dialogue, a response to the energy of the object, and you have to be there to tap into that. It is the equivalent of holding a pebble in your hand, turning it over and over until you suddenly see it in a new light. You can't do that from a picture or a drawing; you need the tactile connection, and in the end I find that I need to build it myself. What I mean is that I need to guide the making; in fact, the shop crew is much better at this than I, and I learn from them every day. This part of the process is a team effort. We play with the piece, we turn it over, trying to find the moment when our imagination discovers some hidden potential. Often, the hardest part is knowing when to stop.

My friend Andy Goldsworthy makes many of his sculptures this way. He finds streams, downed trees, piles of stone, thorns, leaves, even raindrops, and then he manipulates them. He adds a line, a geometric gesture, a pattern, and in doing so, he often makes, for the briefest of moments, a work of art in collaboration with nature. But so much of his work is about him first finding the right objects.

top
A Table for Mauree

above
Steel pipe scraps cut into uniform lengths

opposite
Hourglass Winery entrance, reclaimed wine bottles

FOUND OBJECTS 123

below
Hourglass Winery entrance, details

opposite
Repurposed shipping containers

Sometimes you find things that are just too strong on their own, and you have to leave them alone. Sometimes you can incorporate these pieces into something larger, and in doing so, harness their energy. For me, these are usually natural objects, not human-made things. A stone, a piece of a tree, or a weathered bone are objects I often notice on my walks in the woods. Fundamentally they all represent some stage of decay—the bone is from an animal long gone, the stick from a tree now fallen, the stone from a mountain ground down to tiny pieces. Perhaps in this realization lies my attraction to the reclaimed object. It is about celebrating the beauty of decay, the momentary arresting of that inexorable march. Perhaps the beauty lies in the cycle of life, death, and rebirth—and in the expression of that fundamental reality.

FOUND OBJECTS 125

126 PART II. MATERIAL PALETTES

opposite
Sunnyvale interior, 56 Blocks, reclaimed circuit boards

right
Odin's palm, found redwood log

below
Manifold tables

bottom left
Peg-leg table and bowl, turbine vane and cylinder cap

bottom right
Detail, reclaimed turbine vane

FOUND OBJECTS 127

> *I remember rooms that have had their part*
> *In the steady slowing down of the heart.*"
> —Charlotte Mew, "Rooms," ca. 1920s

FIVE PROJECTS

ROLLING WALL MUSEUM

LAVA HOUSE

CURLY'S COVE

DOGLEG HOUSE

THE CABIN

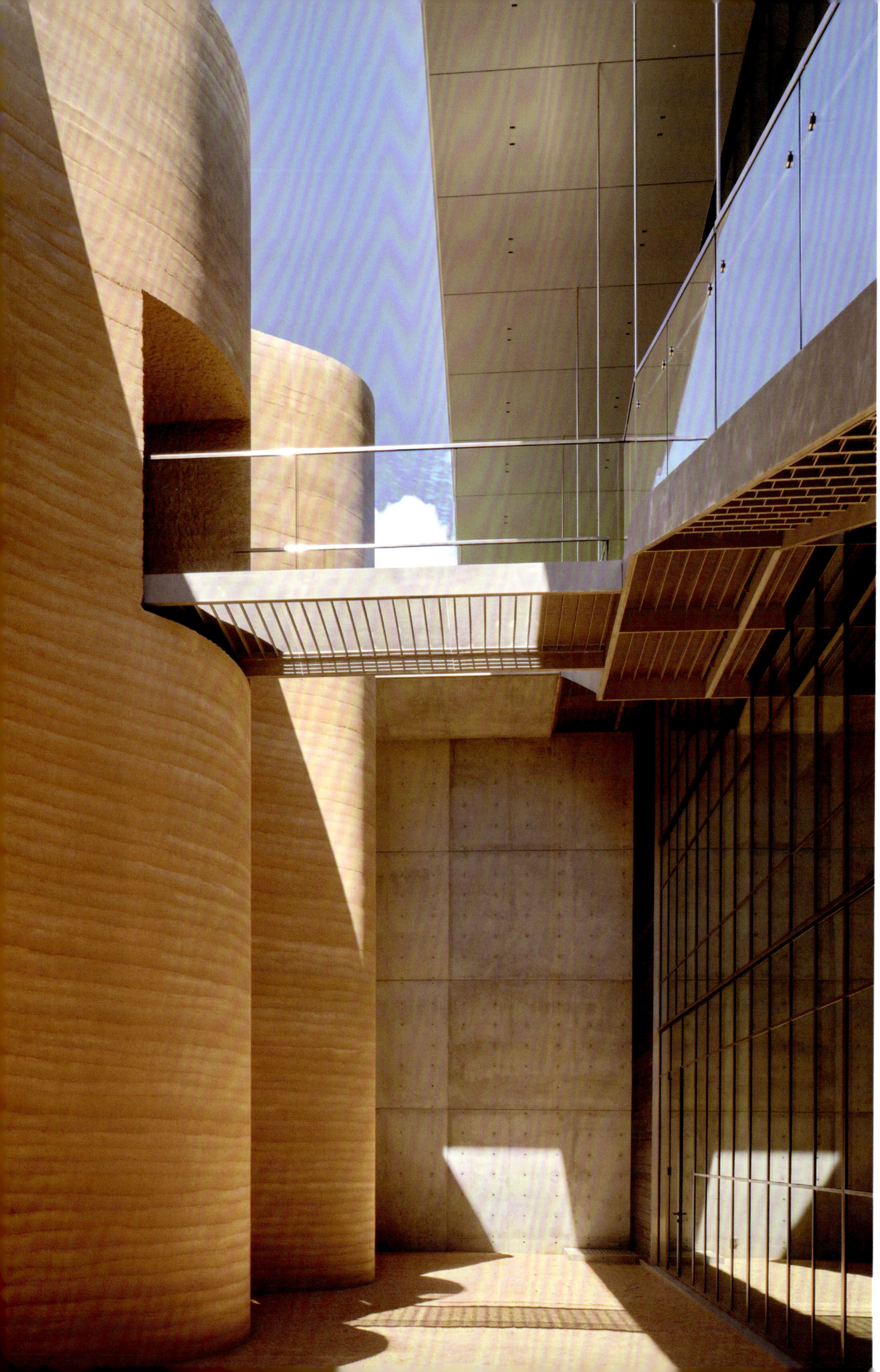

ROLLING WALL MUSEUM
2014–19

This is a private museum, built for a couple with an extraordinary calligraphy collection. It allows them to exhibit the work, and it enables scholars to stay at the museum as they study the collection. The site is in a residential neighborhood in the rolling hills overlooking San Francisco Bay.

Calligraphy is an extremely fragile art; the paper will decay with exposure to light, so exhibiting it can be a challenge. Our solution was to bury the exhibit area underground, but to create a "light canyon" on the south side that would block direct sunlight but allow reflected light into the space. The building has five stories, three of which are subterranean, and from the street it appears to be a single-story flat-roofed structure. It actually sits lower than the two-story ranch house that used to occupy the site. The top level (level 5), at which you enter, is an entertainment area with a view of the Bay, a large dining table, a commercial kitchen, and a conference room. The next level down (level 4) has two guest rooms, a traditional tea ceremony room and garden by Hiroshi Sugimoto, and a bridge to the subterranean parking garage. The next two levels (levels 3 and 2) are the exhibit hall levels, and the bottom level is collection storage and mechanical space.

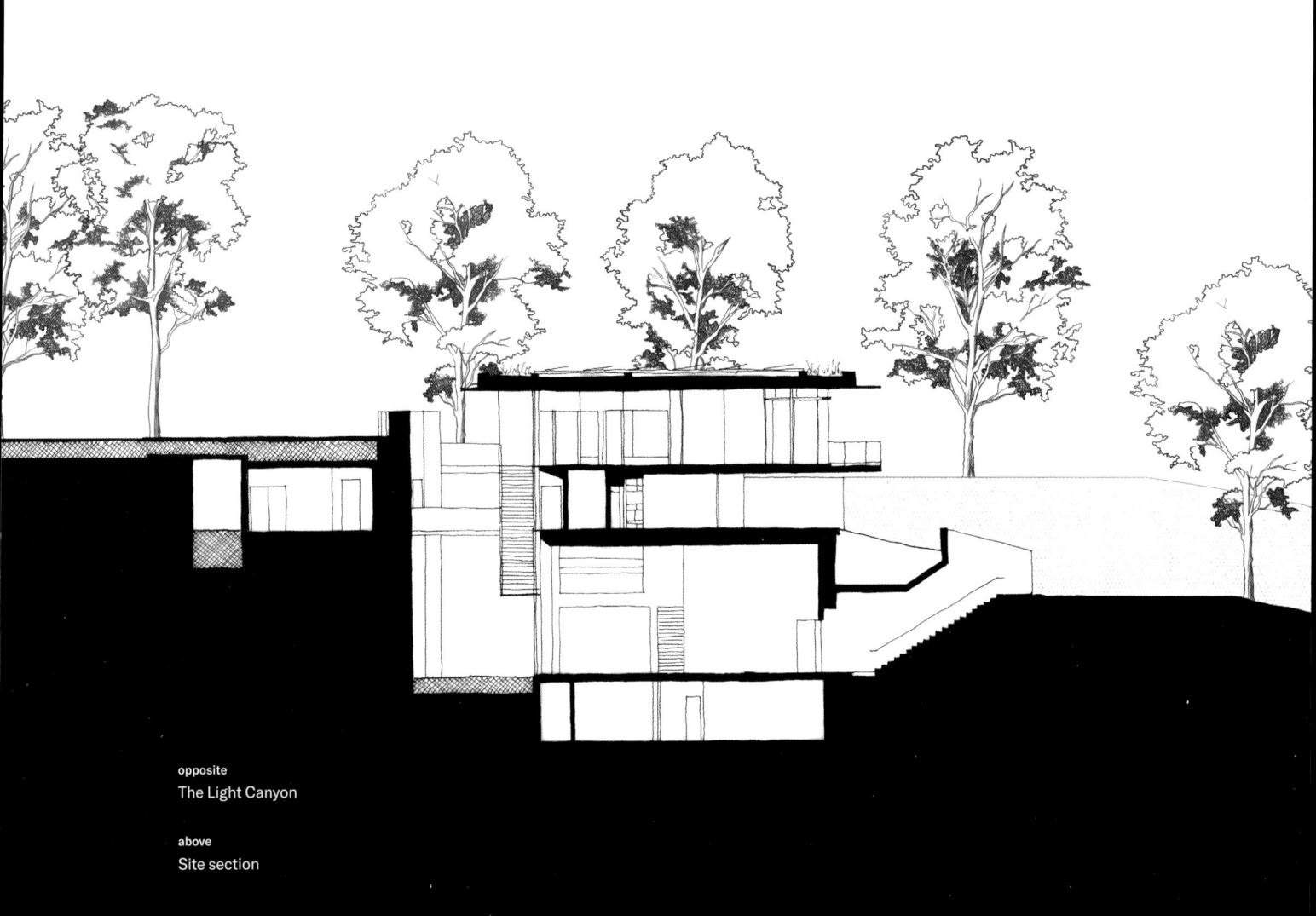

opposite
The Light Canyon

above
Site section

132   PART III.   FIVE PROJECTS

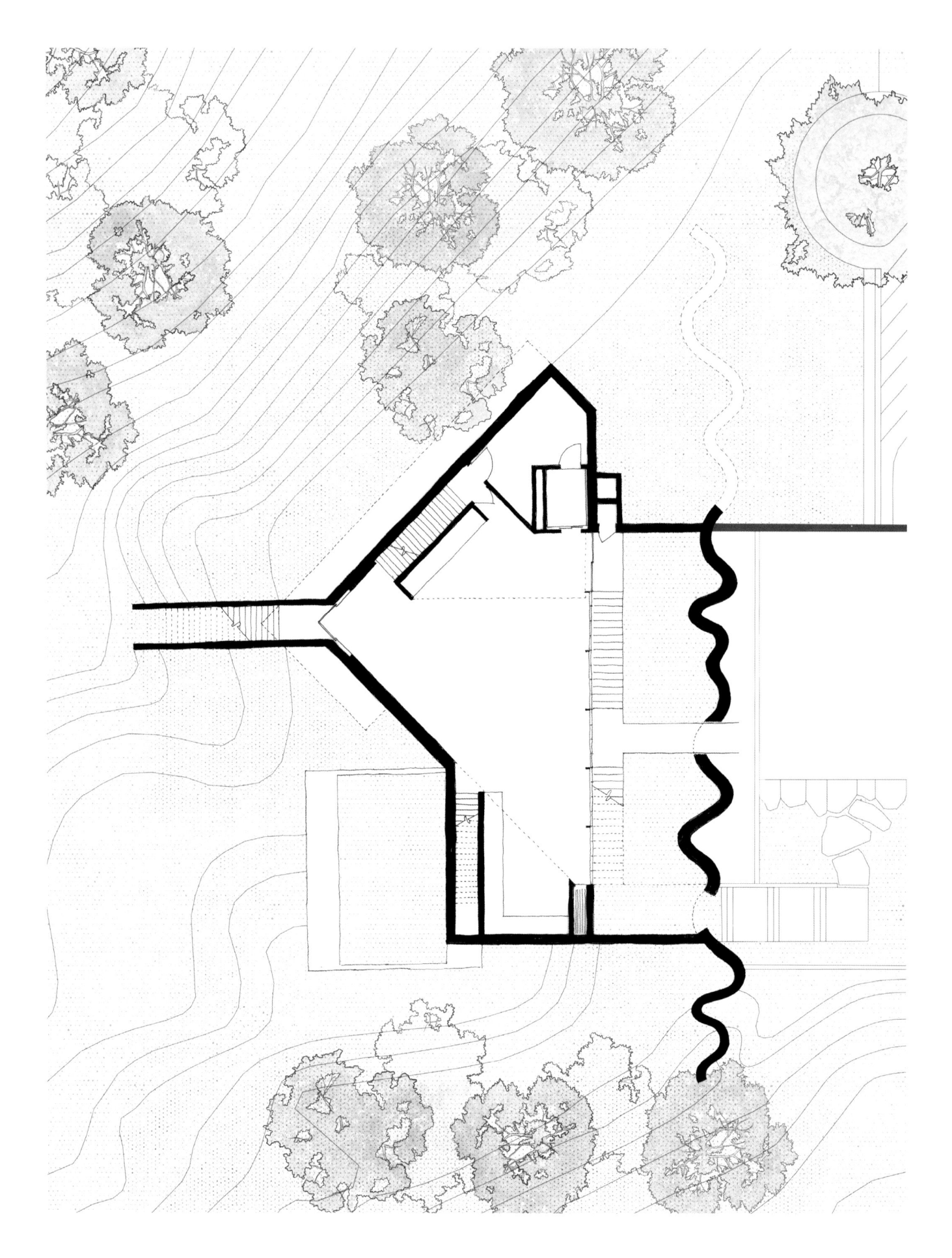

This basic design concept was being developed when the general contractor, David Warner of Redhorse Constructors, suggested that perhaps we might want to consider contacting Andy Goldsworthy about designing the retaining wall for the light canyon. Now, this is not just any retaining wall; it is 40 feet tall and more than 80 feet long, and it is in earthquake country. My original concept had been a perfectly polished concrete wall, like I'd admired in so many of Tadao Ando's undertakings. But I loved Andy Goldsworthy's work, and the opportunity to meet him seemed too good to pass up, although I suspected he wouldn't be interested in doing a piece that was so integral to a building, a piece that would not stand alone. Luckily, I was wrong.

We visited Andy at a site in Marin where he was making a stone piece that diverted a seasonal creek into a chamber housing a stone cairn. All of the stones were from the adjacent creek bed, and he had his crew of UK stonemasons with him. This crew is a wonder to watch. They understand the stone, and can shape it with an economy of effort, then fit it with remarkable precision. We'd made an appointment, but Andy was working with a grinder and didn't look up for an hour. That was fine; it was a treat to watch them all work. Now, Andy can be a bit of a curmudgeon (many of my favorite people are), and when he finally acknowledged me, he said he needed to shower but that if I wanted to stick around, he'd meet with me after that. He seemed a little suspicious of this architect poking around, and I could tell he thought this was probably a waste of time. But I had surmised that he might be hard to convince, so I'd brought a bottle of bourbon, a twelve-year-old Willett that I thought might make a nice introduction for him to American whiskey. He brightened up considerably when I pulled out the bottle, and over a glass we had a lively and provocative discussion about the wall. It is not the first time I've made friends over a glass of bourbon, but it might be the most memorable. I try to send him a bottle every year as a thank-you.

opposite
Site plan: gallery level

right
Olle and Andy during construction

overleaf
Rear facade

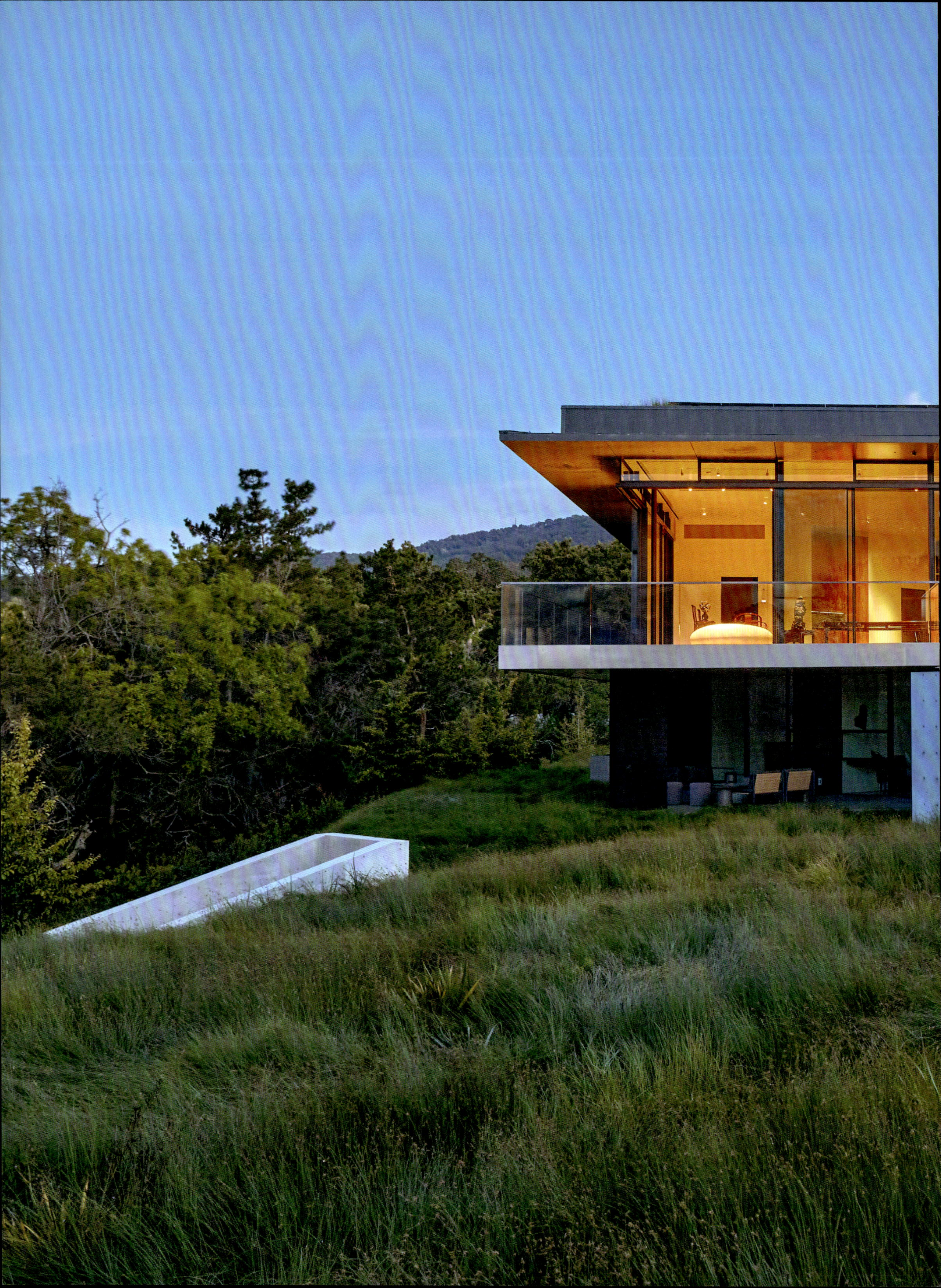

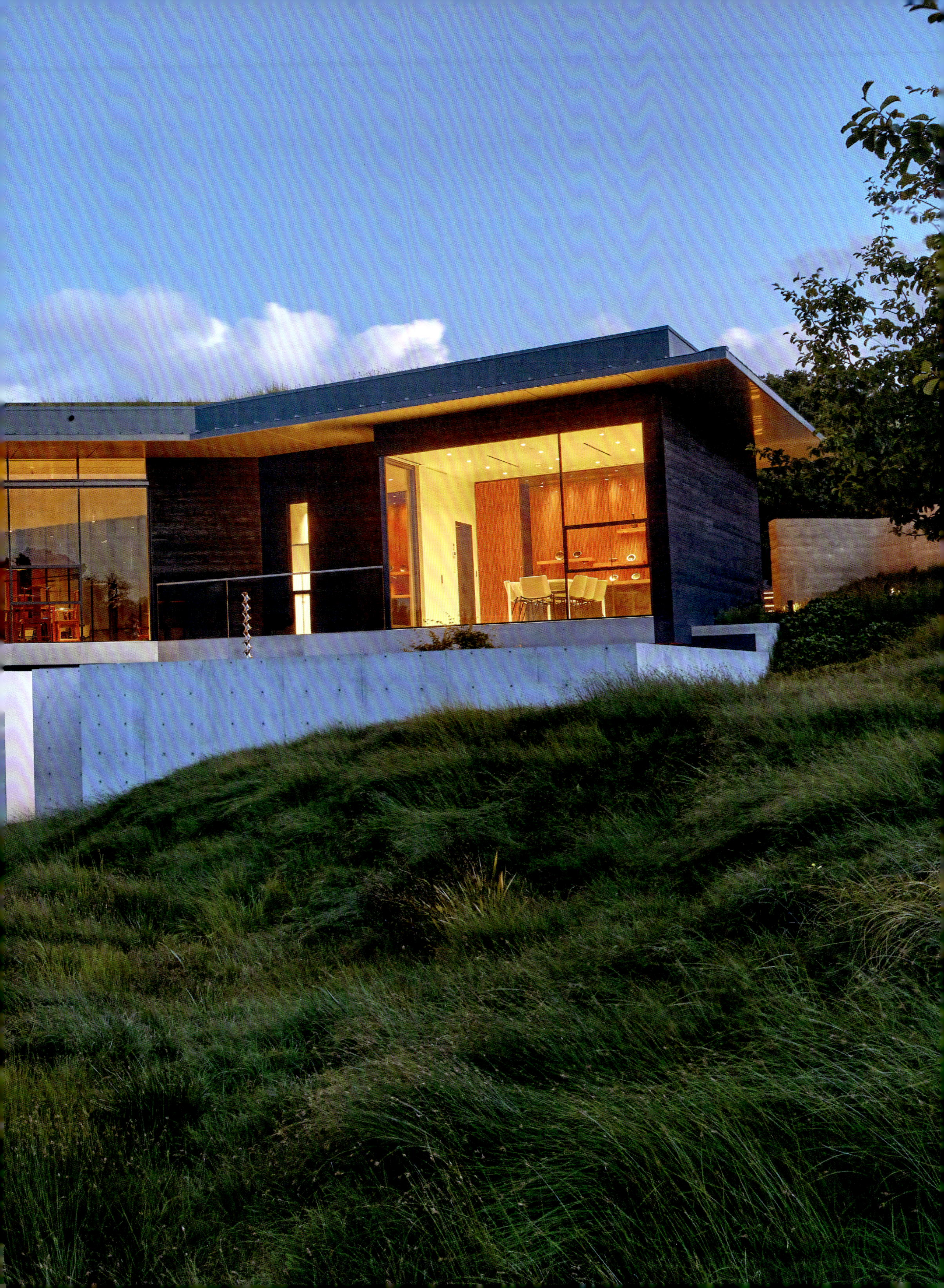

Most of the museum design was completed before Andy became involved, but I knew that the wall of the light canyon needed to be special, so in a way I was designing in anticipation of the gift he gave us. Despite the fact that we very deliberately made it, our idea was to treat it like a kind of found object—something extraordinary discovered on the site that we reacted to. The glass facade that faces his wall is an enlarged version of steel industrial sash windows. I wanted the tiling effect of the window mullions, for each pane frames a different piece of the wall, making each rectangle a unique piece of art in and of itself. In certain light conditions, the glazing will reflect back the grid pattern onto the wall. While there is an indoor elevator that can take you to the various levels, the staircase is outside the glazed wall and puts you in the light canyon, between the glass and the wall, so you are constantly aware of the effect of the wall on the building: the form, the colors of the earth, the shadows it casts, and its sheer weight, both actual and implied.

above
Top-level view of the wall

opposite
Main stair

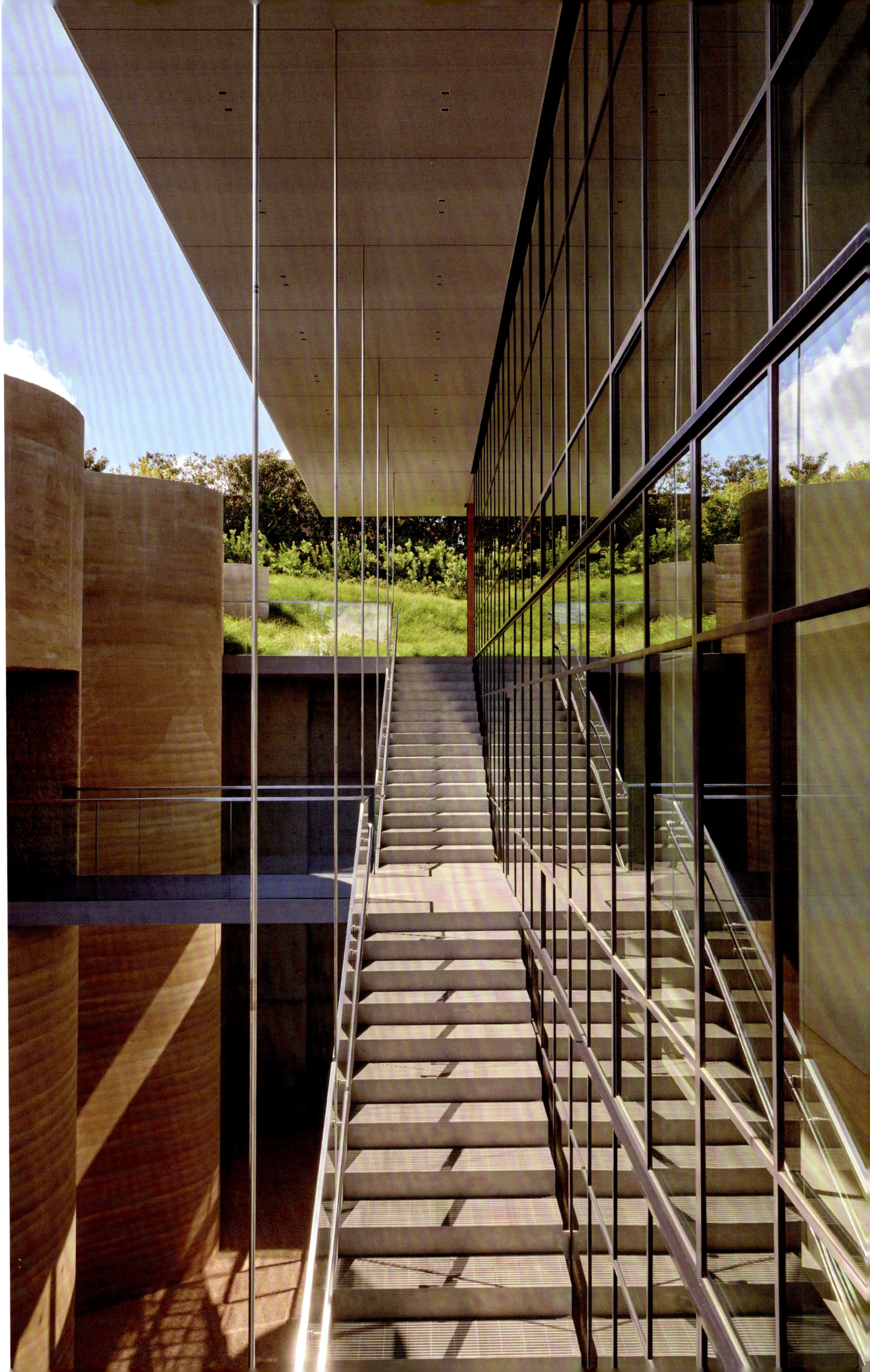

PART III. FIVE PROJECTS

The top floor, devoted to meetings and entertainment, barely peeps over the top of the wall. When you look down from this level into the canyon, you are struck by the scale. As you enter from the parking area, only the top few feet of the wall are visible, with one notch revealing a path leading to the front door. As you pass through the notch, you step onto a bridge that spans the canyon 35 feet below, and suddenly what appeared to be a one-story building is clearly four stories tall. It is a rather dramatic moment.

At the next level down, the guest level, the focus turns north to the view of the hillside and the Bay beyond. The function is more private, so only the circulation hallway looks out to the canyon.

The two levels below are the museum. When you reach the lower of the two, you can walk out into the light of the canyon, you can touch the wall, and you can feel the solidity of the rammed earth on one side versus the transparency of the glazing on the other. For me, the experience of this building, and Andy's wall, is about that sense of pressure. The wall is so solid, so compressed. It is the hillside that the building has broken free of, yet they still cling to each other, bound by light. The building and the wall are two separate things, yet they define each other. That is also as good a description as any of our collaboration.

opposite
Rolling wall from above

above
Bridge to garage, shadow pattern
from window wall reflection

right
Rear deck with gallery stair below

below
View from main level toward San Francisco Bay

opposite
Staircase from gallery level to rear landscape

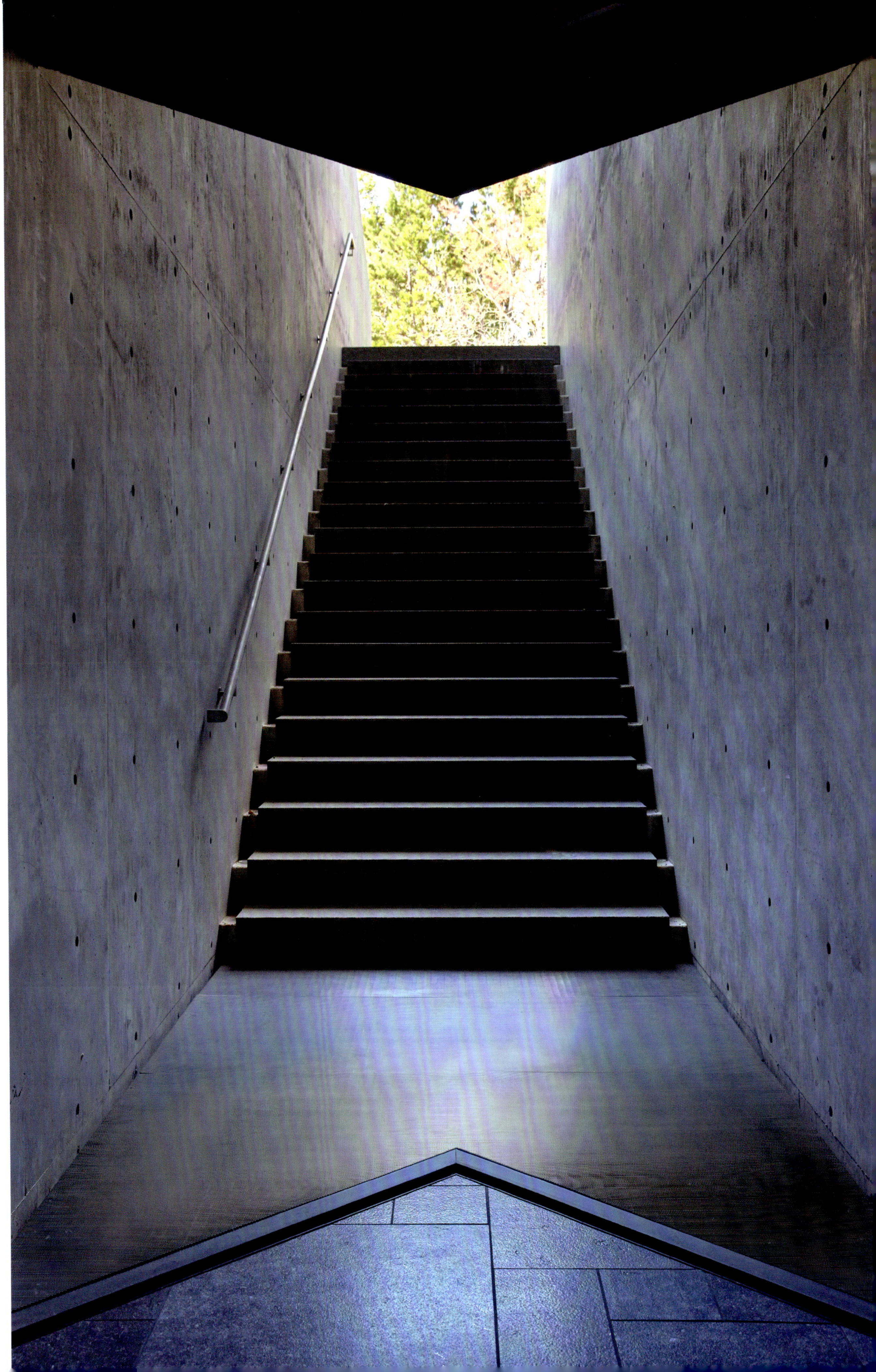

top
Gallery main level

bottom
Goldsworthy exhibit

opposite top
Gallery level, reflected light on wall

opposite bottom
Gallery, Goldsworthy exhibit

142 PART III. FIVE PROJECTS

ROLLING WALL MUSEUM 143

PART III. FIVE PROJECTS

The greatest challenge for the wall was not the design—Andy had plenty of ideas—but rather the material. His work is about the place where it is made, typically from materials gathered locally. Our site had almost nothing—no stones, no harvestable trees—but we did have a lot of soil (40 feet of excavation for the building). So he settled on the idea of using the soil to make rammed earth, a process in which soil is mixed with cement powder, then compacted in 8-inch lifts. He had done a small rammed-earth work in the Presidio a year or so earlier, at which time he'd met David Easton, the worldwide expert on rammed-earth technology, who also happened to have his studio in Napa. We had our team.

Andy had two initial ideas for the wall, the first being a series of root spheres buried and then partially exposed, and the second a version of the serpentine forms that recur in his works. The spheres spoke to the idea of display and collection, but they would have to be made from wood gathered elsewhere, and in the end, I think that bothered him. The serpentine wall would involve using the detritus of the construction process, and the purity of that idea won out. I suggested that he come to my studio and we could clear out the shop for him to work on the design. We moved much of the machinery and made a space where we could roll out butcher paper on the floor and he could draw the wall at one-third scale.

If I had to pick a favorite day I've ever had in the studio, it would be the first day of Andy working there. I stayed out of his way, only looking in on occasion, but it all felt so collaborative. We'd talked about how I wanted the light to modulate and change as it reflected off the wall, and how critical the play of light across it would be. But that was probably my only comment. Watching him work on hands and knees, drawing and erasing, then running upstairs to look down on the drawing, then running back quickly to make a change—it was a rare window into the process of a master, and once again our studio rewarded us.

Then we had the problem of building a rammed-earth wall at a scale beyond anything that had been done before. David Warner and David Easton deserve most of the credit for figuring it out. Because of the wall's location on the site, we had to build it first, for the building would otherwise have been in the way of the giant excavators and crane needed to set and pull the forms. The Davids came up with the idea of using huge Styrofoam blocks cut with resistance wire as the curved face formwork, but given the considerable forces put on the formwork during the ramming phase, those blocks had to be reinforced with steel and tied together. Then once the work had hardened, the form had to be removed without damaging the piece. David Warner came up with the idea of placing all the Styrofoam blocks on Teflon pads, and then having two excavators pull the entire formwork away from the wall in one dramatic tug. When it released, it sounded like a bolt of lightning (perhaps Thor's approval), and it worked perfectly.

I felt curiously, strangely ambivalent about the wall once it was stripped. The scale was odd—it was too large standing by itself, and looked out of place. It needed the building to work. I think that is why this was such a great collaboration: neither the wall nor the building would have worked independently. It was the marriage of the two that made this project so special. I will be forever grateful to Andy, our clients, and the Davids for making that happen. What a treat the entire process was.

opposite
Andy Goldsworthy at LD studio

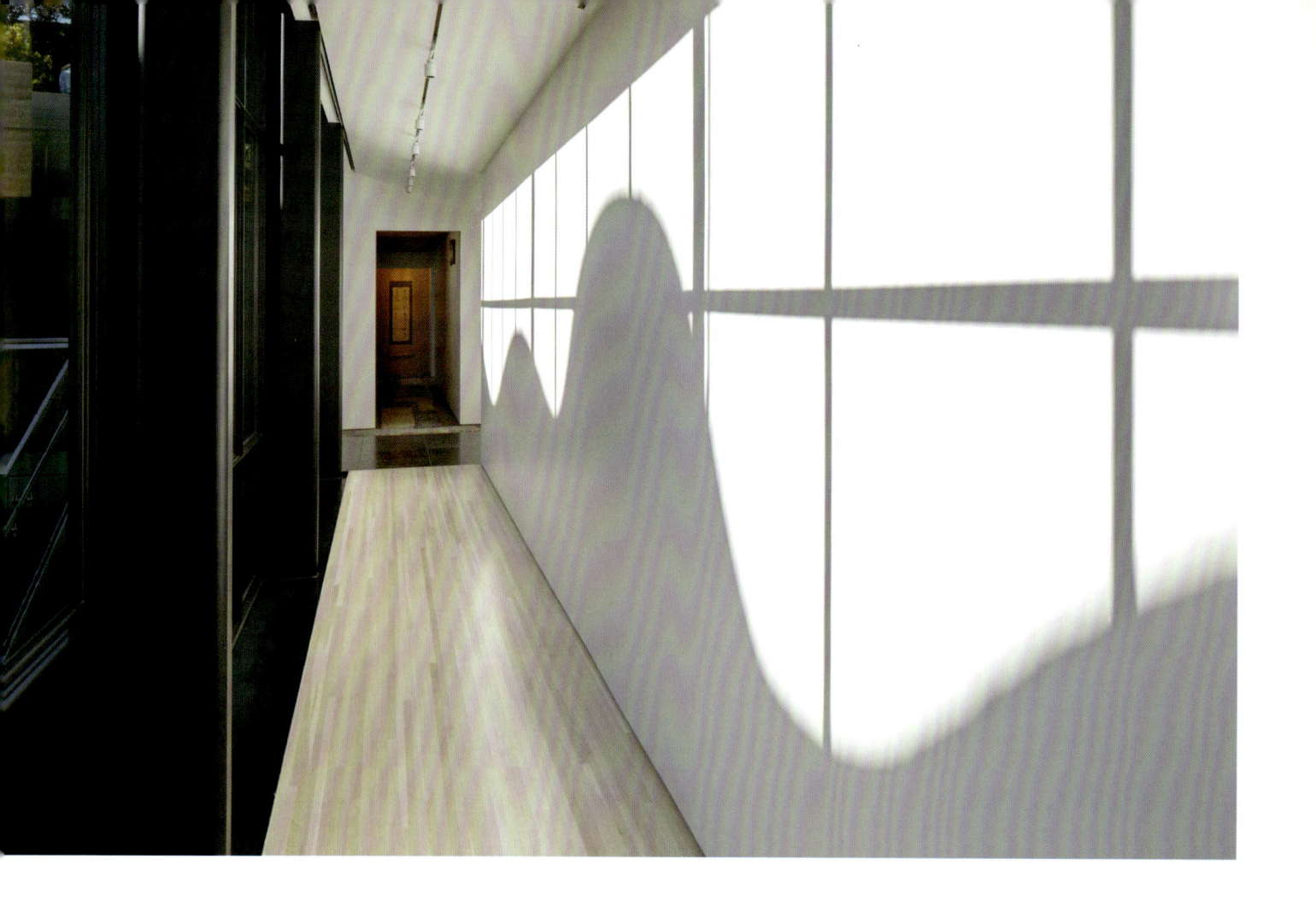

above
Top of wall shadow

opposite top
Bridge to garage level and bourbon bunker

opposite bottom row
Building formwork; outside form being removed; completed wall

146   PART III.   FIVE PROJECTS

ROLLING WALL MUSEUM 147

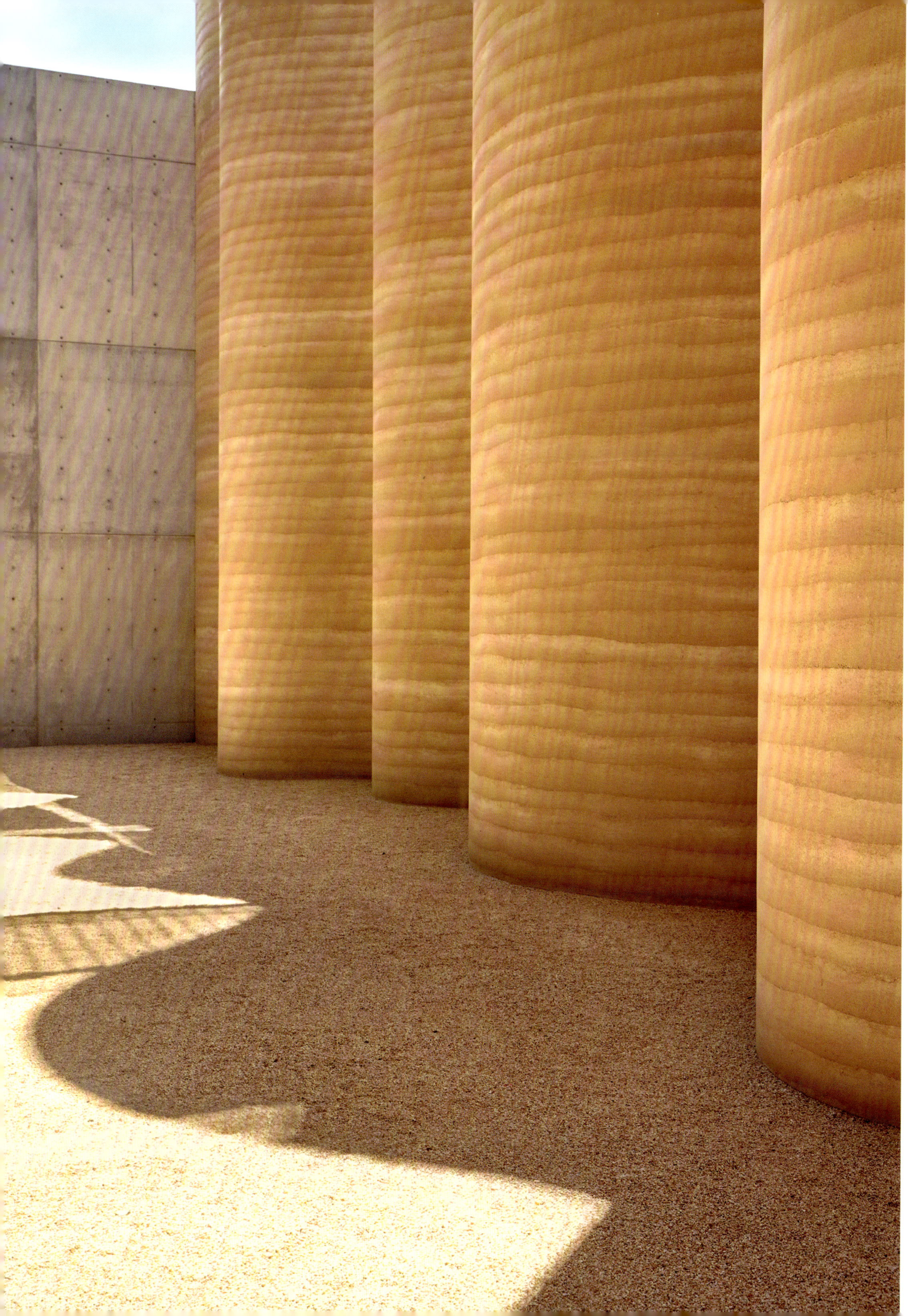

The wall has now been in place for a few years. Rammed earth initially looks quite perfect, almost polished, but it is relatively soft compared to concrete. It weathers. Cracks appear, the surface begins to erode, and its appearance begins to soften. The last two winters have been wet in Northern California, and with that we have a surprise gift: moss! It will be interesting to see how this evolves. As winter ends, the moss will die back, but I suspect in wet conditions it will return ever stronger. Beyond being beautiful, I love that nature is taking possession of the wall. If you squint, the moss pattern almost reads like calligraphy.

opposite
Wall shadow slightly after noon

above
Rolling wall moss and moss detail

ROLLING WALL MUSEUM   149

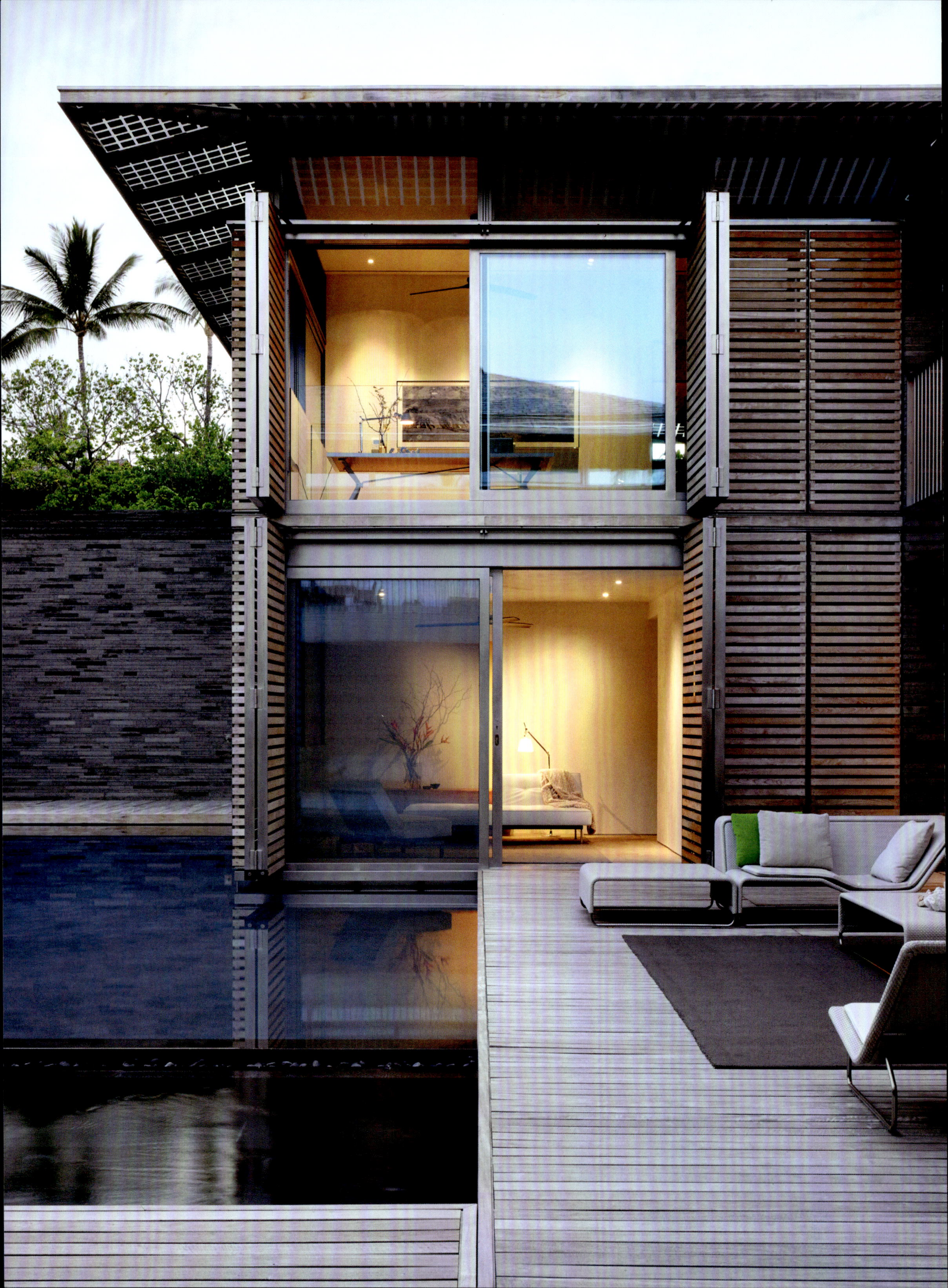

LAVA HOUSE
2006–12

The site for Lava House was an oceanfront lot on Hawai'i, the Big Island. The setbacks and height limit dictated a one-story structure, but the program would have completely filled the site, allowing very little room for landscaping. So that was the first challenge. The typical contemporary Hawaiian beachfront home is generally some version of a U-shaped plan, with an auto court in the center of the U. Within the center wing is the entry and great room; one side wing is the garage and kitchen and other service areas; and in the other wing are the bedrooms. One enters through the front door directly into the great room, on axis with the view to the ocean, and that room opens out to the pool terrace beyond, often with an infinity pool.

Now, there are a few things that I find problematic with this diagram. First, it places too much emphasis on the car, whose formal entry dictates the house shape. All the wings have windows that look out onto the auto court, which then have to be screened with vegetation, essentially blocking any sort of depth within the view beyond. Second, I've never liked walking directly into the main space of a house. There should be a moment after one enters the front door that compresses space—that welcomes you inside and sets you up for a drama waiting to unfold. Third, there is the location of the pool, which sits in the foreground of the view out toward the water. The concept of this placement is borrowed from modern bungalows in Indonesia and the like, where the vanishing-edge pool blends into the horizon, creating the illusion of an infinite expanse of water. In theory and in architectural photographs, that works, but the reality of outdoor kitchens and poolside furniture and toys puts objects in the foreground that disturb the illusion. You are always looking at a bunch of stuff instead of the beauty beyond. Finally, there is the issue of the wind. Off the ocean is typically the most exposed part of the site, and with the pool sitting where it does, the structure of the house does not provide any windbreak.

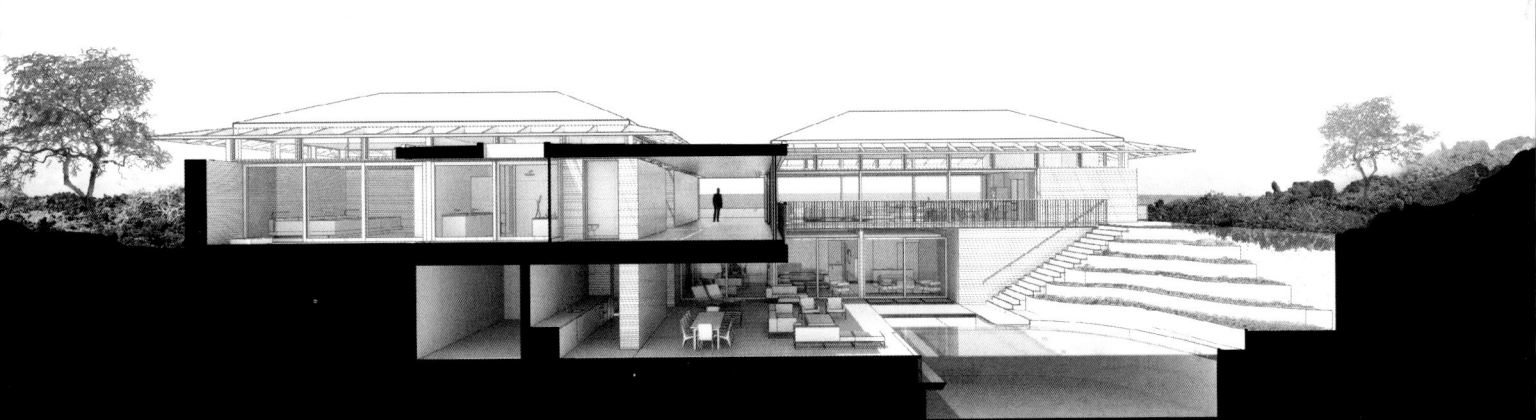

PART III. FIVE PROJECTS

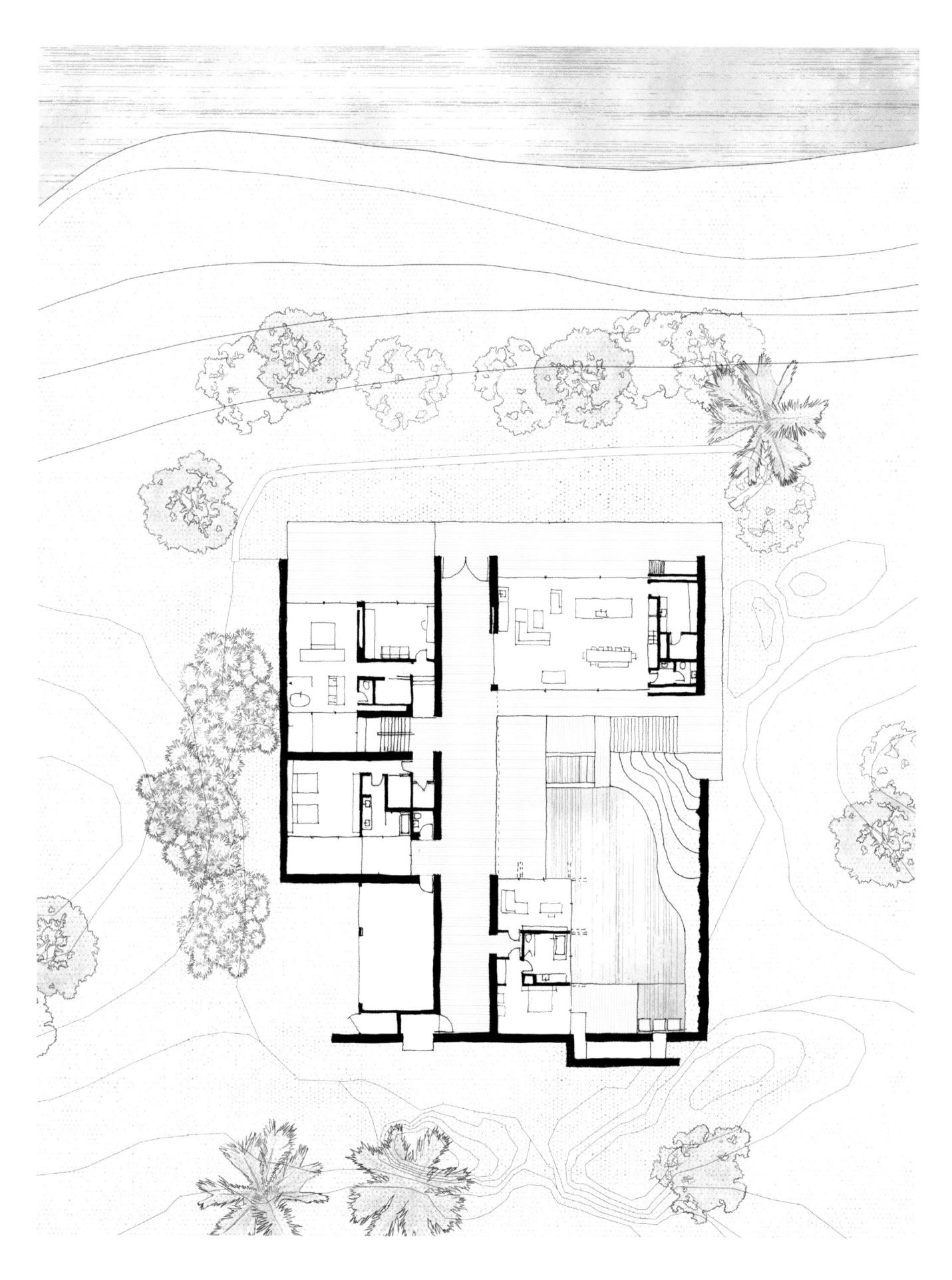

The idea for Lava House emerged from those challenges. We would excavate most of the site down an entire level, 12 feet below the existing ground plane, so the mass of the house could surround an interior courtyard one story below the entrance level. When you dig near the coast, you often hit water; the lava is porous and the groundwater near the shore is typically seawater. So here we placed the pool, as though we had uncovered a subterranean water source. With the house surrounding it, and it being one level down, the pool is completely sheltered from the prevailing winds off the ocean. This also gave us a "basement" level that would look out onto the pool area, effectively giving us a two-story house where we were allowed to build only 16 feet above the original grade, including the mandatory pitched roof.

The climate in Hawai'i makes you want to live outside. A little shelter is nice, but you want to feel that moist, warm air caress your skin; it is the softest air I've ever experienced. So we designed all of the circulation spaces to be covered, but outside, with large, motorized sliding-glass doors opening up both the poolside and ocean-side walls of the main living space. The goal was to make the main rooms feel like they were covered outdoor spaces—lanais.

opposite
Site plan

above
View from guest wing toward main pavilion

top
Living room

above
Lanai

opposite
Office view toward main pavilion

154 PART III. FIVE PROJECTS

LAVA HOUSE 155

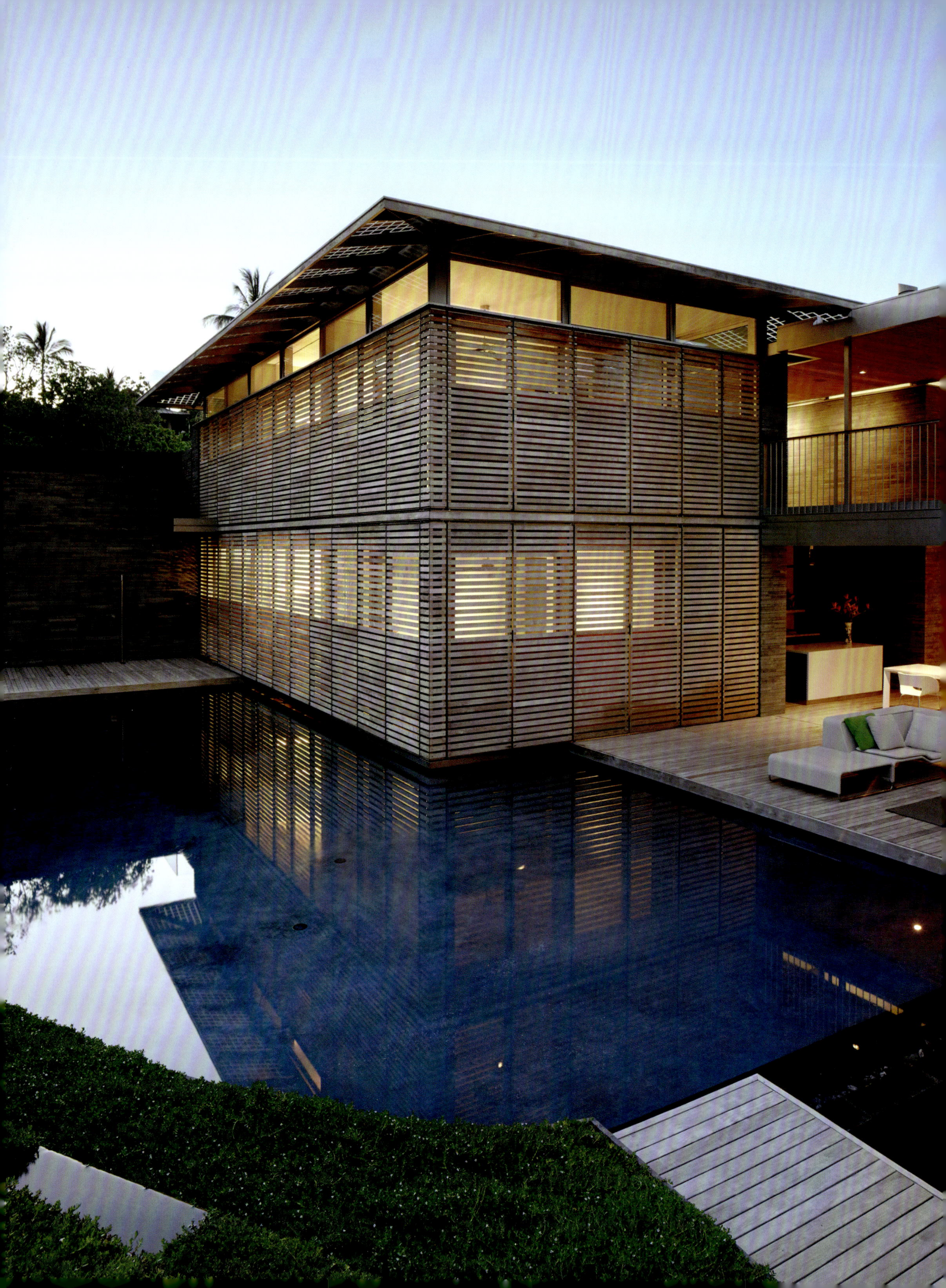

opposite
Guest wing with shutters closed

below
Shutters open at pool

LAVA HOUSE

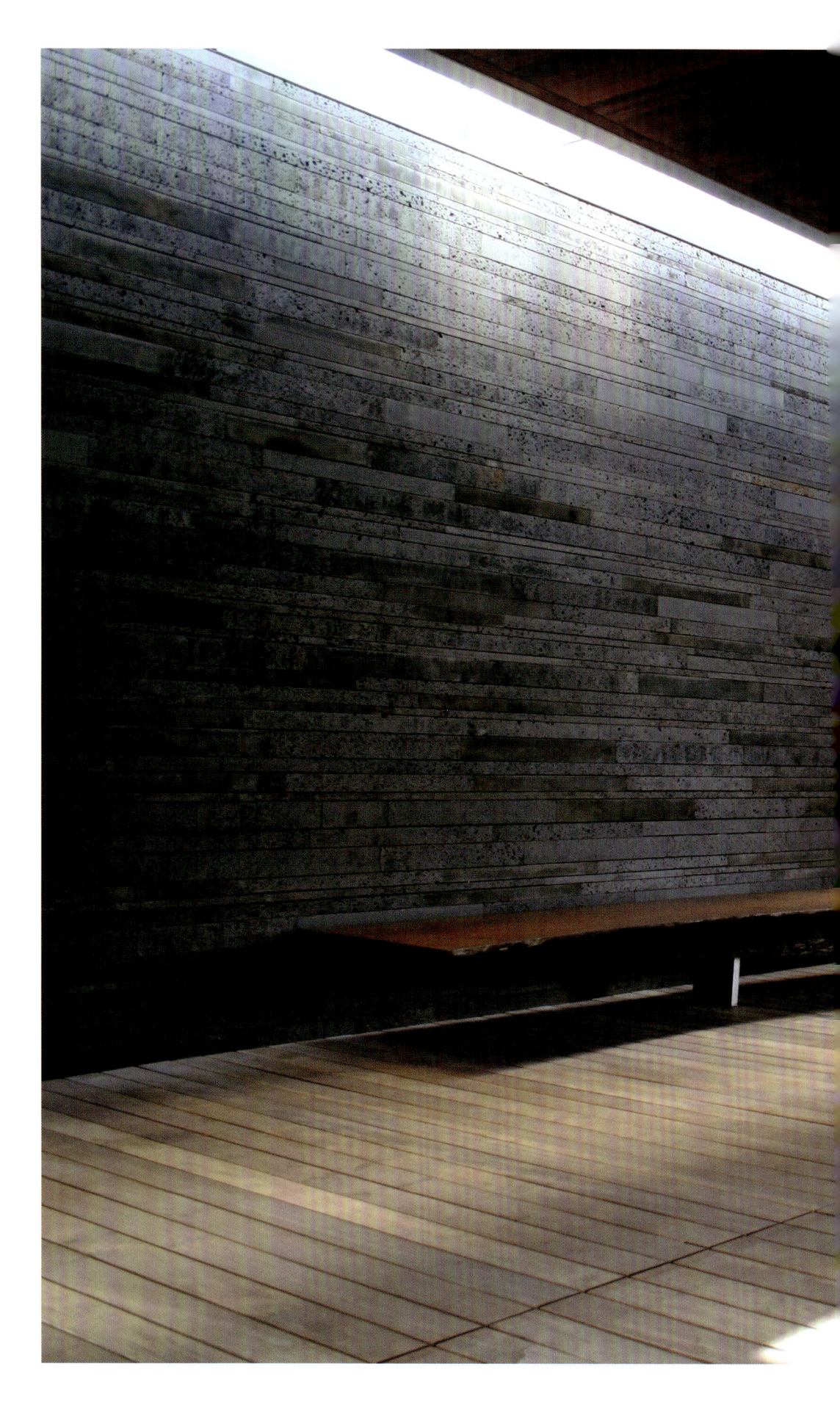

Entry lanai

LAVA HOUSE 159

To date this is the only stone building I've designed, and I loved the chance to use the lava. I had recently visited Peter Zumthor's Therme Vals outside Zurich, and I was captivated by his use of the local stone, stacked slabs of which make up the walls. It was like the building had been extruded out of the ground, out of the landscape, in a way that made it feel like part of the mountain. I wanted that sensation of my building having been pulled out of the heroic excavation we had done, and that excavation was in fact out of solid lava. Unlike the stone in Switzerland, which fractures along a plane (like slate), lava has no linear grain. When one applies force to a lava block, it breaks up into gravel. But lava boulders are often processed, like most building stone, into slabs. So the approach we used was to cut the lava into a variety of slab thicknesses and then stack those slabs, exposing the edges of the slabs, not the faces. When the lava was interior, we exposed the saw-cut face, basically a honed finish, and when the stone was exterior, we exposed a "broken" face. So, while the stone is the same inside and out, the texture and effect are completely different.

above
Driveway paving using edge-laid lava slabs

right
Lava block edge detail

far right
Lava wall installation

opposite
Gate and "wall jewels" at entry

160   PART III.   FIVE PROJECTS

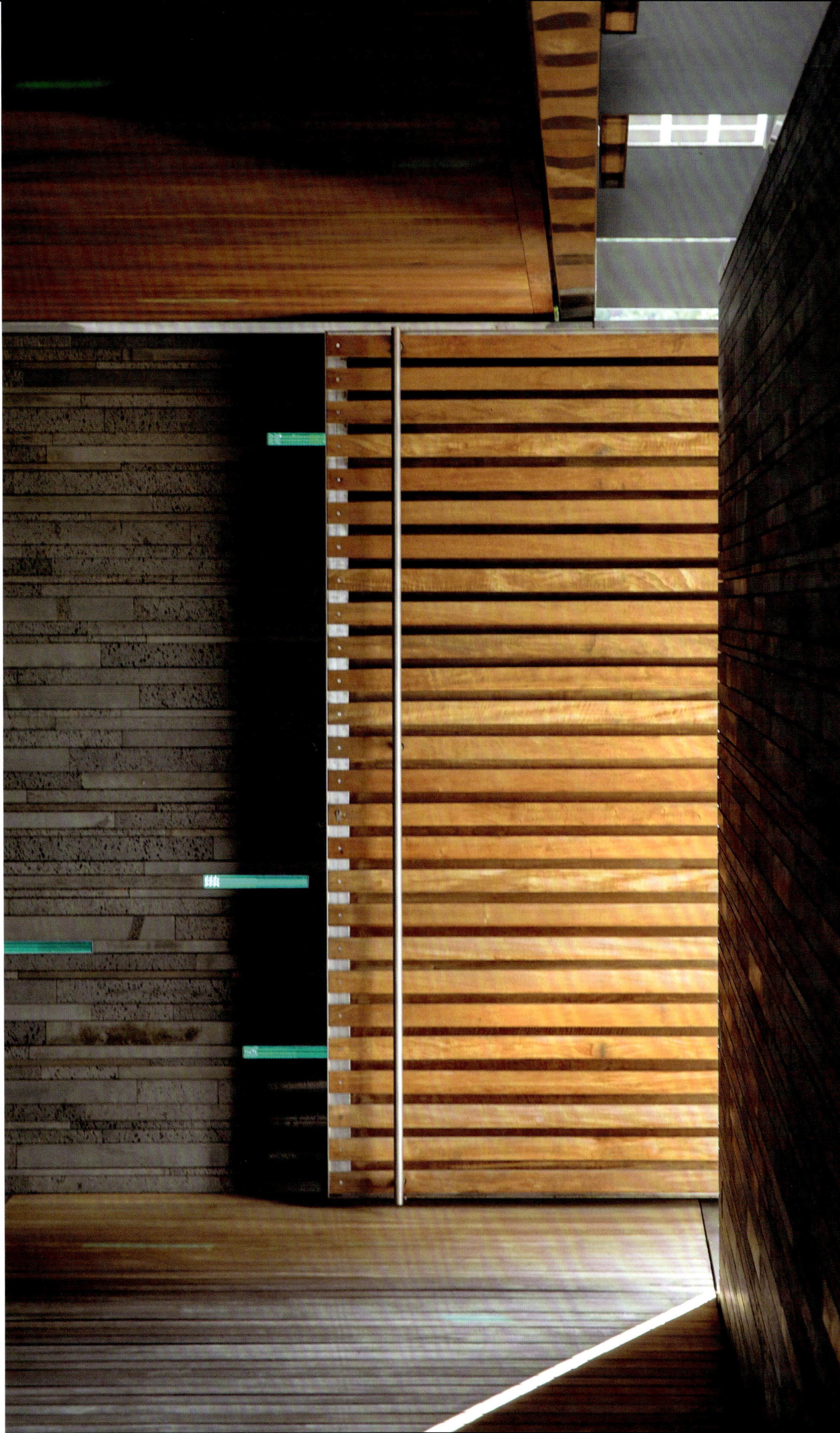

Within the stacked lava walls we placed, in a few special locations, an invention we came up with called "wall jewels." These were stainless steel sleeves that encapsulated stacked plate glass, allowing a stripe of light to penetrate the 2-foot-thick masonry walls. The beveled edges of the stacked glass pieces form prisms, which in certain light conditions refract a prismatic effect across the stone. At night, when the interior is lit, these stripes of light reveal themselves on the exterior, creating a light show where one would expect to see only a dark, solid mass.

The entrance to the house is one of those special spots. In the shop we built the wall jewels, the front door, and the bench—that last with an extraordinary piece of walnut from Arborica, a sawmill in Marshall, California. Of all the spaces I've designed over the years, this may be my favorite. The play of light, the drama of that long lanai leading to the main living area, the beach beyond, and the craftsmanship that surrounds you in that moment—it's as fine a space as we have ever made.

But my favorite lava story is about the blocks we used to build the retaining wall for the pool

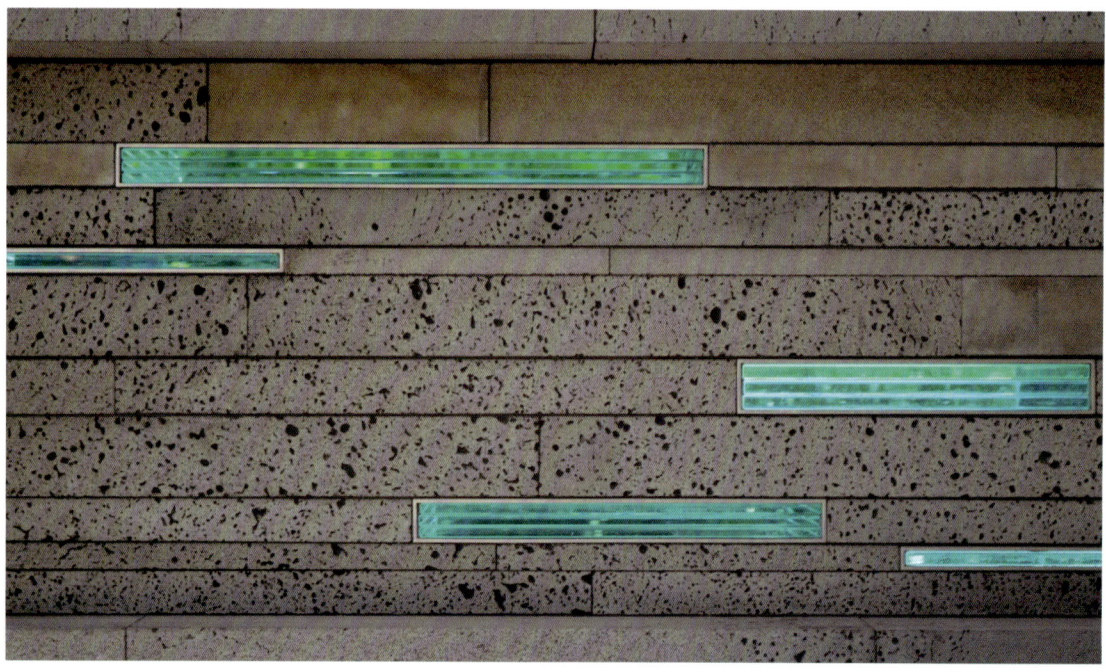

above
"Wall jewels," detail

right
Lava scrap pile at quarry

far right
Lava blocks arranged prior to installation

opposite
Lava block retaining wall at grotto

162   PART III.   FIVE PROJECTS

grotto. In doing our research for the lava slabs, we visited a quarry on the Big Island, where they were cutting slabs for the new Apple Store in Waikiki. Now this was a big project. The easiest way to mine lava is to take it from the surface, where the top face reflects however the molten lava cooled. There are four typologies of lava in Hawai'i—Pahoehoe, 'A'ā, Block, and Pillow—but the visual variety is almost infinite. The temperature of the flow, the speed of cooling, and the elements and minerals within all contribute to different surfaces and colors.

When we visited the quarry, they were cutting the Apple slabs. Apple's aesthetic, really Steve Jobs's aesthetic, is about perfection. Apple wanted very uniform slabs with essentially no flaws or natural imperfections, each 3 by 6 feet. Thus, outside the saw shed was an enormous pile of offcuts, the outsides of the blocks that they were cutting. They were going to make gravel out of them. I started climbing around the pile and quickly realized the amazing collection of lava surfaces it contained. I asked how much they would charge for the pile, and the response was by weight, the same price as gravel. With a handshake I bought it on the spot. The pieces had just been dumped, so they were chipped and fractured. We settled on a deal where they would trim each piece to 24 inches wide and get as much length as they could out of it. The saw time would be charged hourly.

We were so fortunate to get that lava. We happened to be in the right place at the right time, where someone else's junk pile turned out to be our treasure. But of course, we make that luck too. The shop and the activity within have opened for us many material possibilities, and it helps make Lundberg Design unique. We just see things a little differently. It is so satisfying to find something that has been discarded and turn it into a moment of beauty. And it makes for an even better story when the person throwing it away is Steve Jobs.

above left
Lava textures: split face and honed

above right
Lava textures: natural face and split

opposite
Three walls at pool level

164   PART III.   FIVE PROJECTS

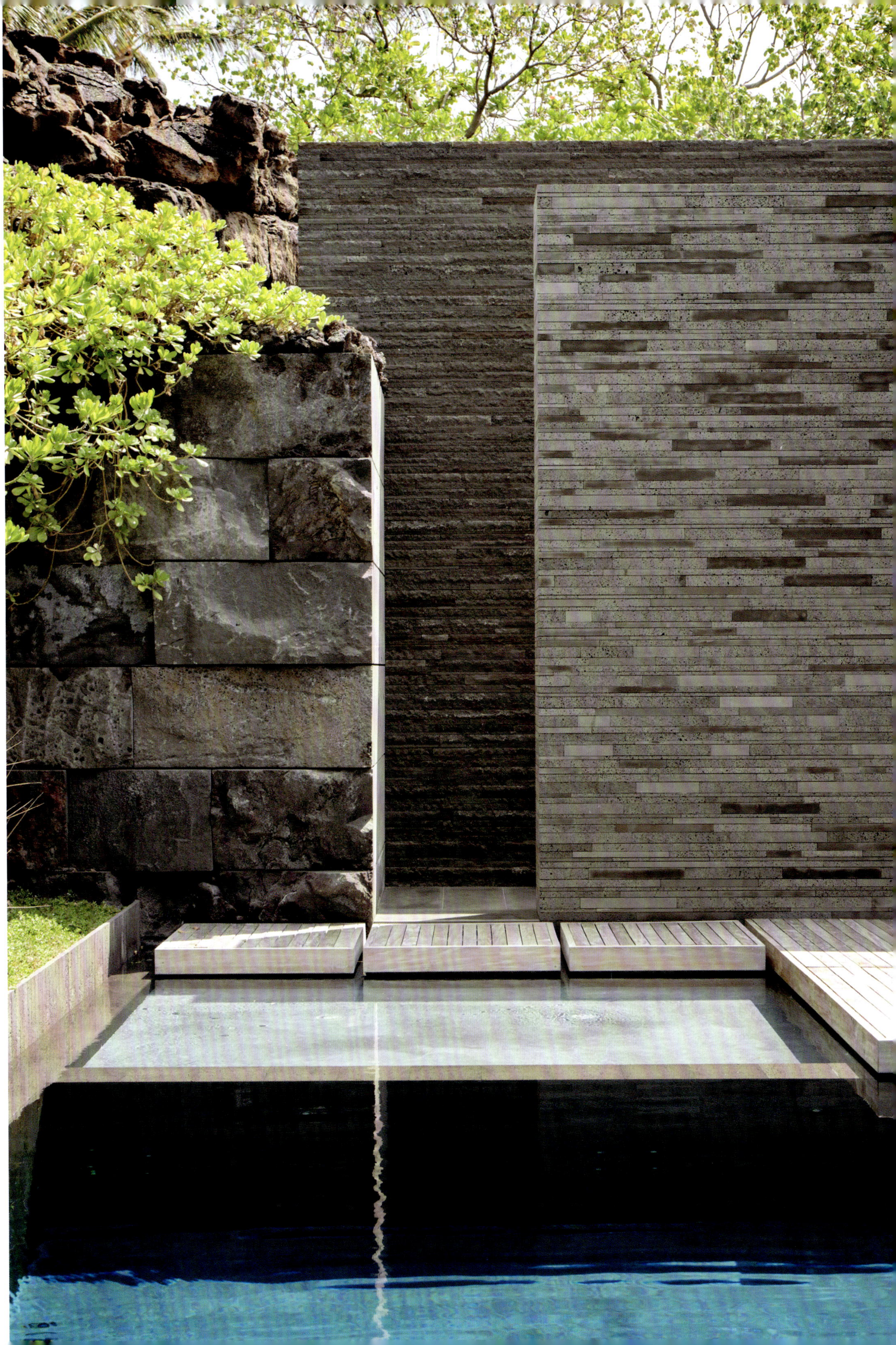

PART III. FIVE PROJECTS

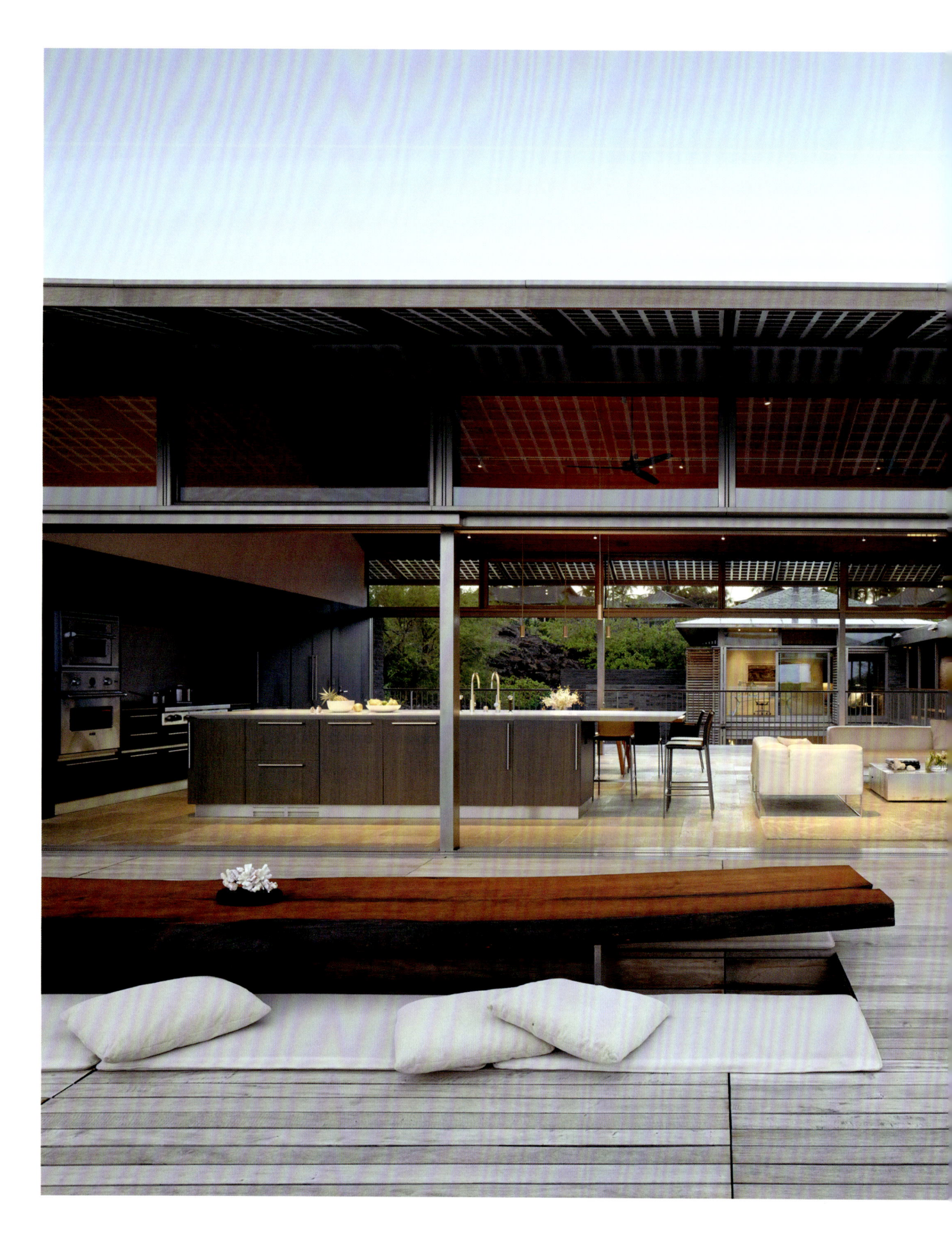

left
Deck at main pavilion

below
Horigotatsu teak slab

LAVA HOUSE 167

top
Main pavilion with
glass walls retracted

above
Installing (very heavy) root ball

right
Charred teak root ball

opposite
Living room

LAVA HOUSE 169

above left and right
Staircase

right
Guest room detail

opposite
Main bath outdoor shower

PART III. FIVE PROJECTS

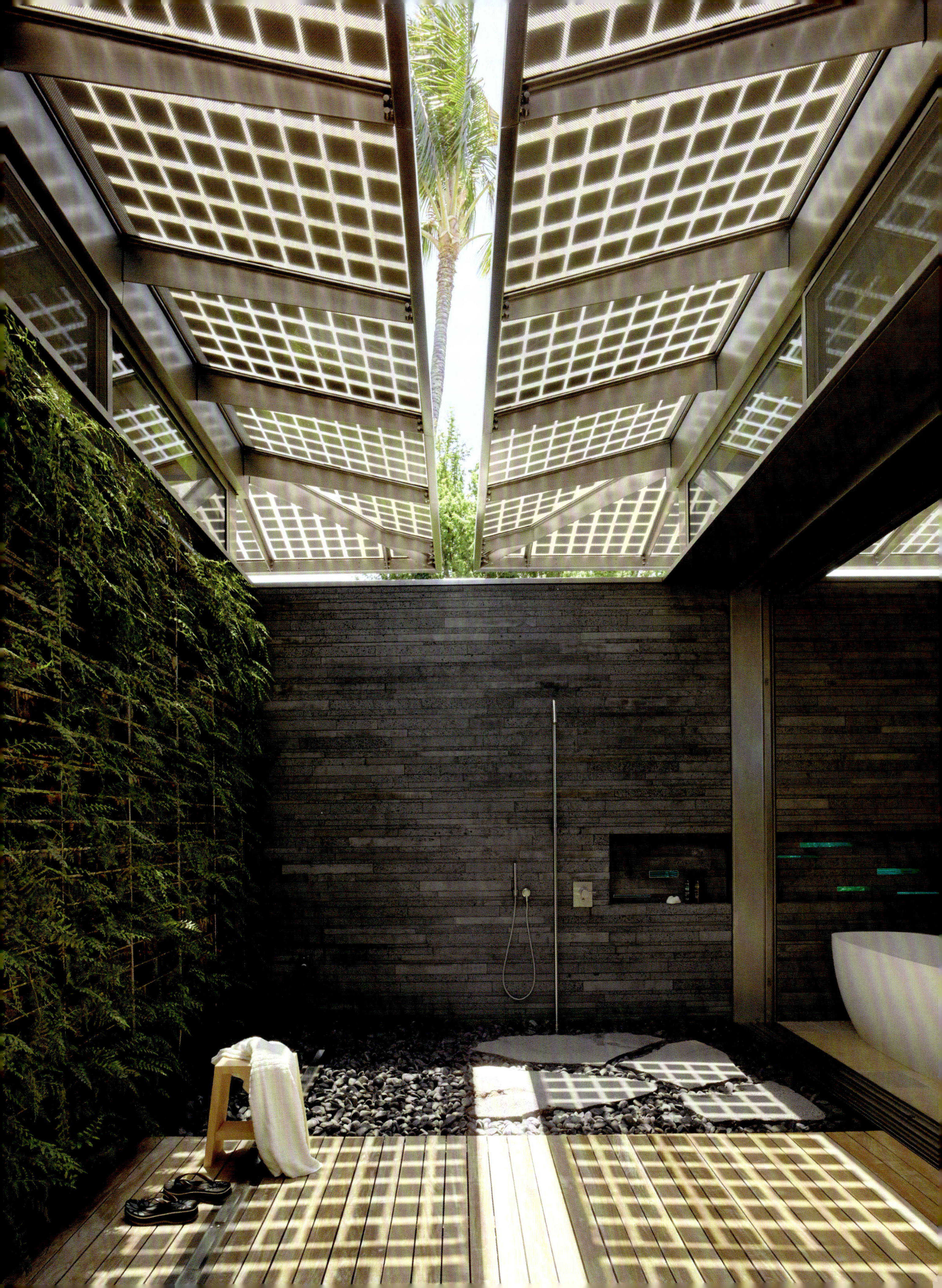

172 PART III. FIVE PROJECTS

opposite
Site prior to construction;
during construction

above
Structure from beach

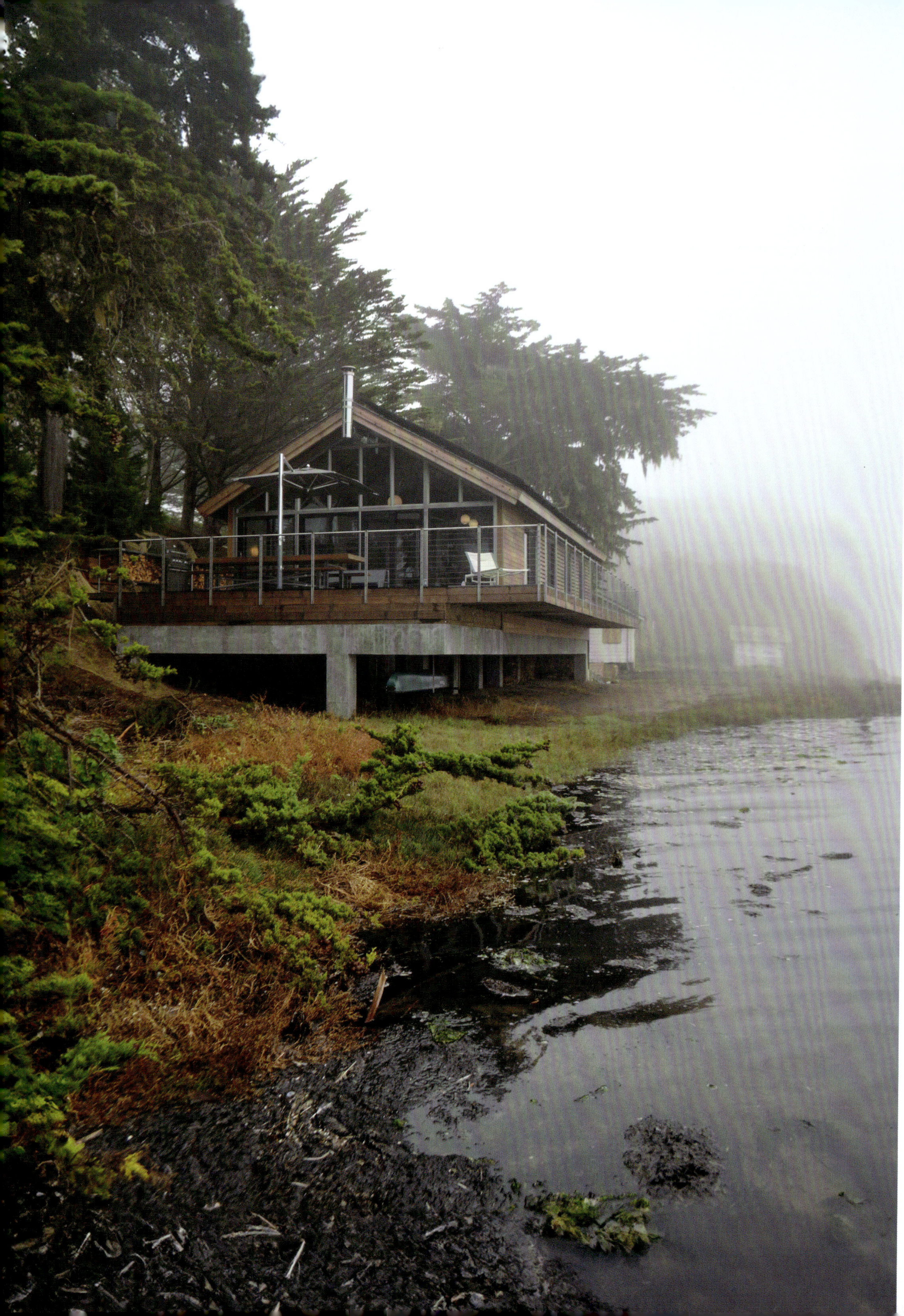

CURLY'S COVE
2013–16

Curly's Cove is in the southeast corner of Bodega Bay in Sonoma County, California. In 2011 Mary and I were looking for a fixer-upper to invest money and sweat equity into, and she found a dilapidated fisherman's shack that was for sale. There was not much value in the existing building. It had fallen off its foundation, every exterior surface was eroded beyond repair, and the interior was a rabbit warren of tiny spaces with a bathroom that had been added on the exterior deck, probably so that originally it could drain directly into the bay. But what a site! It sat partially in the water and had a view that revealed the bay and the adjacent Doran Regional Park exclusively; not another structure was visible except for a similar dilapidated structure next door (whose reclamation we are now just finishing). It was the kind of coastal building site that no longer exists in California, as Coastal Commission mandates ensure that such pieces of land remain undeveloped (a policy that I completely support). But this was an existing home, not condemned (although it certainly could have been), and as the homeowners, we had a right to bring it up to current building code standards. Not that this was going to be easy.

opposite
West facade viewed from water

below
Site section

South shore of Bodega Bay

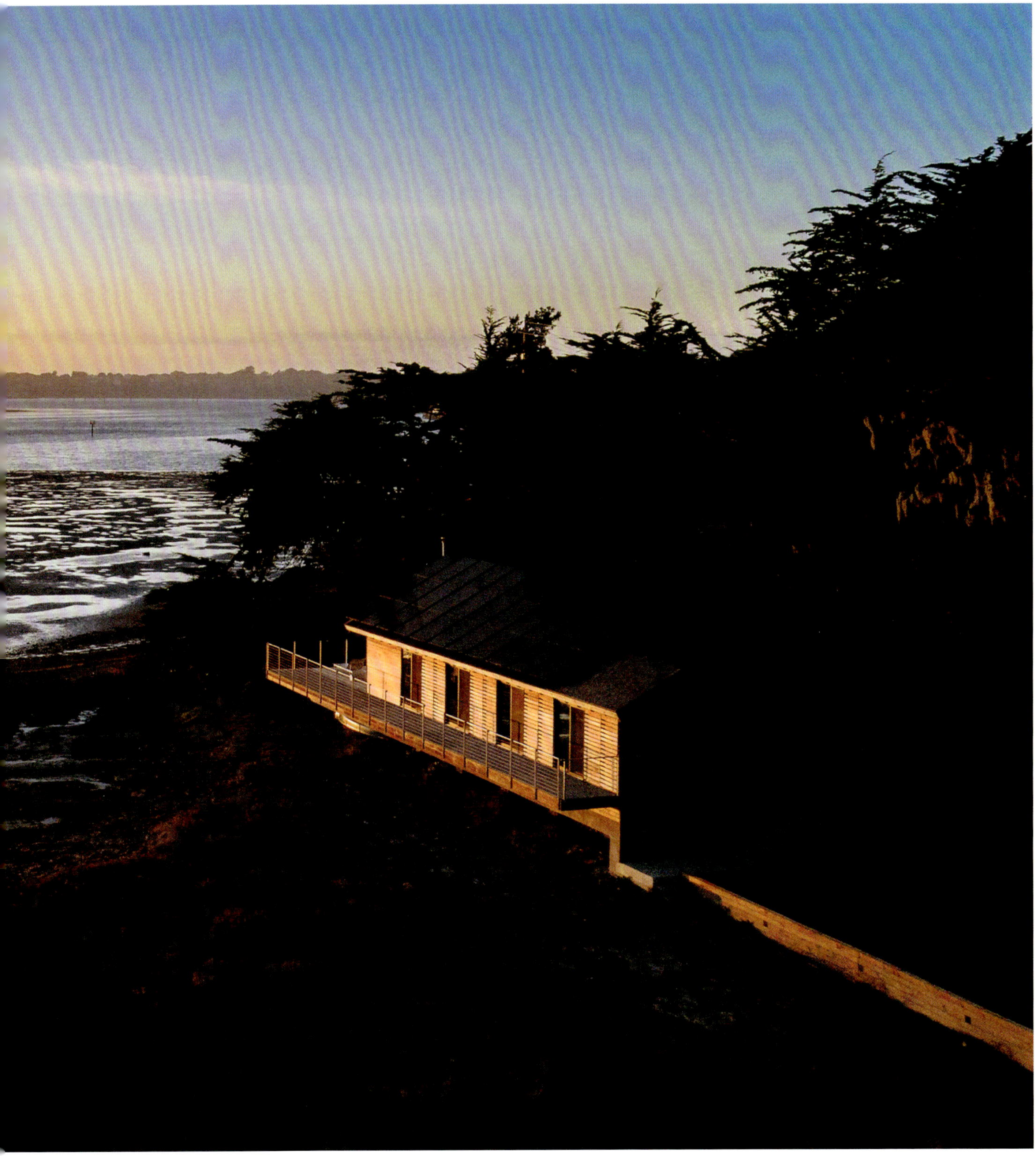

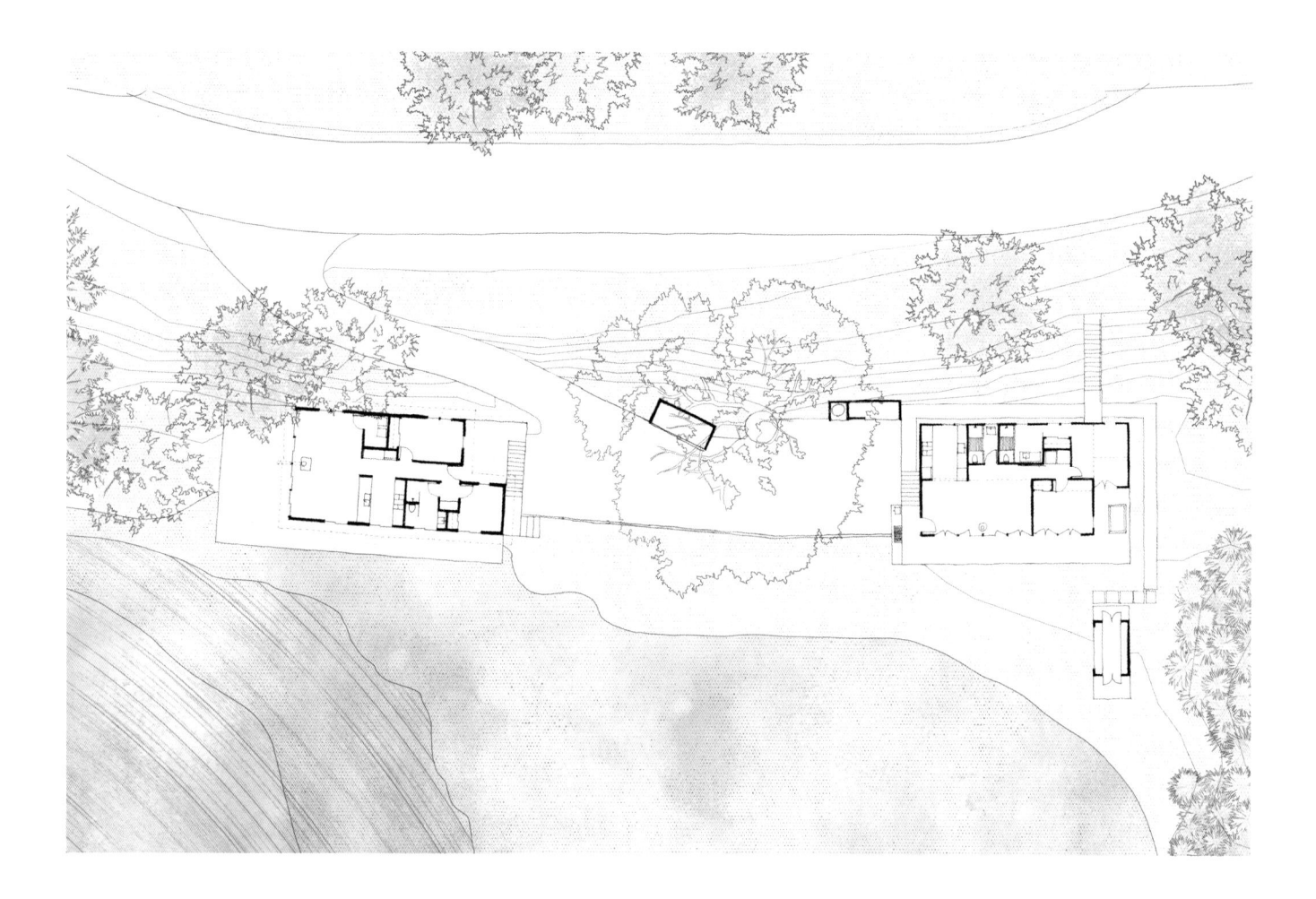

After a year of negotiation, we came up with a compromise proposal that the Coastal Commission approved. We would raise the house by 7 feet to situate it above the anticipated seventy-five-year mark for sea-level rise, and we would move the house 10 feet toward the road, which enabled us, with a double cantilever on the foundation, to avoid putting any foundation piers in the designated wetlands. In exchange we were allowed to completely remodel the structure, although no new massing could be added (we actually reduced the footprint slightly by removing the offending bathroom addition).

It would have been far easier to tear it down and build it from scratch, but we couldn't do that, because once the existing structure was gone, we'd have no right to build. The existing structure was what was grandfathered in, and its presence gave us the opportunity to build on that extraordinary site. So we jacked up the building and removed everything except the structural framework. We then built a complex foundation framework of drilled piers into bedrock (the San Andreas fault is a mere 200 yards out in the Bay), concrete grade beams and cantilevers, then a pressure-treated timber joist system that performed a second cantilever for the deck. It may be the most complicated foundation ever built for a 1,100-square-foot house. But now we were above the water instead of almost in it, and the views became far more expansive.

opposite
Site plan

top
West facade from road

above left
Before remodel

above right
South facade from the flats

CURLY'S COVE

180   PART III.   FIVE PROJECTS

While we had to retain the original massing, the county and the Coastal Commission gave us quite a bit of leeway with the exterior design, and total leeway on the interior. They wanted the facades that faced the road to respect the original pattern of fenestration, which were a variety of double-hung windows, but on the view facades they allowed a more modern expression. The plan called for a perfectly centered hallway, underneath the ridge beam and on axis with the front door. That hallway ends up in the living and dining area, and the axis is terminated by a wood stove. The end of the building, the gable, is completely glass, and looks out onto an old cypress tree that frames the view of the Bay. Along the southern facade, each room has a glass sliding door, with sliding wooden shutters to modulate the natural light. The original structure had been clad in redwood siding and shingles, which we discovered after tearing off the bilious green asphalt shingles that had at some point been added. I wanted to recall the history of the building—to have it read, from the water, as similar to what had been there for a hundred years, so for the siding I chose Ipe, a tropical hardwood that can be sustainably harvested, and for the shingles, dark gray slate. The Ipe weathers to a gray color very similar to aged redwood. I wanted the structure to be a little of both old and new, to honor its survival and past while expressing its second life as a contemporary house.

Inside, we opened up to the roof with cathedral ceilings in all the main spaces, exposing the old skip sheathing in the process. We reclaimed all the old beadboard interior paneling for the interior walls. I did put in variegated slate floors, which hold up nicely to dogs and beachgoers, and white subway tile in the bathroom and kitchen.

The end result was rather stunning and quite the transformation, in large part thanks to my contractor, Pat Clark, and my shop crew. The Lundberg Design shop built the glass gable facade, the sliding shutters, the outdoor entry stair, the deck railing, the dining table, the outside table, the canoe support, and the world's heaviest coffee table—a teak root ball that looks like it might have floated up on a high tide, except for the fact that it weighs about half a ton. All of the detail those pieces add make a huge difference. The attention to detail and the quality of the work really celebrate that special spot.

The original plan was to sell the house once we finished, but it was just too special to give up. Apparently being a developer is just not in my blood, so we now use it as a vacation rental.

opposite
The deck

top
Kitchen

above
Living room with root-ball table

opposite
Glass wall facing west

182 PART III. FIVE PROJECTS

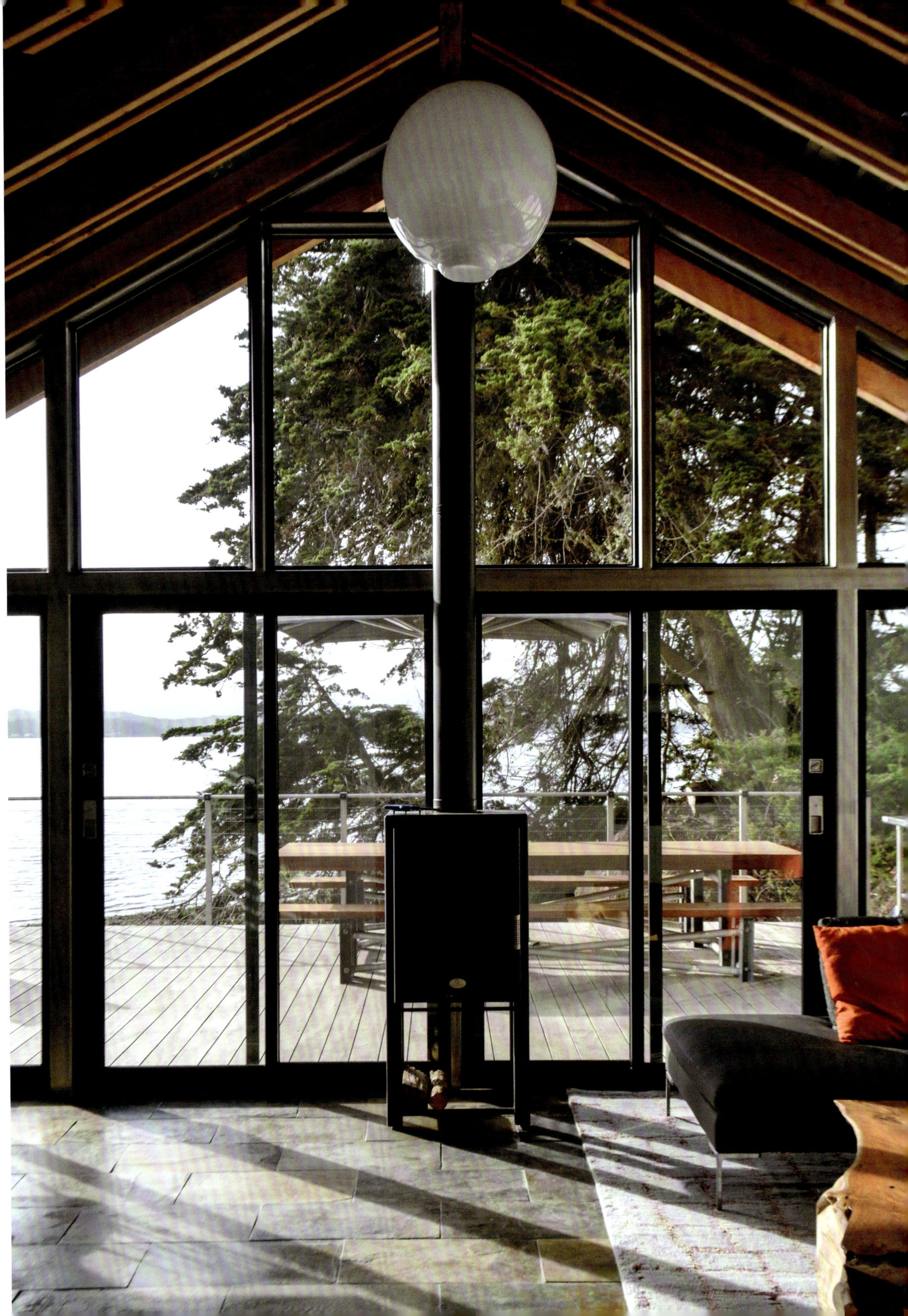

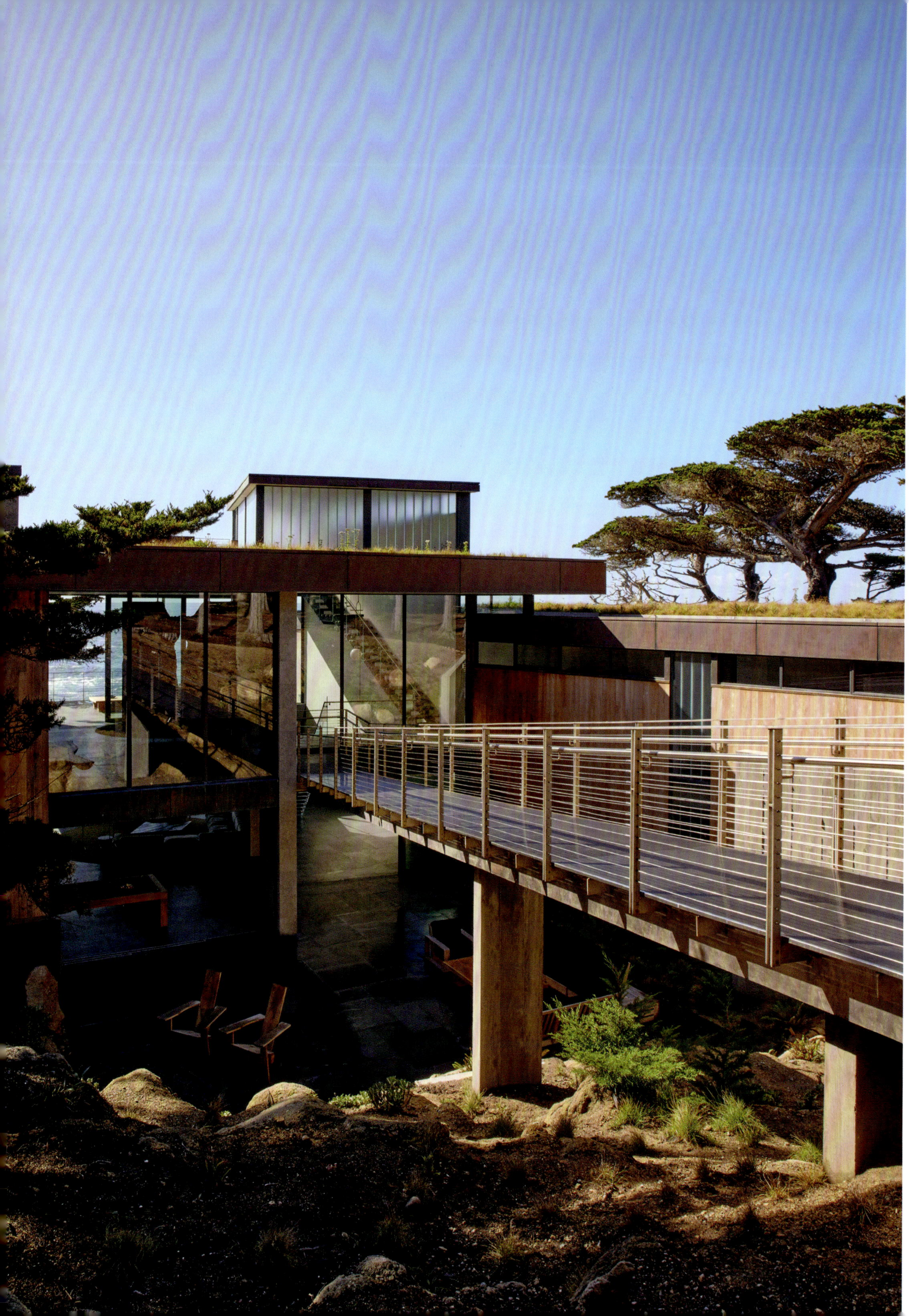

DOGLEG HOUSE
2016–2023

Dogleg House is on the California coast, a few hundred yards away from one of the greatest golf courses in the world. Four friends, one of whom was a previous client, asked us to design a house that they could individually or collectively utilize to come play golf and entertain. Essentially a boutique hotel with great party facilities.

The site, which is as dramatic a site as I will ever get to work on, had an existing one-story ranch house on it. The house was built closer to the water than would now be permitted, and while the house was not considered historic, the surrounding cypress forest was protected. We could demolish the existing structure, but we had to replace it on the same footprint, and we could not touch the trees. Fortunately, the site had been well maintained, and the trees had been pruned over the years so that they did not overhang the roof, for the very realistic reason that they might break in a Pacific gale and crash through the building. That pruning made the option for a two-story structure possible per code.

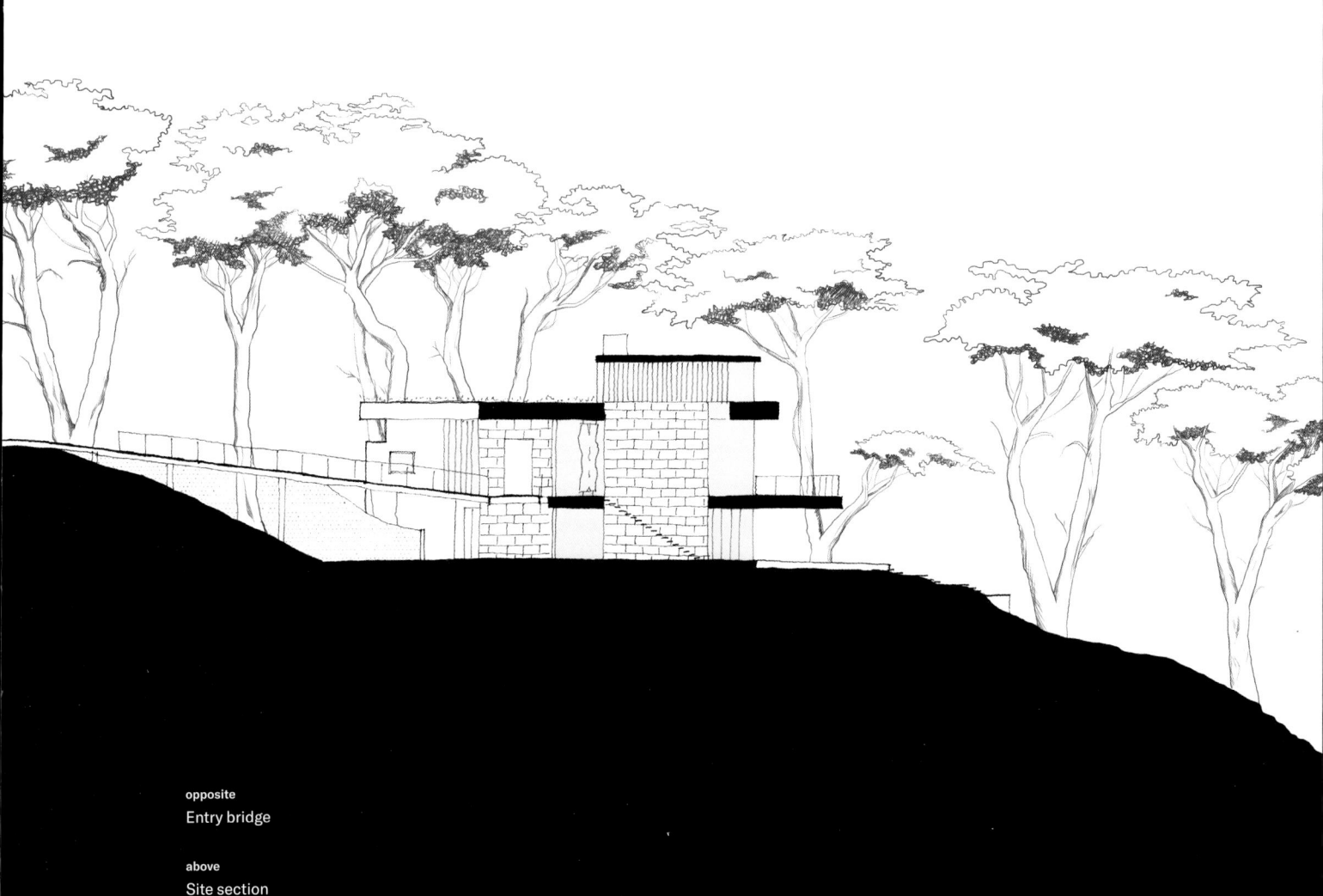

opposite
Entry bridge

above
Site section

PART III. FIVE PROJECTS

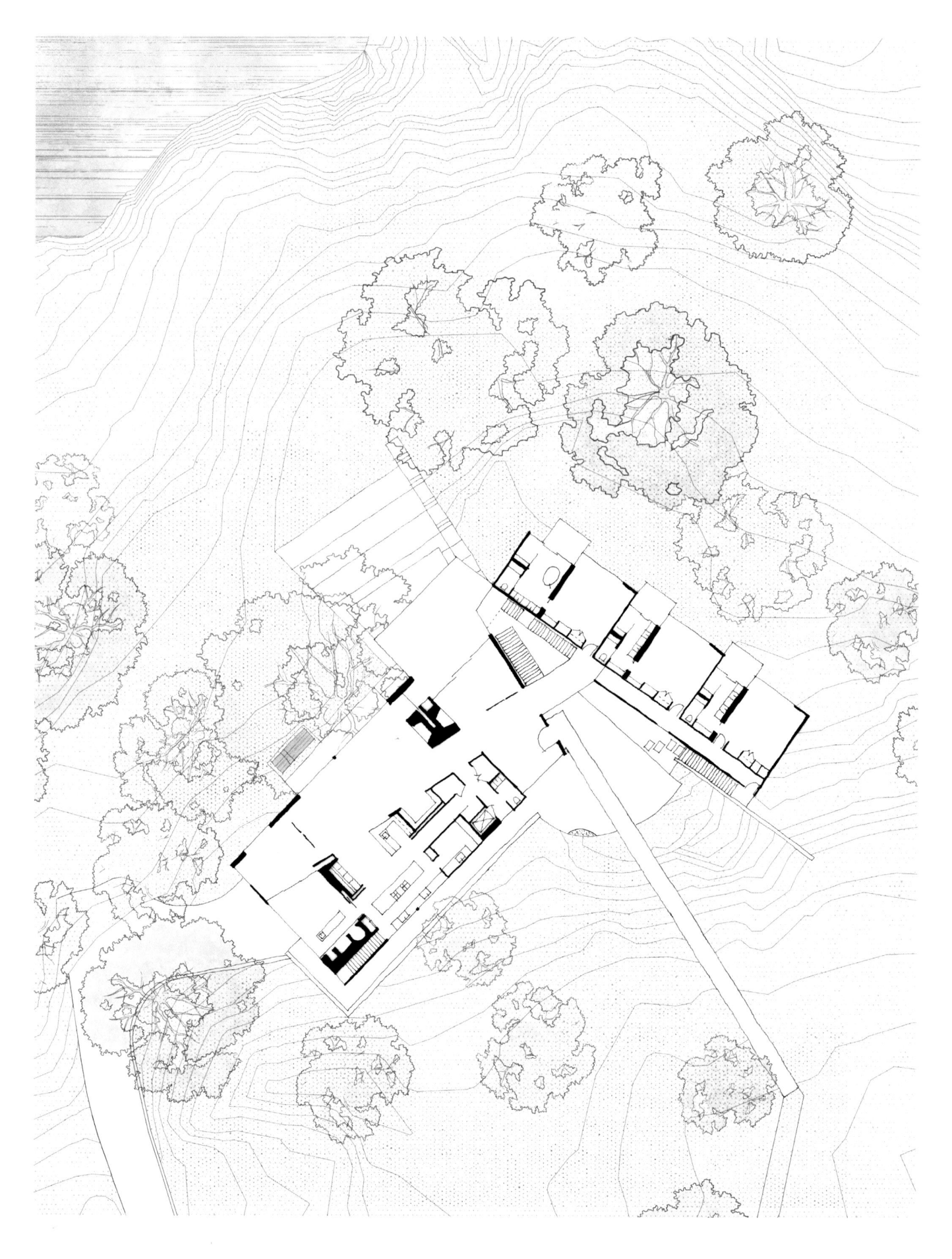

opposite
Site plan

right
Main wing, south end

below
House as seen from the road

overleaf
House as seen from parking

The site has essentially three levels. The street and front half of the site are about 50 feet above sea level. Then there is a steep drop to the original house level, which is 25 feet lower, and then at the far end of the lot is a rocky cliff that drops directly into the Pacific Ocean. The cross section through the site revealed an opportunity to design a two-floor structure, which could be entered via a bridge on the upper level. All of the car parking could stay on the upper level, so that no asphalt or cars would sit in the foreground view from the house—an unfortunate characteristic of the original design. The original plan was L-shaped, a "dogleg" in golfing terminology, although the intersection of the two rectangles was slightly splayed, at about 100 rather than 90 degrees.

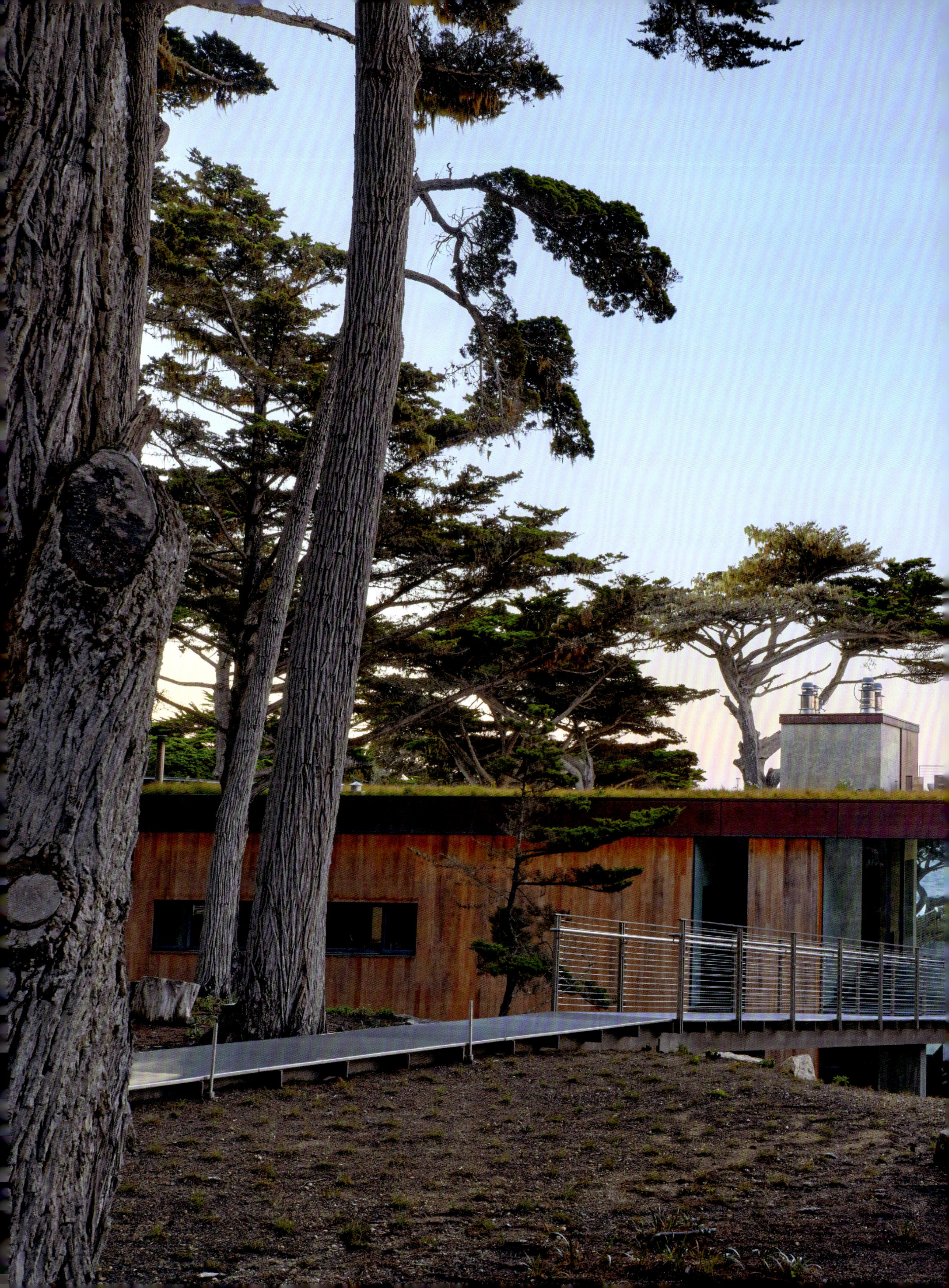

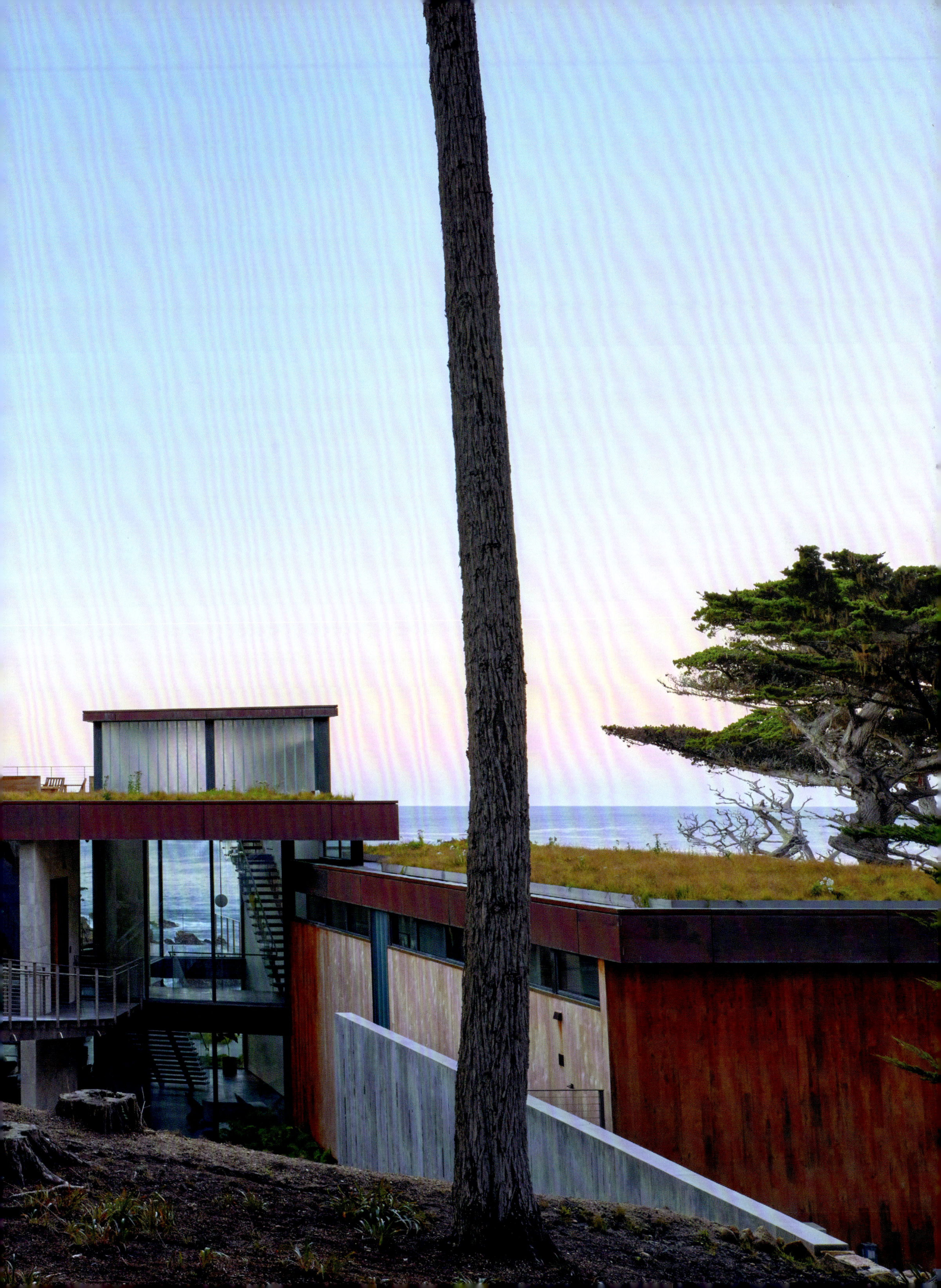

The new design has the bridge entrance intersecting at the junction of the two forms. The left rectangle, which is parallel to the coastline, is the public or entertainment wing, and the right rectangle is the bedroom wing. From the entry, the two wings appear relatively solid, while the intersection is almost completely transparent, forming an actual and visual gateway to the crashing surf beyond. This middle joint/intersection also contains the stair, which goes both to the lower level and to the rooftop, upon which is a cocktail terrace. On the upper level is a large, cantilevered deck that projects out toward the water, and the lower level features both a front terrace and a more protected rear courtyard.

above
View through entry "knuckle" to ocean

right
Channel glass detail

opposite
Bedroom wing corner

DOGLEG HOUSE 191

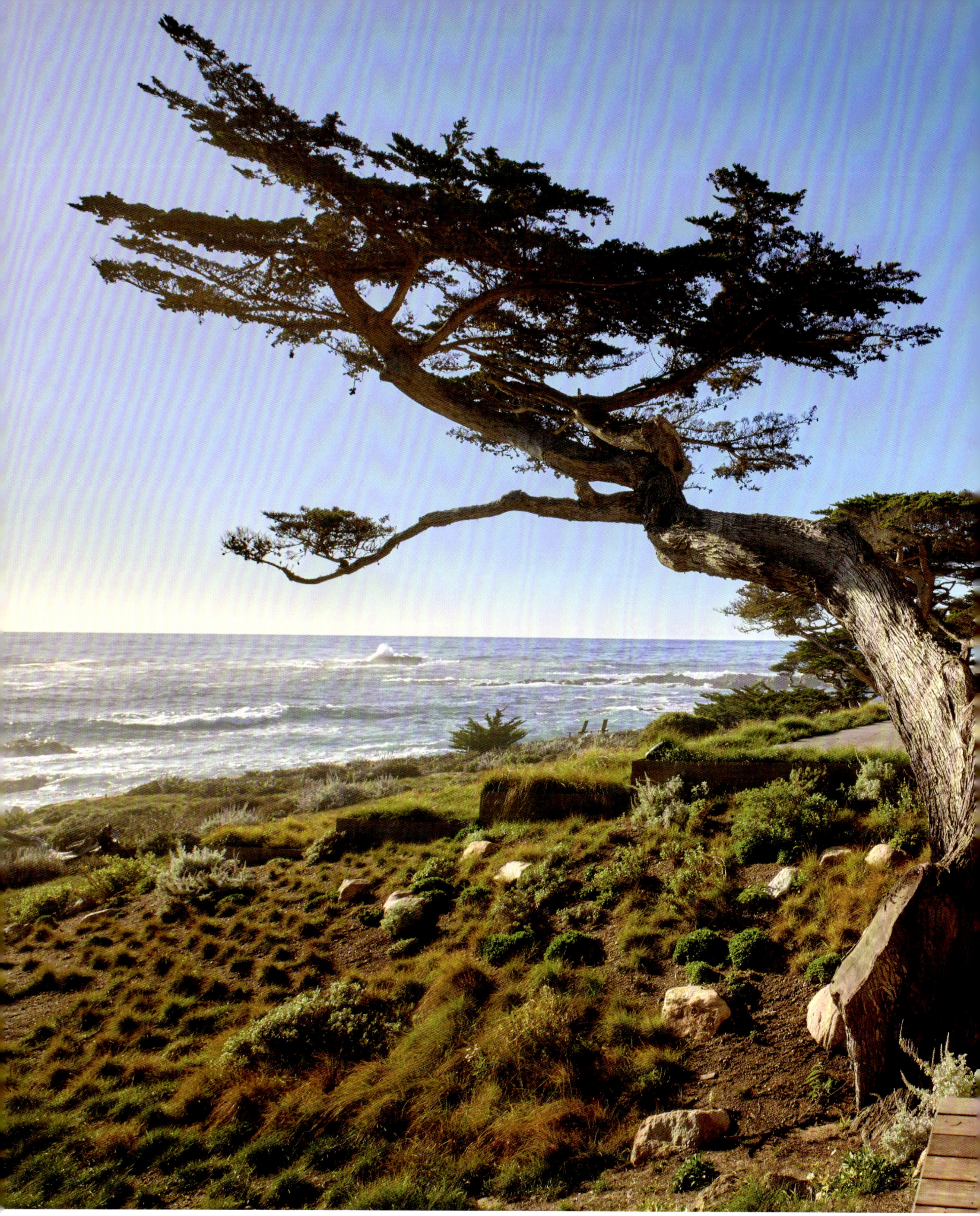

left
Coastline at house

below
Cypress trees at house edge

DOGLEG HOUSE   193

above
Main deck with ocean terrace below

opposite
Fire pit; coastline

194   PART III.   FIVE PROJECTS

DOGLEG HOUSE **195**

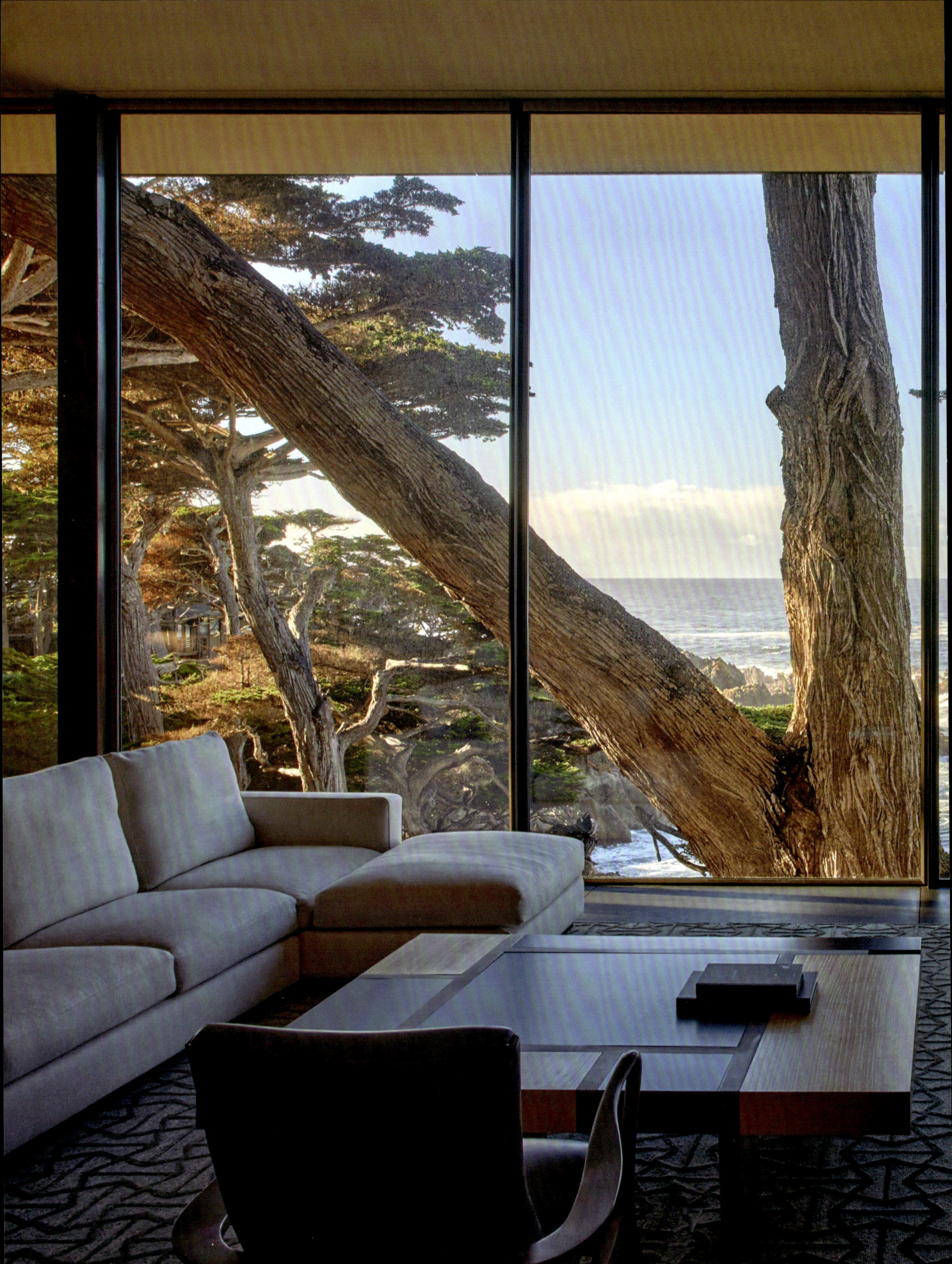

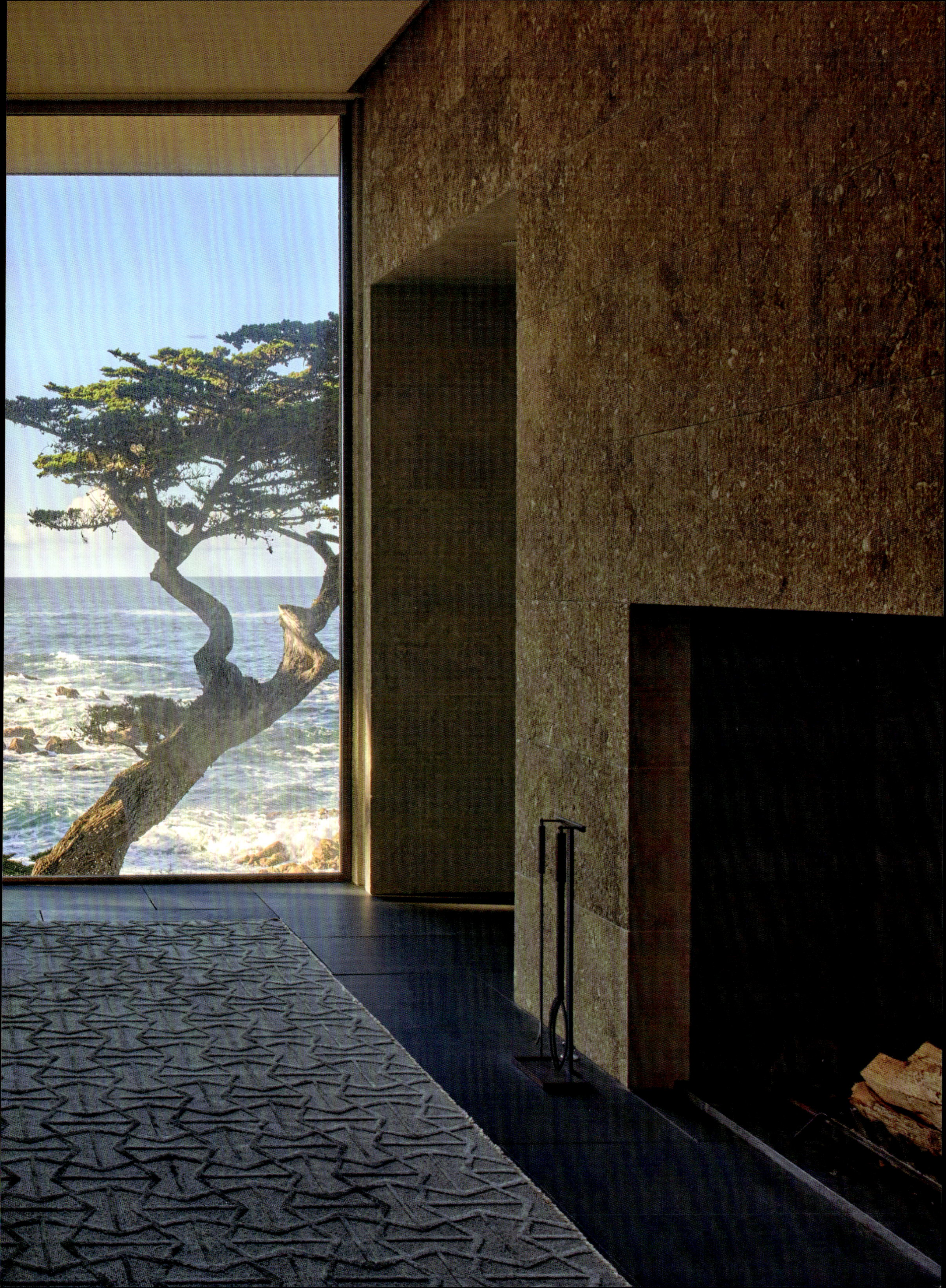

I have never designed for a site with such dramatic trees. These old cypresses are so battered by winds and rain that their resulting twisted forms are as sculptural a tree shape as you will find. Framing views of the trees and the coastline was a delightful opportunity, and almost every room in the house experiences one or both of those vistas. But it is a harsh environment. The rain can come in horizontally, the salt fog is extremely corrosive, and the wind can be hurricane strength. Consequently, we chose exterior materials that could withstand those elements and not require significant ongoing maintenance. The siding is finger-jointed teak boards made from short pieces of reclaimed teak lumber epoxied together to form long pieces. Teak, which still is the preferred wood for yachts, can handle saltwater conditions quite nicely, and we were able to use pieces that otherwise would probably have ended up as firewood.

The fireplaces, large masonry masses that extend up through the structure, are clad in limestone. On the exterior we "eroded" the surface of the stone with a water-jet process that revealed the grain and fossils within. On the interior we left the smooth, honed surface exposed. The windows and doorframes are bronze, which will patina quickly to a blue-green. The fascia and trim are all either bronze or copper, while the bridge and railings are stainless steel.

previous
View from living room

above
Bedroom view

right
Hallway

198   PART III.   FIVE PROJECTS

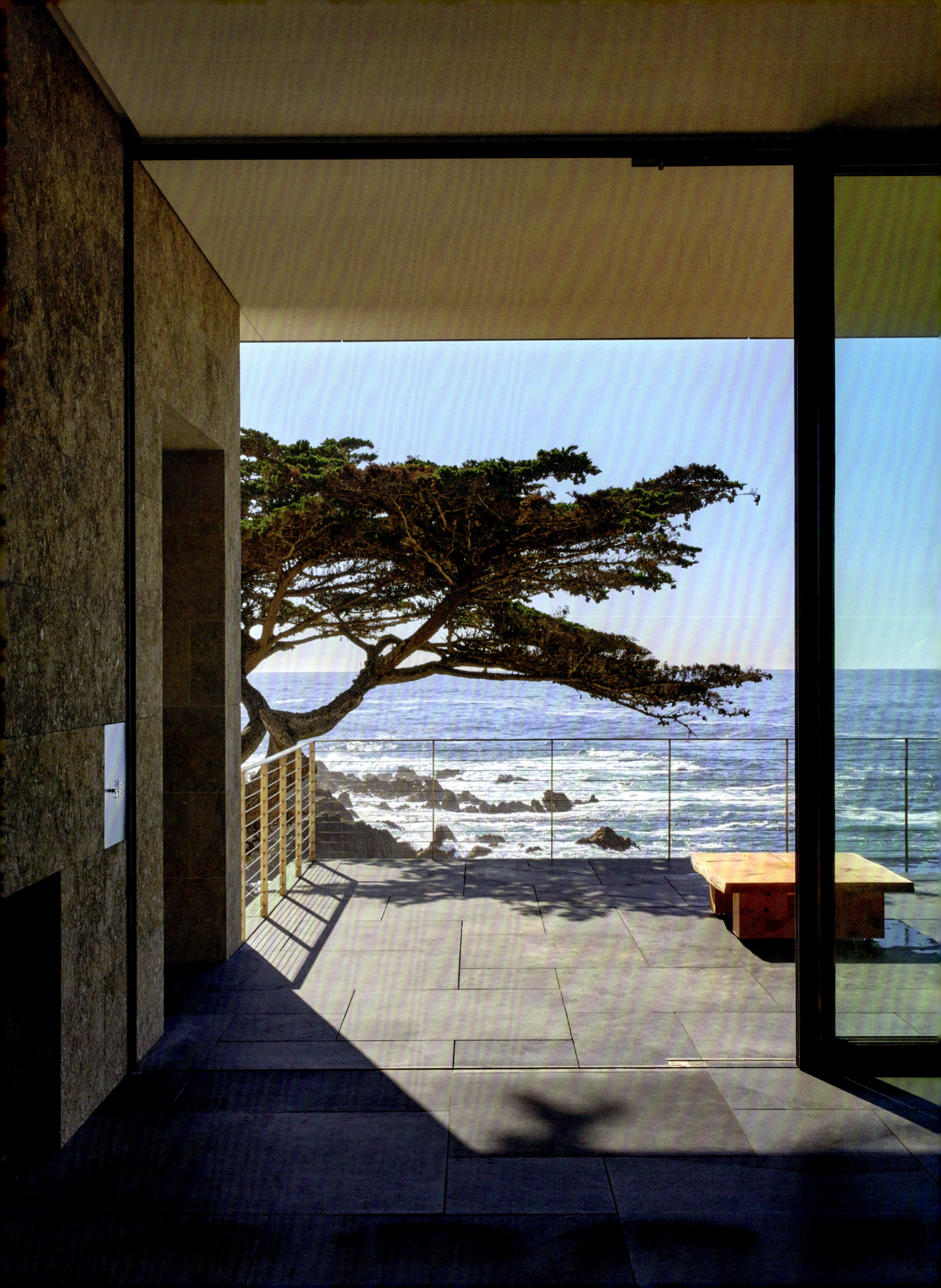

PART III. FIVE PROJECTS

left
Planted roof, bedroom wing

below
Copper with salt spray patina

bottom
Light controls in limestone wall

DOGLEG HOUSE 201

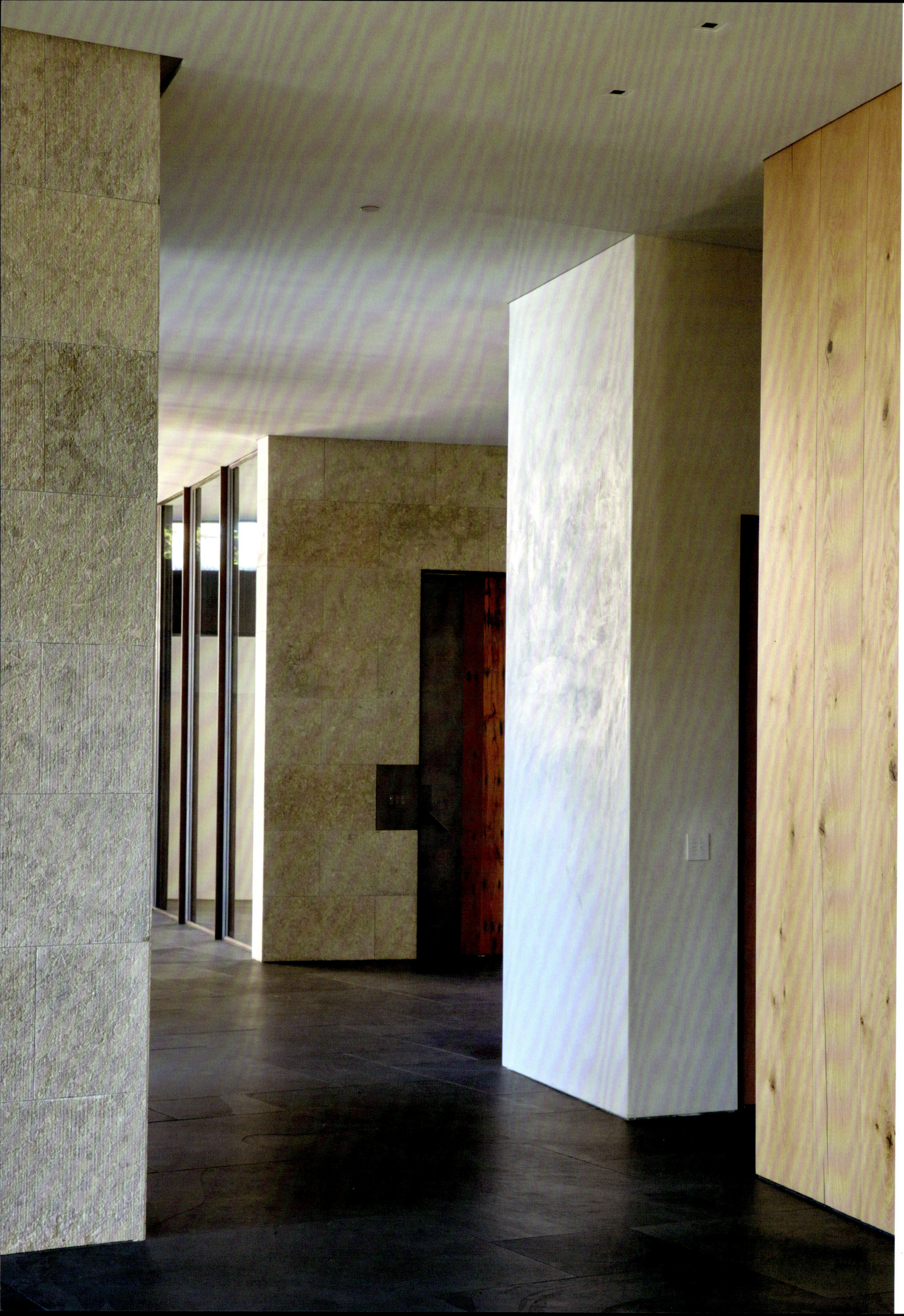

opposite
Hallway toward front door

above
Living room toward deck access

left
White oak millwork detail

DOGLEG HOUSE

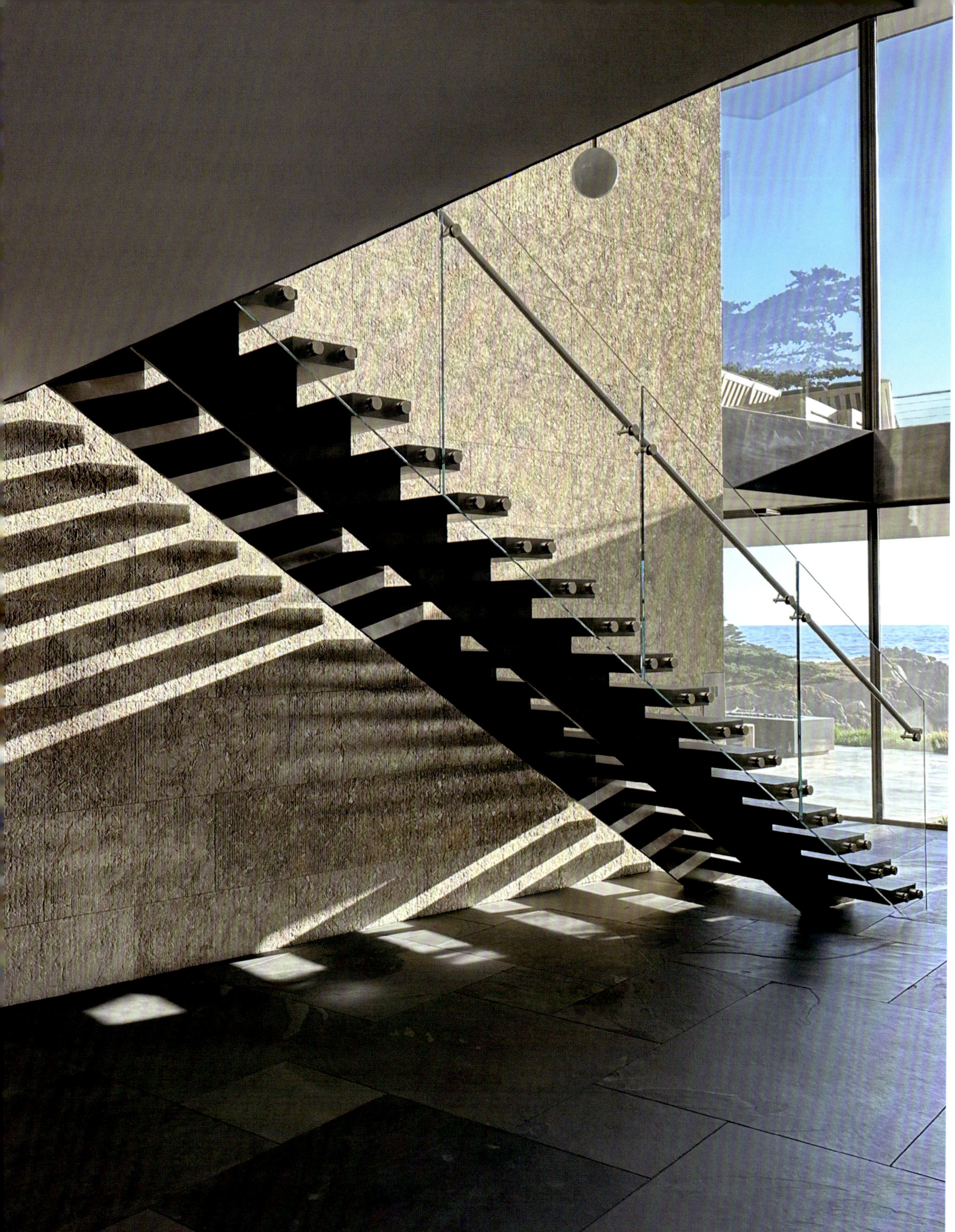

opposite
Staircase

below
Door fabrication

right
Front door

Our shop built several signature elements, including the front door, the entry bench, two room screens, and the fireplace screens. As we were designing the front door, we were offered some teak boards that had been milled from beams salvaged from demolished structures in Indonesia. They were 2 inches thick and about 8 inches wide, with one side smooth (the cut side) and the other side heavily weathered from probably centuries of exposure to the elements. We often utilize materials that can present a smooth side and a rough side, as the differences in texture and appearance reveal the essence of the material; recall that we had already done that with the limestone fireplaces. So here we had a similar opportunity. The outside of the door has a rough, burnished character, while the inside is smooth and polished. We filled old holes and checks in the boards with molten pewter, like little silver jewels. It is my hope that over time, the exterior materials of the house—the teak siding, the limestone, and the bronze windows and trim—will develop a patina of age that softens the overall appearance and gradually transmutes the structure into the color palette of the cypress forest. But the front door is actually already centuries old, and needs no aging. It is already perfect.

DOGLEG HOUSE

That said, my favorite shop-built elements of the house are the two room screens built from claro walnut slabs. The floor plan included two spaces, both more intimate lounges, that were intended to be visually separated from the main space but not completely walled off. Because of my fixation on the forest outside, I'd come up with the idea of creating screens using large wood slabs. But they were going to need to be really big—about 12 feet square. I called my friend Evan Shively, owner of Arborica, the sawmill in Marshall I previously mentioned as the source for the Lava House bench. As Evan has so often done, he proclaimed that he had just what I needed: Uncle Burt! Uncle Burt was a walnut tree from the Central Valley that was so large, it had a name. When drought finally did him in, Evan had purchased the trunk and milled it into slabs 12 feet long and more than 6 feet wide. They were perfect. We squared up the sides, but not to the point of removing all the irregularities, and then bookmatched them to form the screens. They were a little shorter than the floor-to-ceiling dimension, so we were forced to come up with a detail that allowed them to "float," which reinforced the impression of the room continuing beyond them. They are not of the same wood as the cypress outside, but they definitely evoke the scale and presence of the forest, and as slabs they have a lifelike quality. They are wonderful sculptures—nicknamed "Kissing Bears" and "Dancing Fat Men," and I owe Evan an enormous debt of gratitude for saving them for me.

opposite
Arborica sawmill

top left
Cutting slabs at sawmill

top middle
Bookmatching slabs at LD studio

top right
Michael sanding slabs

above left
Jack applying finish to sanded slab

above right
Slab installation

overleaf left
Bookmatched slabs installed

overleaf right
Claro walnut entry bench

DOGLEG HOUSE 207

PART III. FIVE PROJECTS

DOGLEG HOUSE

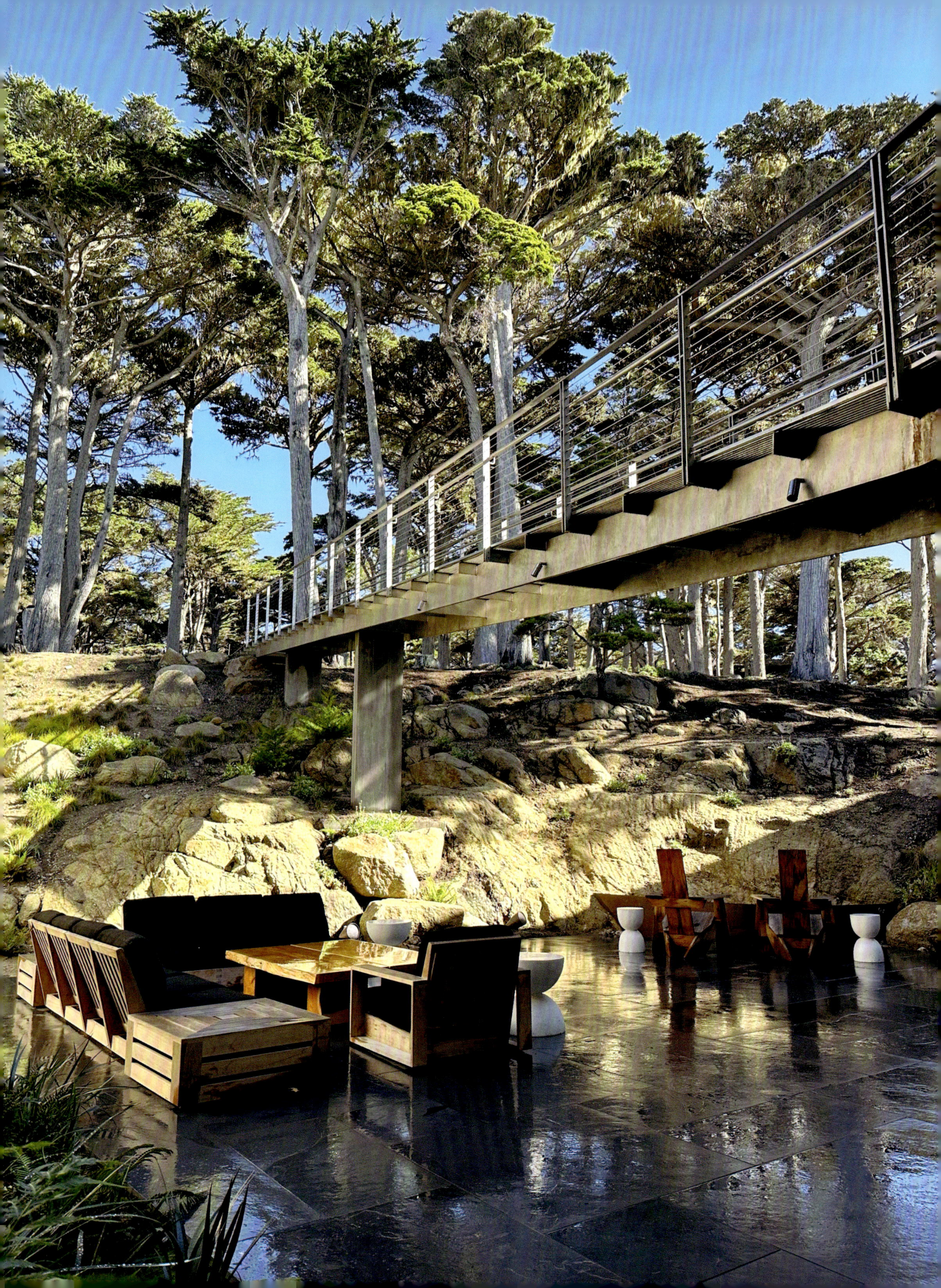

opposite
Back terrace underneath entry bridge

top left
Corten steel firepit installation

top right
Firepit edge detail

bottom
Firepit from above

overleaf
Residence seen from coastline

DOGLEG HOUSE 211

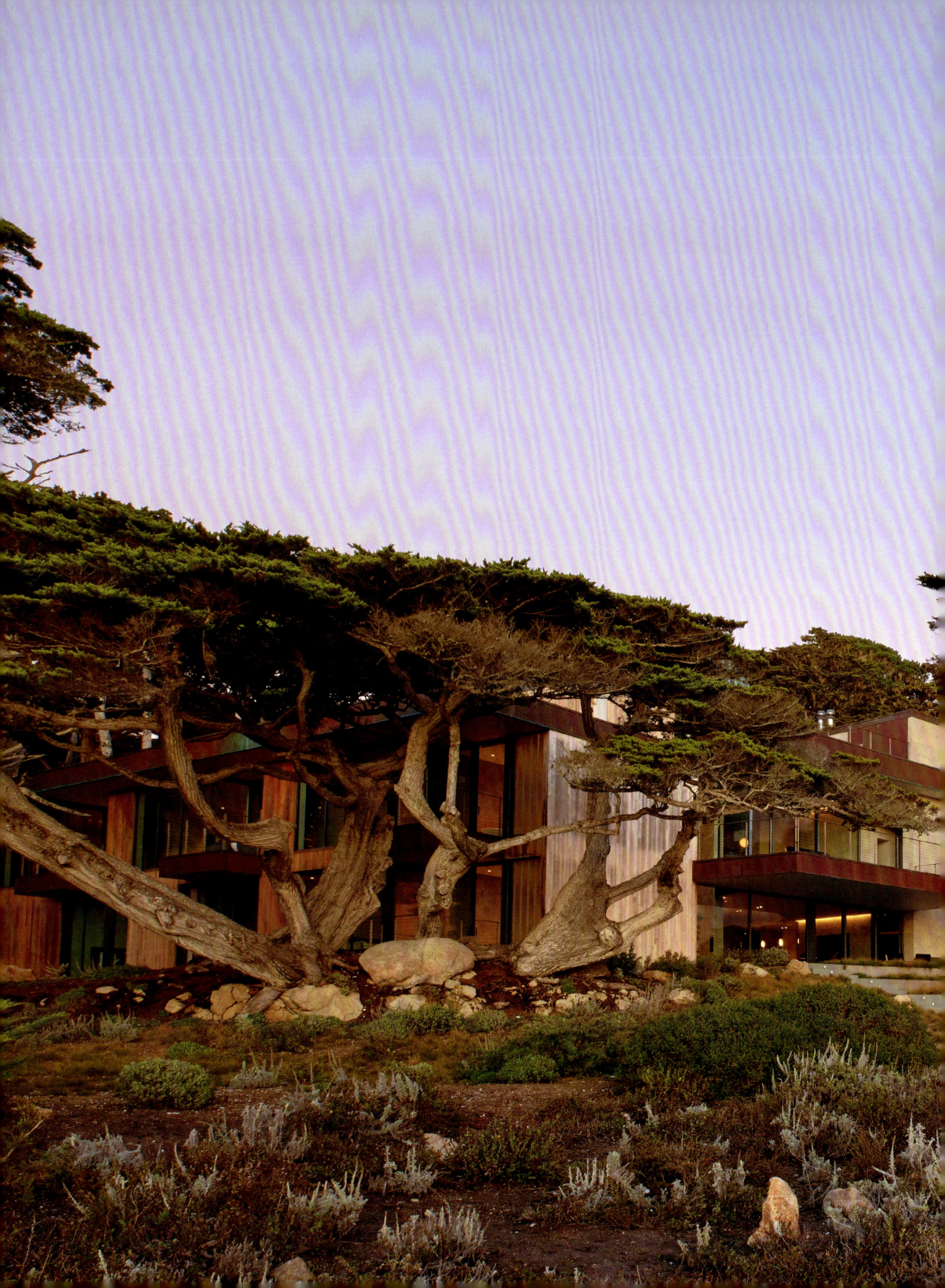

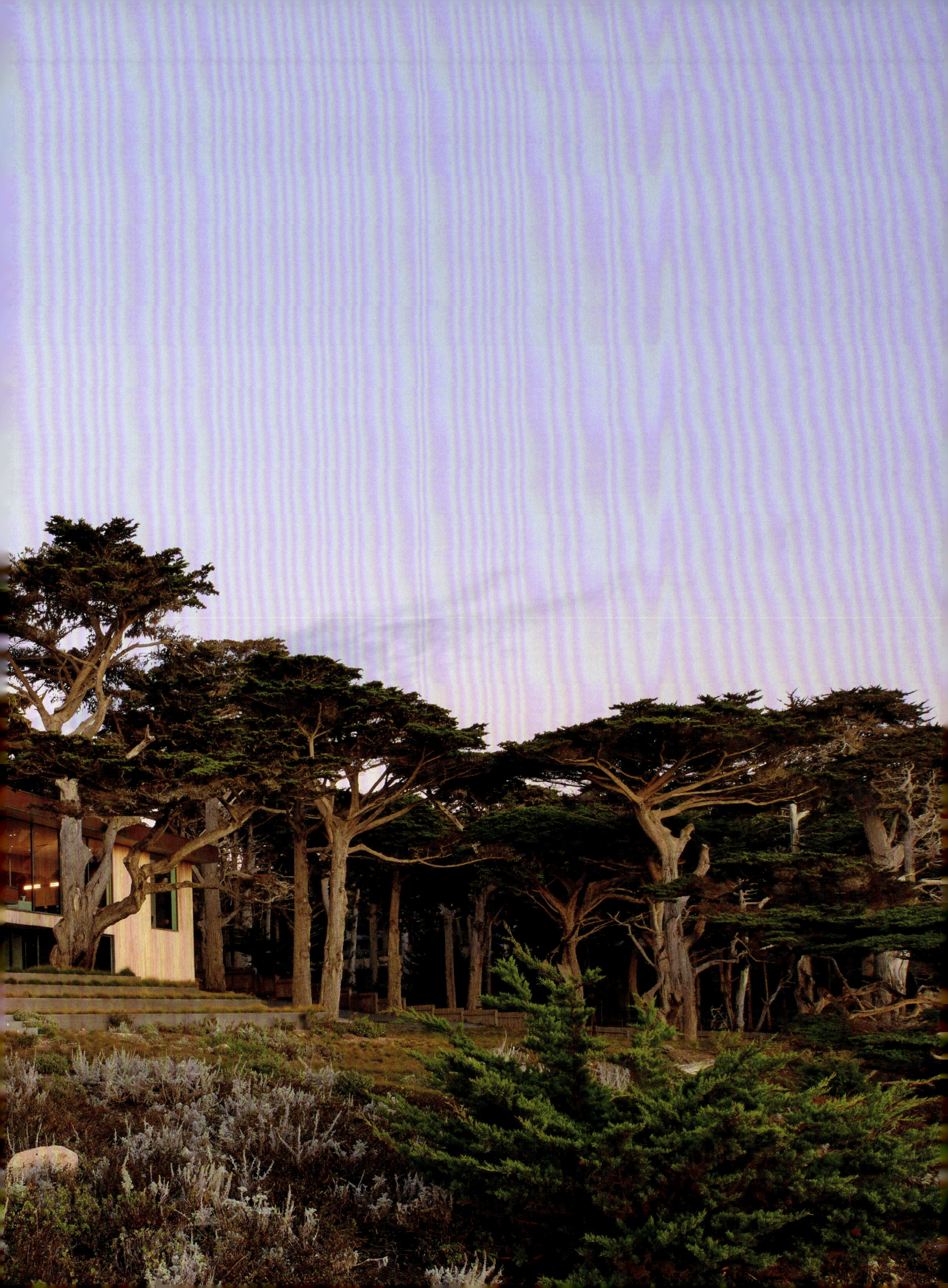

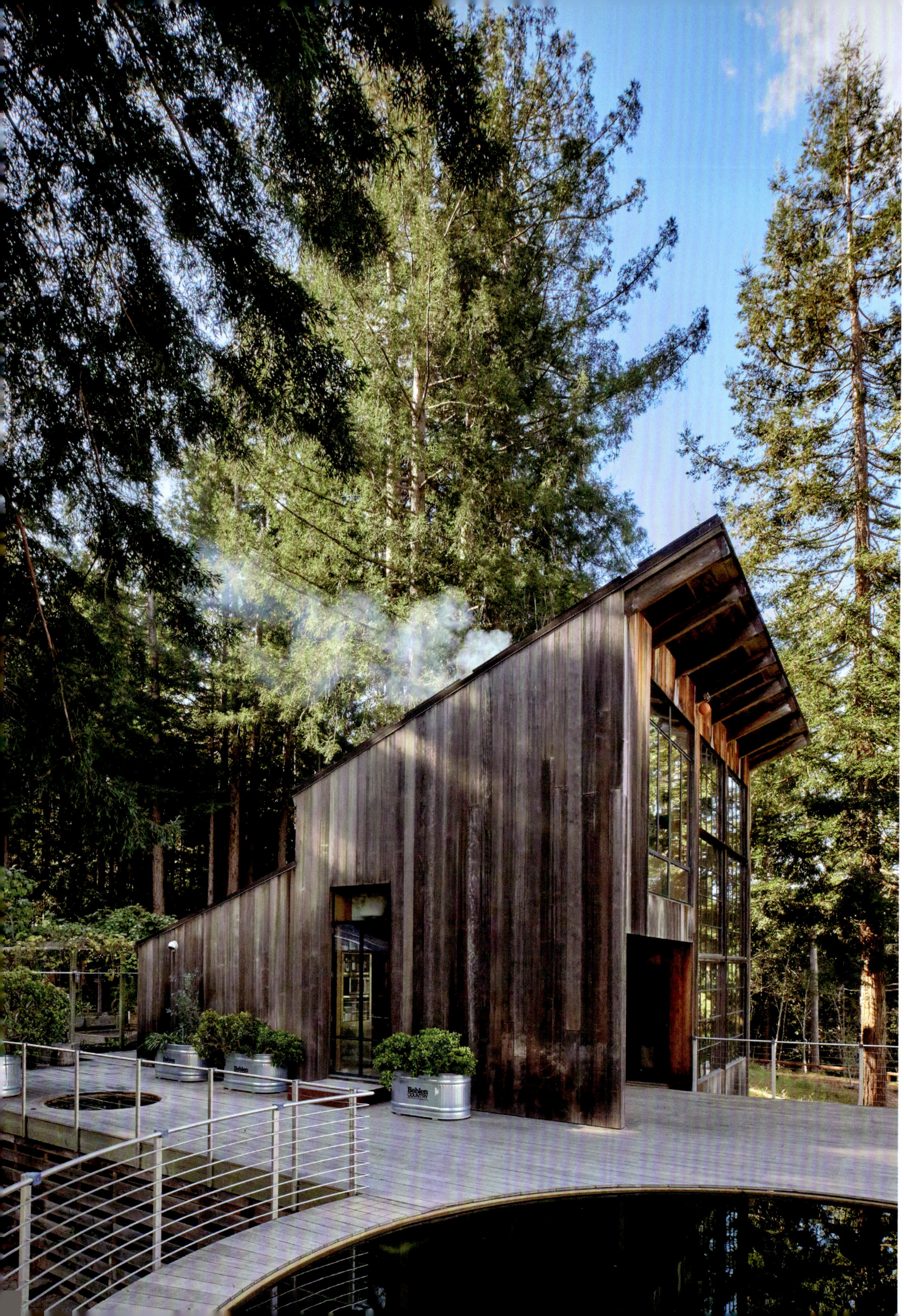
Behlen
COUNTRY

THE CABIN
1996–present

For the last of the finished projects presented in this book, I chose my cabin, the most personal of all my projects. I have attempted to show how personal all of our work is, how our fabrication studio enables us to build unique one-off pieces and details that are special to each project and client. They are in essence expressions of the relationship that exists between architect and client, and the care we take in producing that work I hope reflects how much we treasure our clients' trust and friendship. But the cabin is different—this is for Mary and me, and while Mary does make requests, she is very tolerant about letting me indulge my various ideas.

Here the budgets are smaller, but lots of sweat equity helps balance that. Over the decades I've incorporated a wide variety of salvaged materials and objects; I've lured my staff into helping with construction (usually with the promise of good food); and I have had the incredible luxury of getting to build my own place of refuge over a period spanning three decades. I am afraid this project, likely to Mary's dismay, will never be entirely complete. But in our case, I think that is okay. This place defines us; it is a physical manifestation of who we are. We still make new friends, we cook new foods, we read new books, so the cabin should age with us.

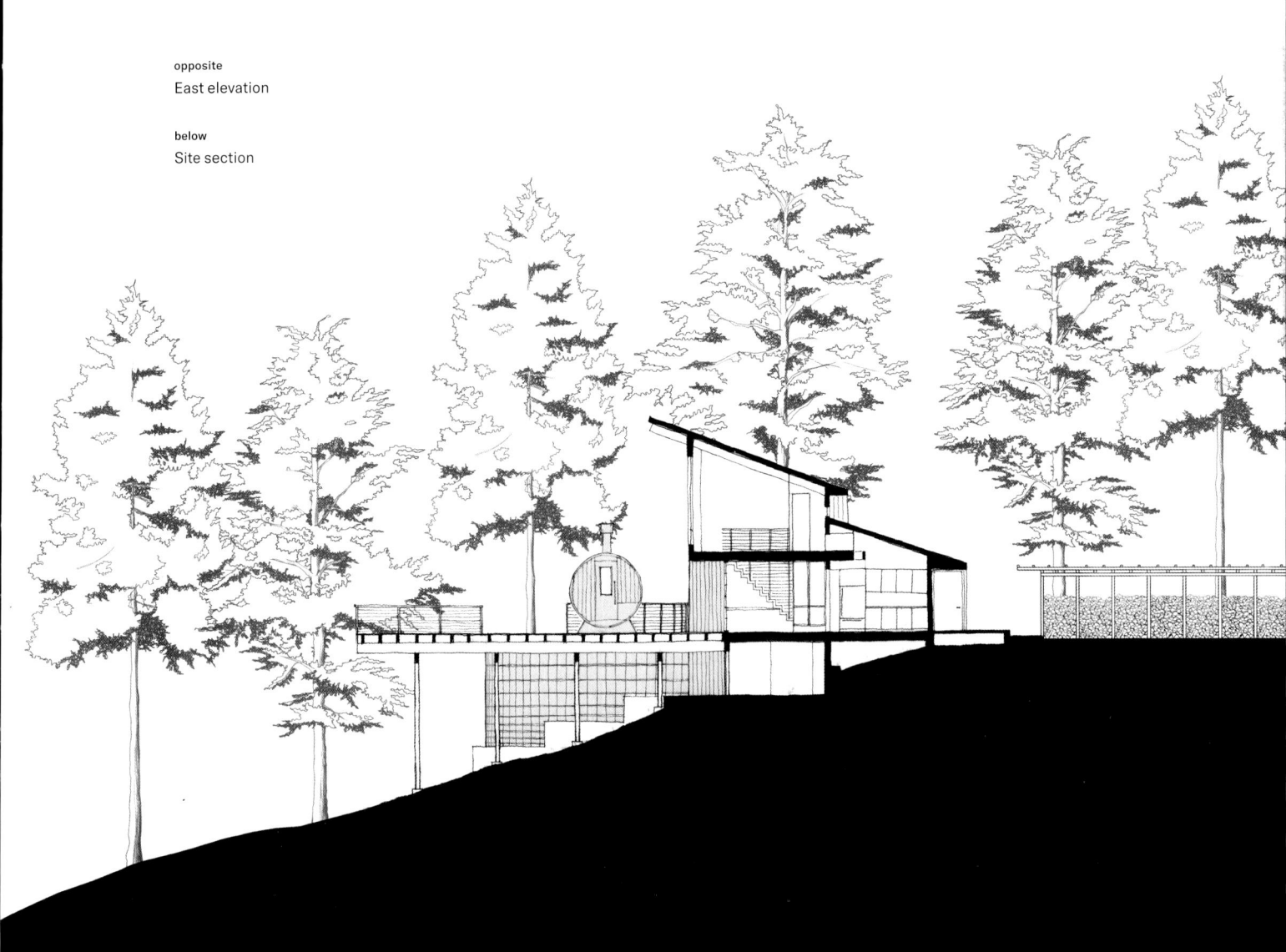

opposite
East elevation

below
Site section

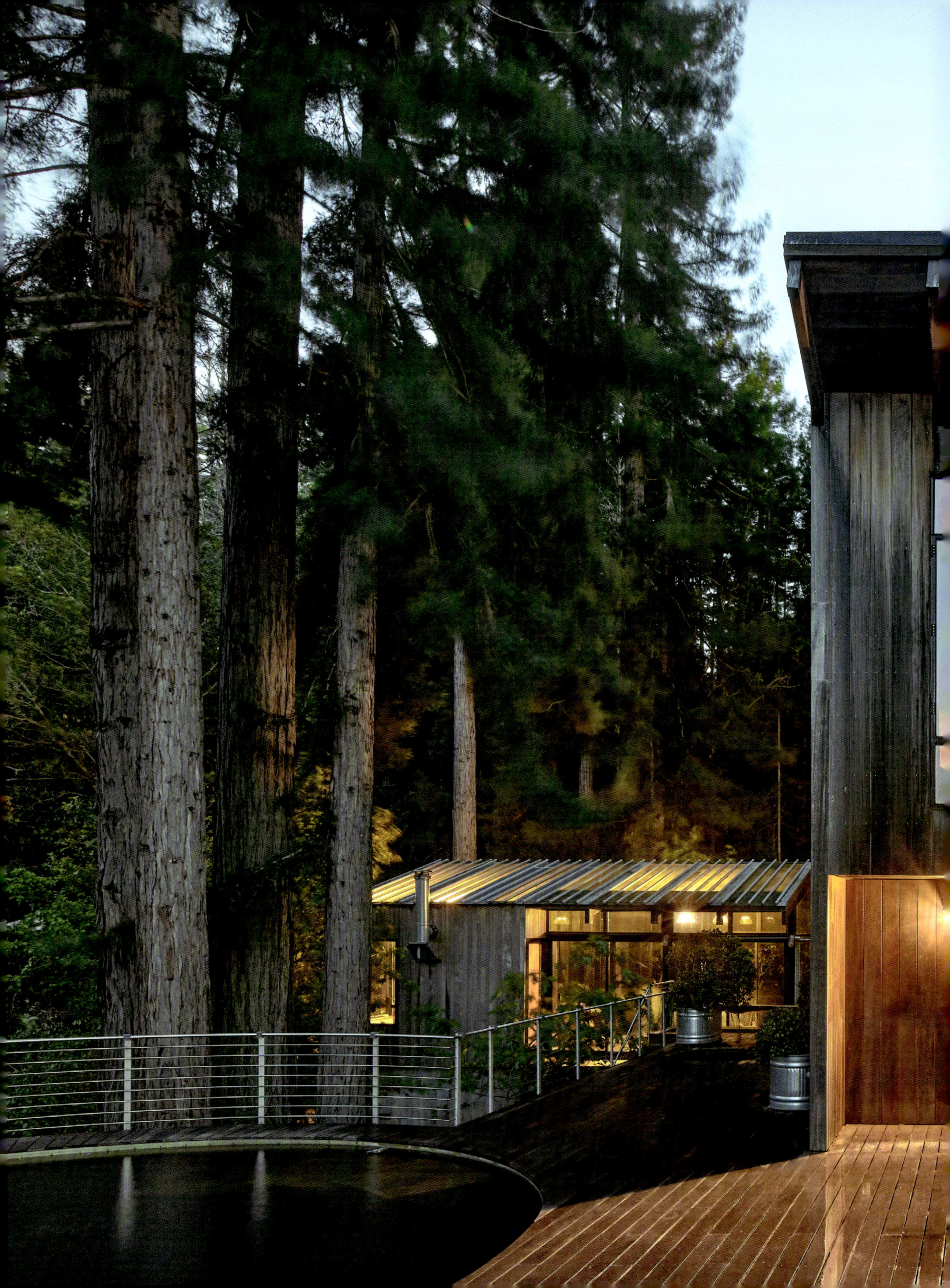

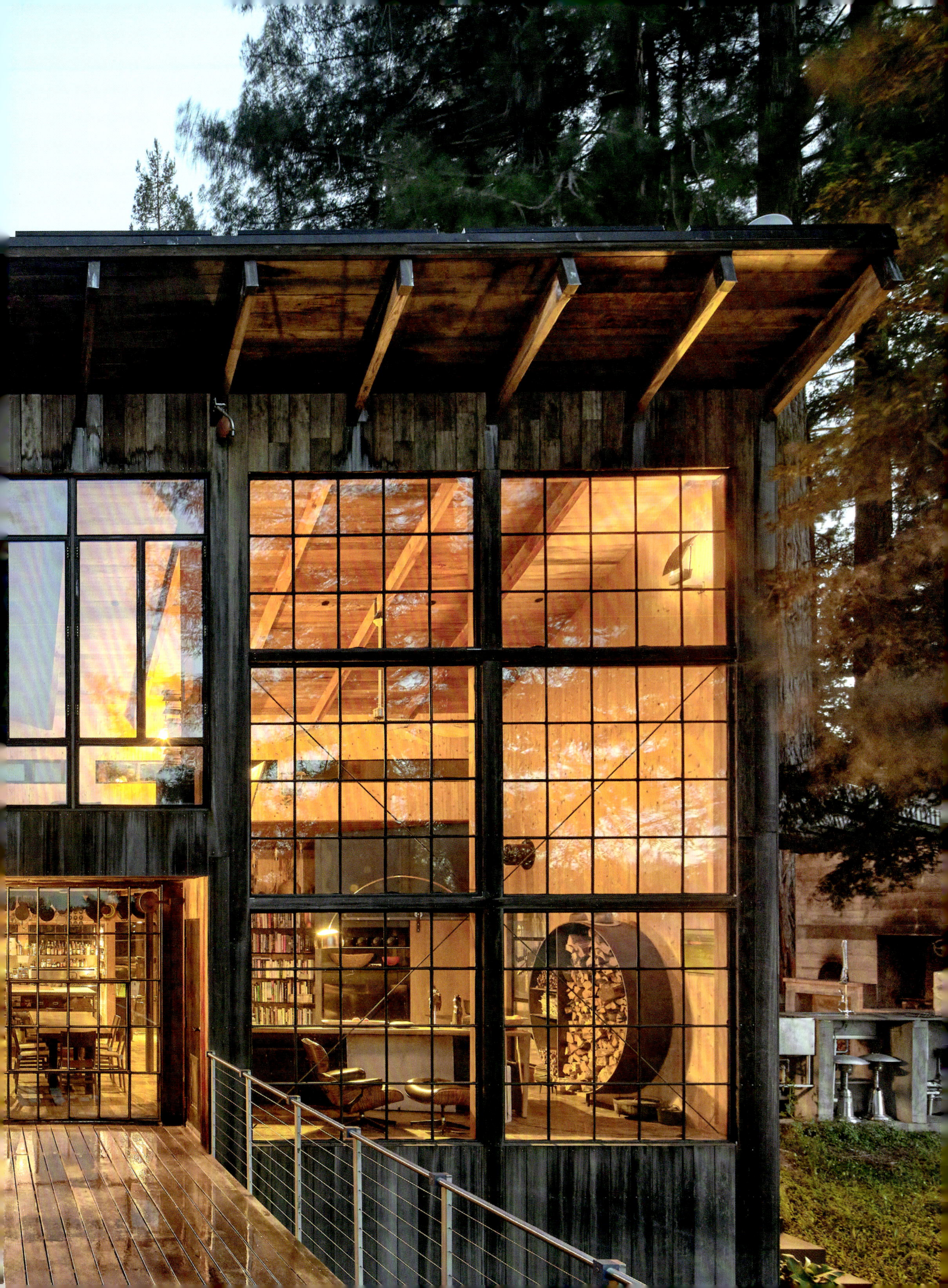

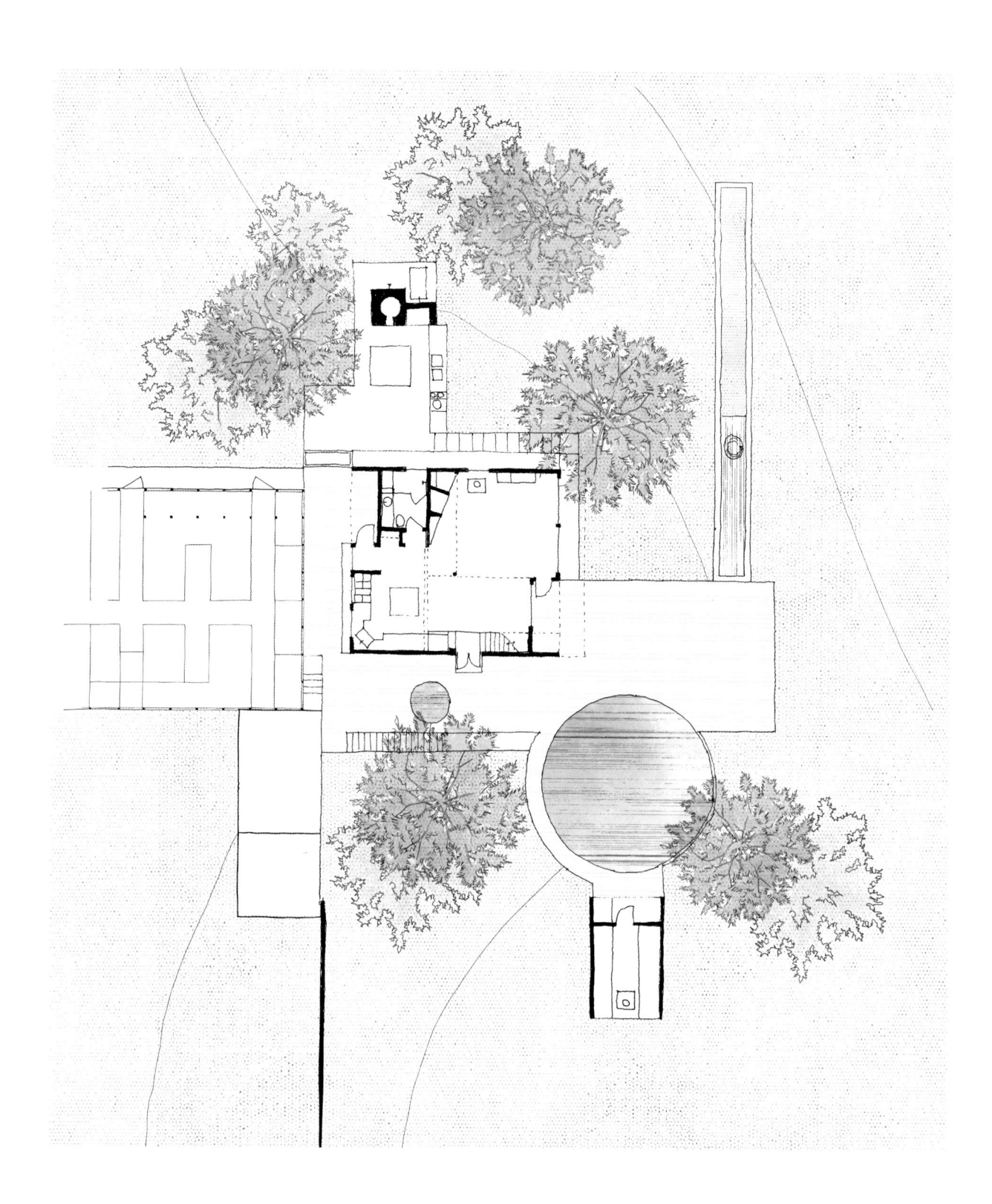

previous
Cabin/office north elevation

above
Site plan

opposite
Olle and Carney looking north

218   PART III.   FIVE PROJECTS

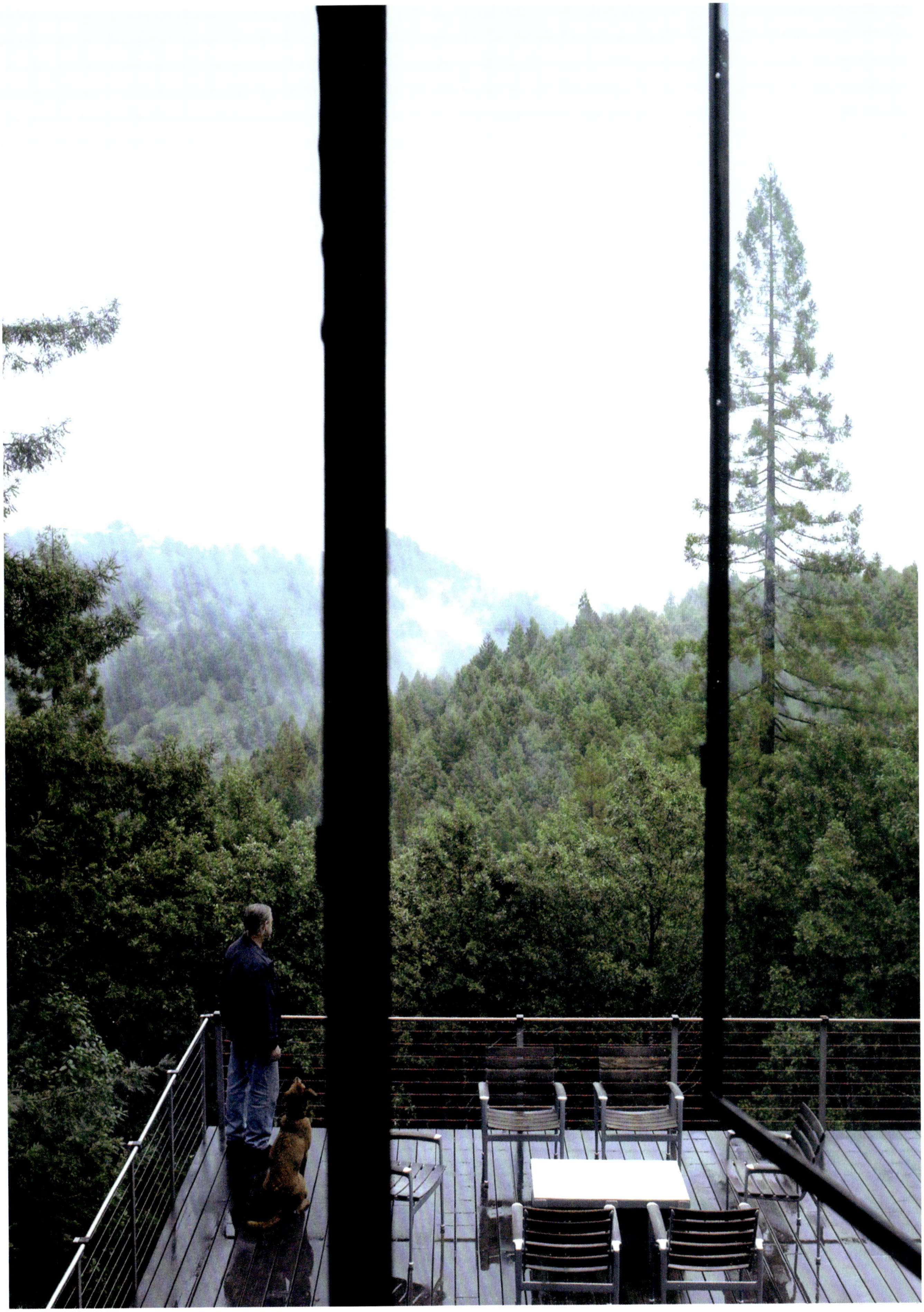

The site is 16 acres of redwood forest, located about a mile inland from the Sonoma coast. We are on a ridge at 1,400 feet of elevation, so the coastal fog usually stays below us, and the ridge harvests the rain as the clouds come in off the ocean. This is why we have redwoods; as you move down into the canyon to the east, the redwoods stop, and Douglas fir and tan oaks take over. The view is to the northeast, overlooking thousands of acres with no other buildings in sight. For the most part the land is too steep to build on or has no water source for habitations, so the view is nicely protected.

We bought the property in 1996. The previous owner had started construction on a cabin but quickly realized he was in over his head. We camped in his structure for a year while we pondered the possibilities, and I put in a garden to keep Mary busy while I was building a house. In the end we decided that the original siting was perfect. This was where we wanted the cabin. But nothing much else was worth saving. We demolished it all except the floor plate, having decided to at least stick with the foundation and the 900-square-foot footprint.

above left
Cabin on day of purchase

above right
Peter Bohlin's house for his parents

opposite
Living room with loft bed cantilever

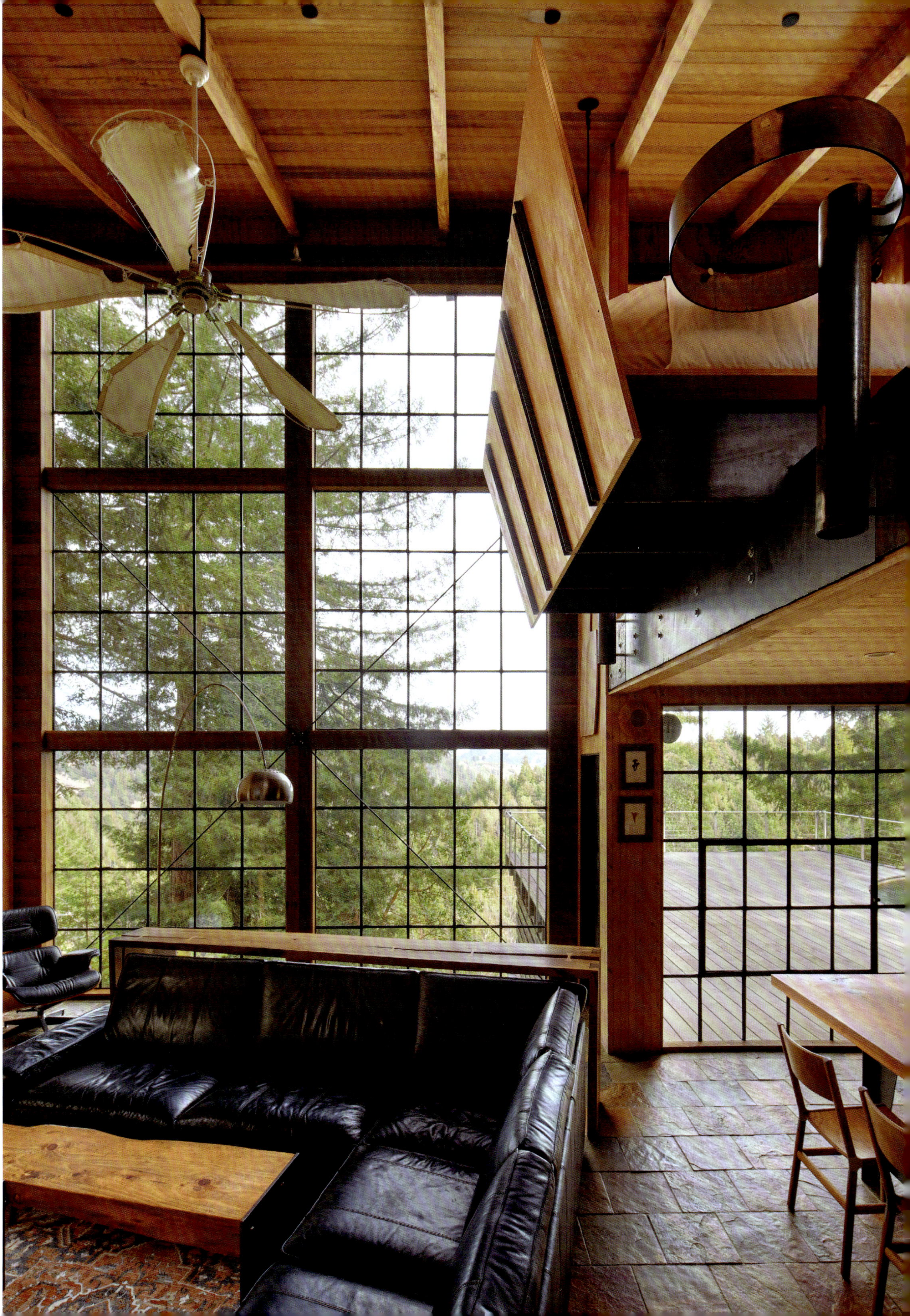

PART III. FIVE PROJECTS

opposite
Loft stair with sauna beyond

above left
Loft bedroom

above right
Bed end table

Ever since the Virginia church project, I'd been longing to build my own place again, this time with perhaps a little more vision than the first attempt. Over the years I'd been collecting steel industrial sash windows for that express purpose, for I'd always had an idea of building a "warehouse in the woods." When I was in architecture school, I read an issue of *The New York Times Magazine* that featured Peter Bohlin's house for his parents. It was a modest, beautiful, wood-clad structure that floated over a forest hillside, but what captivated me was his use of industrial sash windows. They were large units, each broken up in a grid of mullions that collectively "tiled" the view, individually framing pieces of the landscape while also capturing the whole. I loved the artful abstraction of that effect; it seemed to add a layer of interpretation that a single large pane of glass would have missed. That house has influenced the architecture I design for myself perhaps more than any other building, and happily I've been able to meet Peter and thank him for that inspiration. In school, Postmodernism was running rampant, a direction toward which I felt no affinity, and Peter's house gave me the confidence to pursue another expression.

The design of the cabin is quite simple: it is a shed-roof structure that opens out toward the north view, with the higher volume forming a double-height space over the living area, and a bedroom loft over the dining room. The larger challenge was incorporating the windows, salvaged from five different buildings, into a coherent whole. Some came from the Ellison project, which was, if you recall from part 1, "Jumping Off," a complete redo of the Coleman House designed by William Wurster. Mrs. Coleman was a wealthy San Francisco socialite, and I quite like the fact that her windows, designed by Wurster (probably the most famous San Francisco architect of his time), are now in my little Sonoma cabin. The resulting composition of the fenestration, interestingly, works very well. Had I designed all the windows from scratch, the mullions would have shared a common proportion. Yet despite their differences, the arrangement elides their differences. The common detail they share, the slender steel mullion, ties it all together. Perhaps that imperfection makes the end result a little less precious, a little more like a cabin.

opposite
North elevation

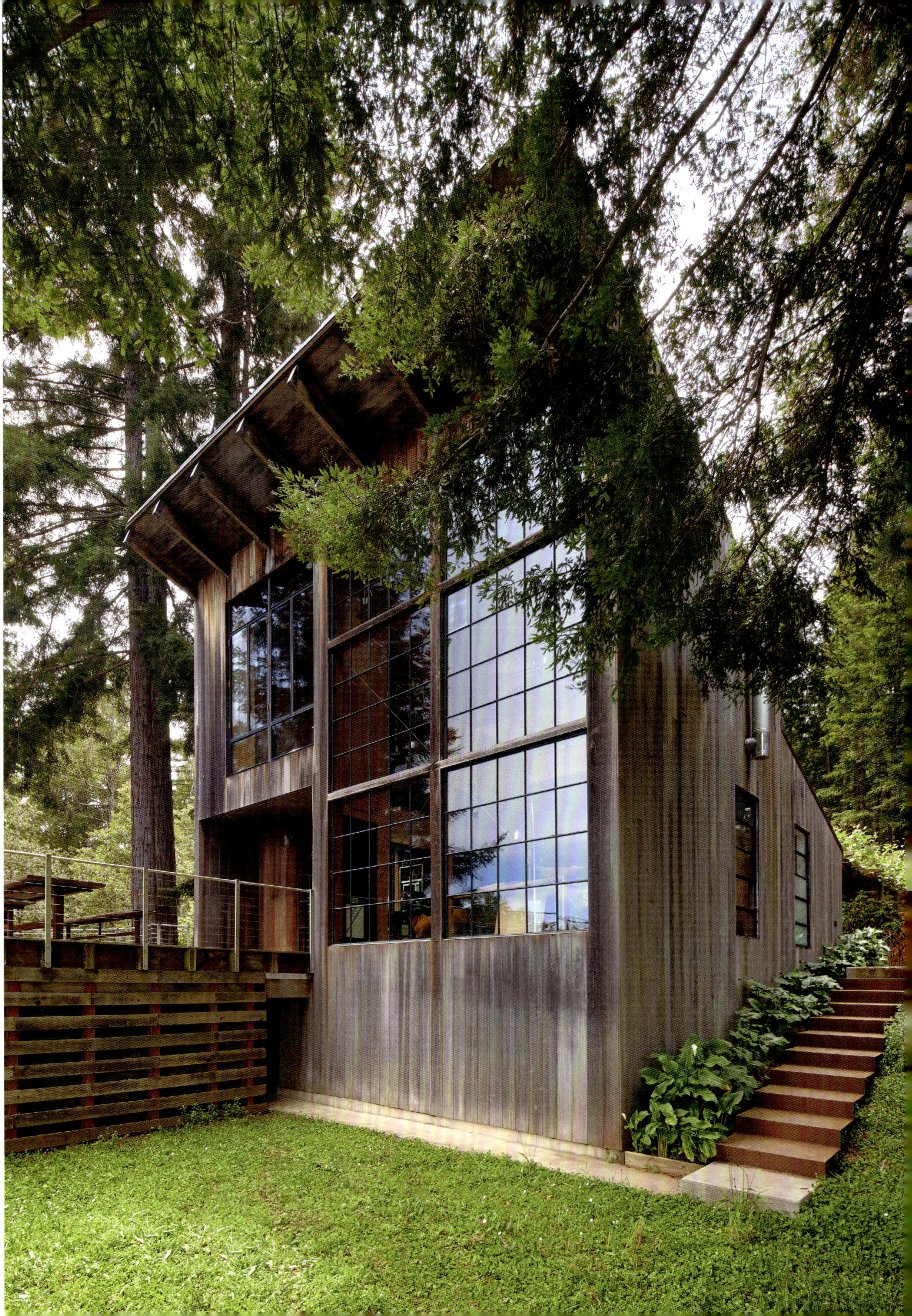

The deck, which extends above the steep hillside beyond, actually has a larger footprint than the cabin itself. My budget dictated that it had to be built after the cabin was at least livable, so it was phase two. As it was starting, I was also working on a project for a client, Linda Lee Harper, who had purchased an old cattle ranch in the hills of Napa and wanted to convert the property into her residence. On that site was an enormous redwood water tank, more than 50,000 gallons in capacity and 25 feet in diameter, which had been used to store water for the cattle. The tank was about a hundred years old, and because it was built from old-growth clear redwood (all heartwood and free of knots), it still functioned perfectly. But she had no use for it, and it was blocking her view, so the thought was to demolish it. I couldn't let that happen, so she graciously offered it to me, with the understanding that I would get it off the site within thirty days. My idea was to incorporate it into my new deck as a swimming pool, perhaps an idea born from childhood memories of the television show *Petticoat Junction*. The challenge was, of course, moving it. Fortunately, there were still builders in Napa with experience with this scale of tank for the wine industry. I was able to hire them to dismantle it, transport it to my site, and then reassemble it—an undertaking requiring no small amount of effort and expenditure.

left
Opening scene from
Petticoat Junction

opposite top
LD staff pouring pool
overflow basin

opposite middle
Assembling tank staves

opposite bottom
Galvanized steel bands

THE CABIN   227

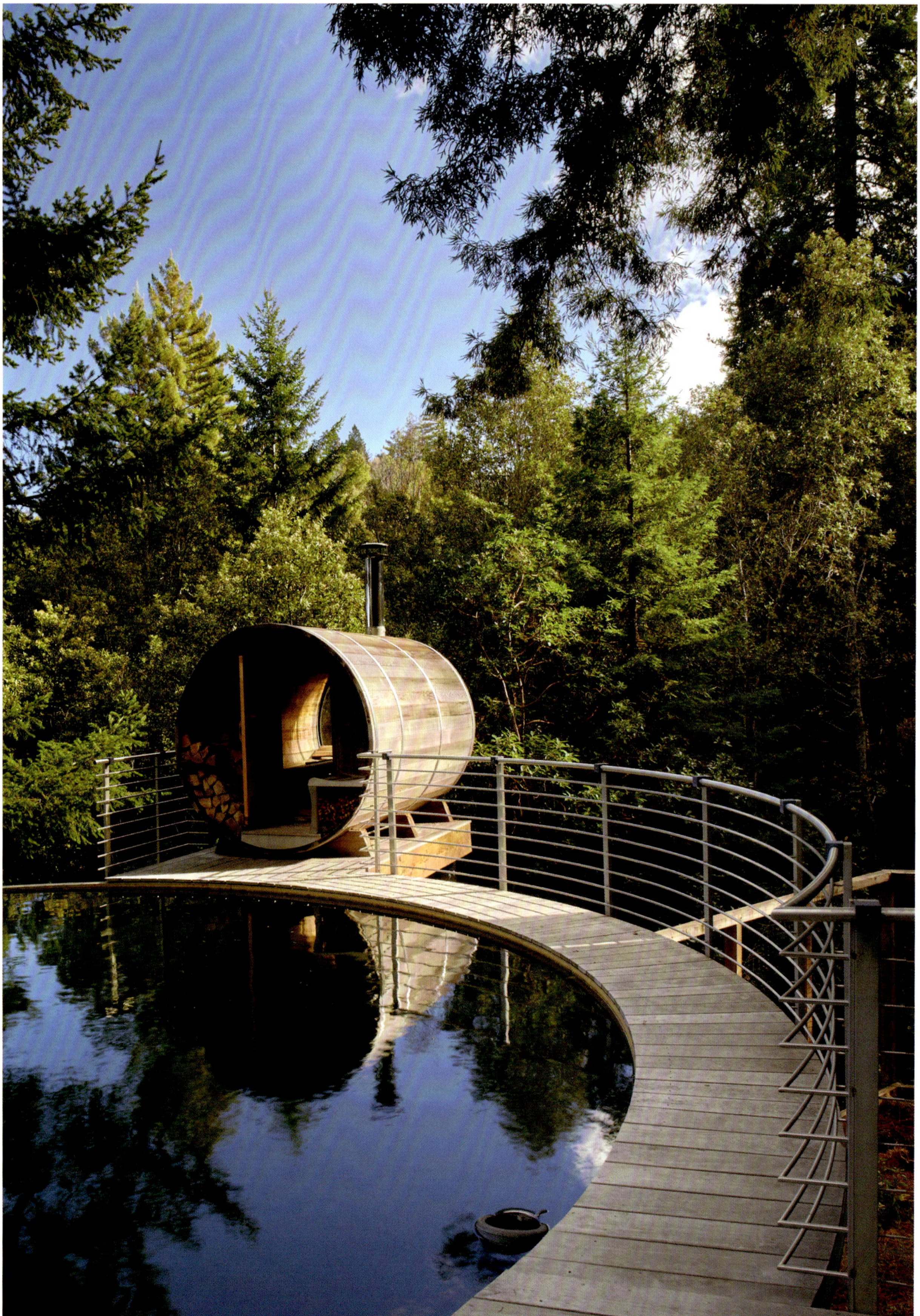

The resulting pool has been quite magical. It is best at night, under a full moon, where it just feels like a black hole in the treetops. Swimming in the forest canopy is quite a sensation; those moments floating in the treetops are the closest I've ever felt to flying. Over time, we added a sauna and a hot tub, with the pool as the cold plunge (it is 14 feet deep, and generally mirrors the temperature of the Pacific Ocean). This has been dubbed the Viking Triathlon, with the prize at the end being a glass of Skåne Akvavit!

opposite
Walkway to sauna

above left
View from sauna

above right
Hot tub and pool

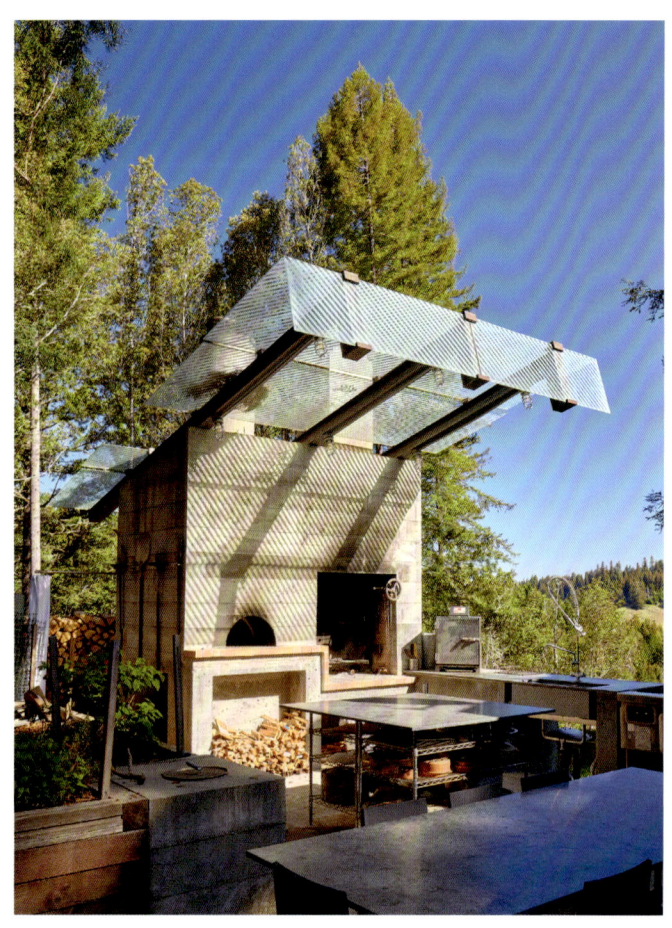

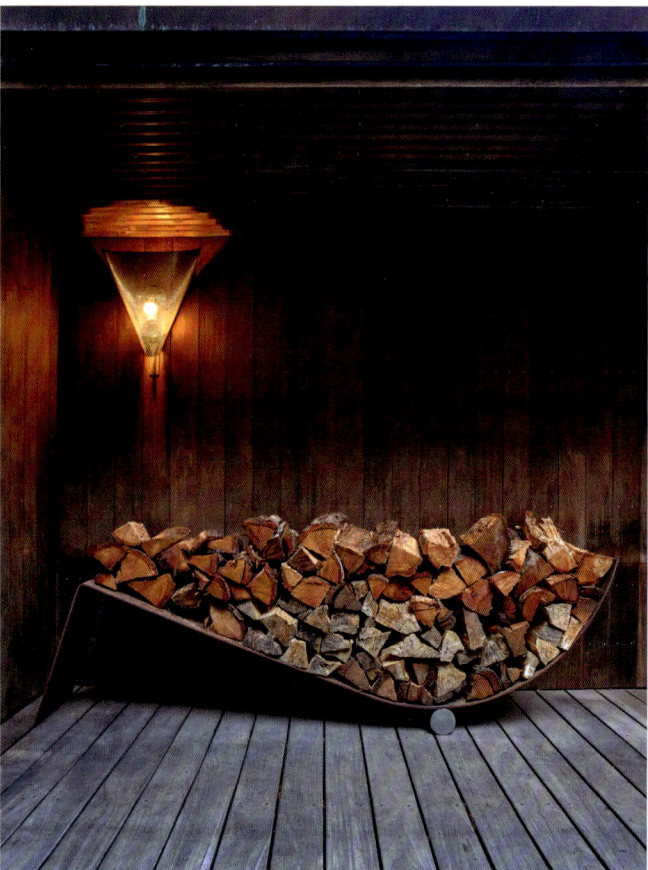

The cabin has always been the place where we prefer to entertain our friends. We have more time here, we are more relaxed, and we have some amazing cooking possibilities. We have designed numerous restaurants—more than twenty in the Bay Area—and many of those chefs have become close friends. There is nothing better than having the opportunity to cook with them; it creates an intimacy that often results in lifelong friendship. I always wanted the cabin to be a place of food. Mary's garden and orchard were the beginning, and now we have the main kitchen, a charcuterie kitchen (where I can make a mess and not destroy the cabin), and an outdoor kitchen with a wood-fired pizza oven, a tandoori oven, a smoker, a cooking hearth, a rotisserie, and an outdoor wok range (to keep my friend Charles Phan happy). There is absolutely no excuse not to cook an extraordinary meal here.

top
Outdoor kitchen

bottom
Firewood holder and custom light

top
LD staff party, Olle making pizza

above left
Paella over cooking hearth

above right
Conner, Sonya, and Olle after
matsutake harvest

THE CABIN   231

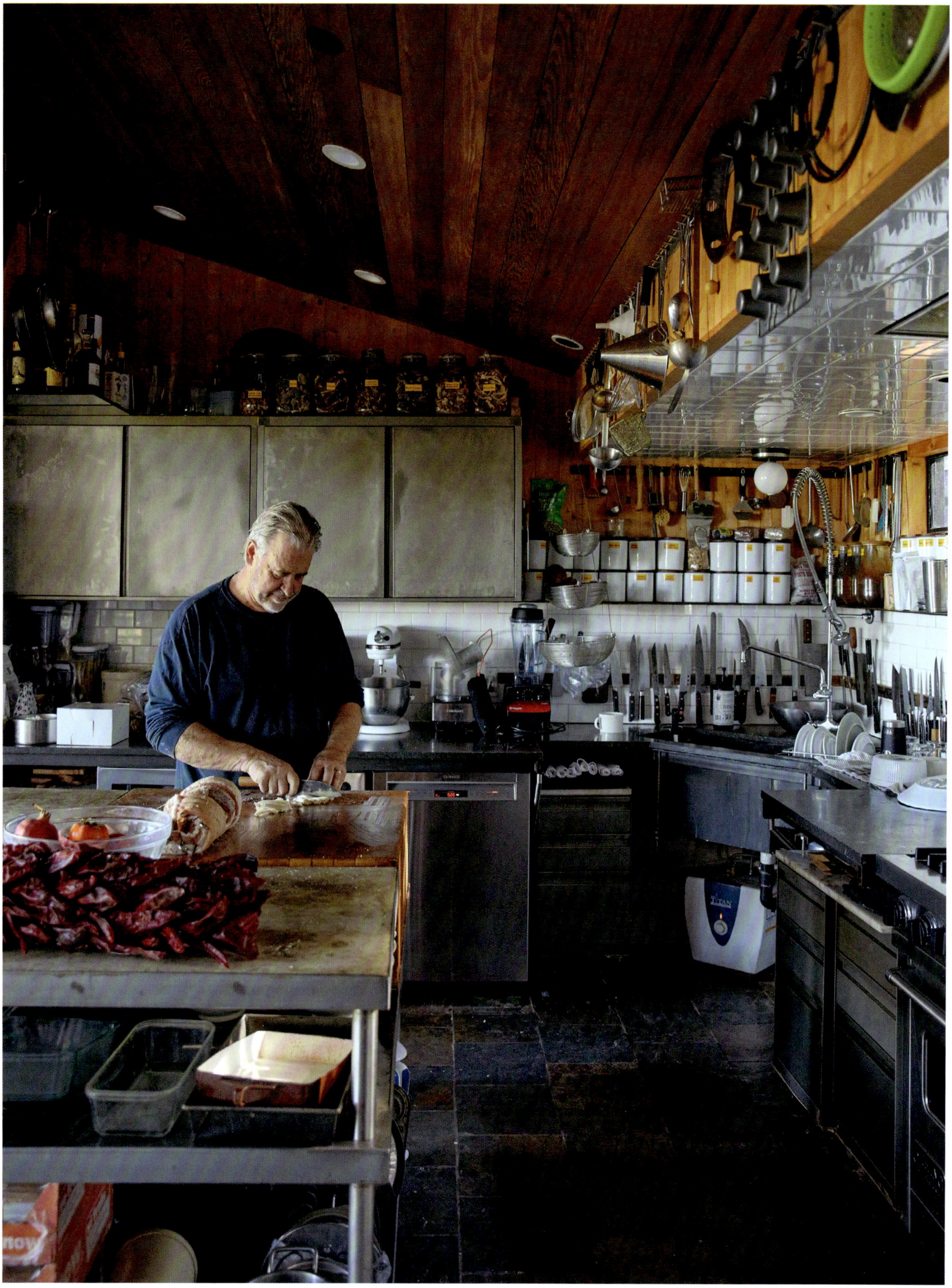

opposite
Olle making
porchetta

top
Pot rack

bottom
Kitchen tools

THE CABIN 233

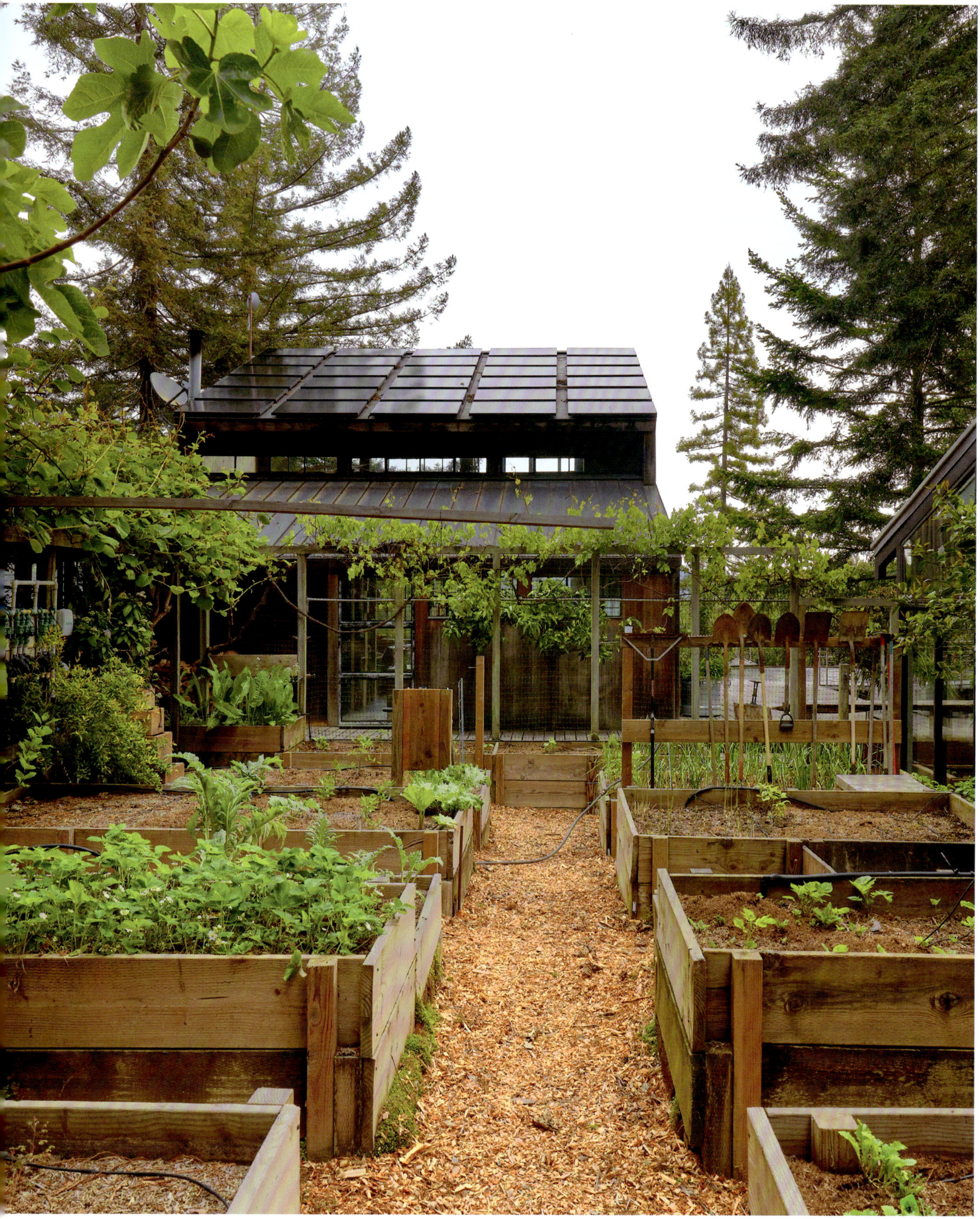

opposite
Cabin garden

top left
Firewood walkway

top right
Garden entry to gym

left
Mary's office woodstove
and firewood holder

THE CABIN   235

Our most recent project was the installation of a sculpture by my brother, Peter. I had been wanting to have him do one of his monumental concrete pieces, but we didn't have a good site for something of that scale; the land is too steep. But in the pandemic Peter started working in bronze, and the scale of his new work gave me an idea. I'd built a rectangular biofilter for the pool, enabling us to treat the water naturally, without chemicals. This pool required a retaining wall that gave us a flat area below the living room windows, as well as a series of cisterns and a bourbon bunker below it. Along the side of the house is an exterior staircase leading to the basement level, and if you were to continue the axis of that stair, it would intersect at a right angle with the biofilter. It was a perfect spot for a vertical sculpture, mounted in the biofilter pool. Peter designed a piece, "just" 20 feet tall and 3,000 pounds (small by his standards), which arrived one day from China in a shipping container. The surrounding architecture and trees prevented the use of a crane, but with some talented local help we managed to pick the piece up with a backhoe and tilt it upright and into position. As large as it is, its presence is dwarfed by the redwoods around it, and it seems to coexist happily with them. They are brothers, just like Peter and me.

top
Biofilter for pool

above
Installing sculpture

opposite
Untitled sculpture by Peter Lundberg

PART III.   FIVE PROJECTS

THE CABIN   237

The major projects at the cabin are probably finished. As I get older, I can physically do less, which is irritating but inevitable. I could have others build things for me, but I quite like that I have, at least in part, been involved in all the construction here. These days, most of us buy and sell homes, and even then, they typically do not last a generation. But our ancestors built their homes, even if our parents or grandparents didn't, and that tied them to a place. To have a place that I have been building for almost half of my lifetime has been a great joy, and the luxury of doing it slowly, over time, has taught me so much about design, and about myself. Most of our lives we are occupied with accomplishing things as quickly as possible, and in that we often miss the journey. Becoming an architect has, for me, been a lifelong pursuit, with potential new discoveries always just around the corner. The cabin has given me a place to express myself on an entirely personal level. It is a work just for me (and Mary and the dogs).

left
Early construction

opposite top
Outdoor living/dining

opposite bottom left
Hardwater redux

opposite bottom right
View from driveway

PART III. FIVE PROJECTS

THE CABIN 239

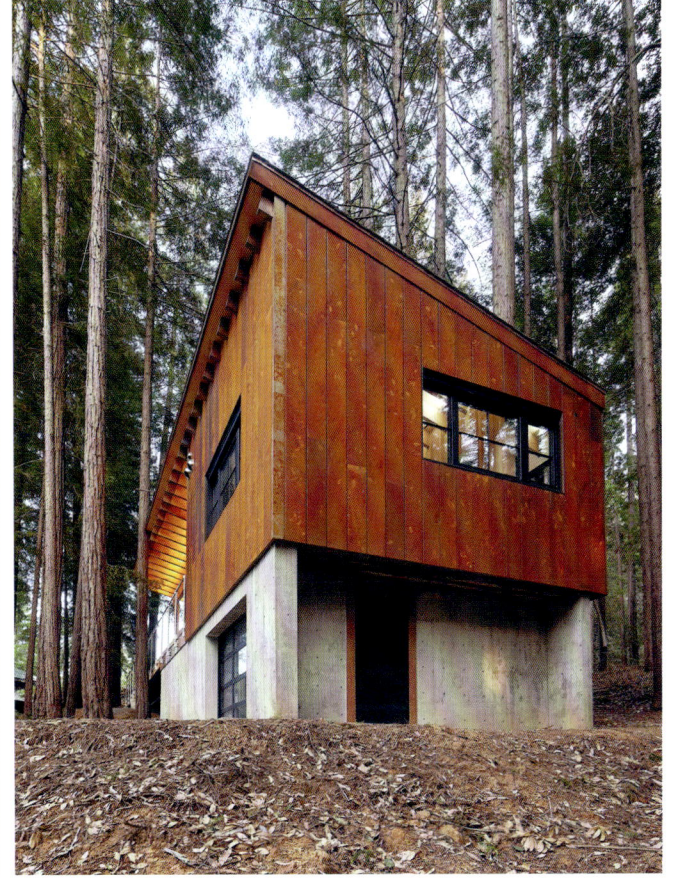

top left
Peter and Olle installing
firewood holder

right
Firewood holder detail

bottom left
Carney at office door

opposite
Firewood holder in place

overleaf
Bird's-eye view of cabin from north

240   PART III.   FIVE PROJECTS

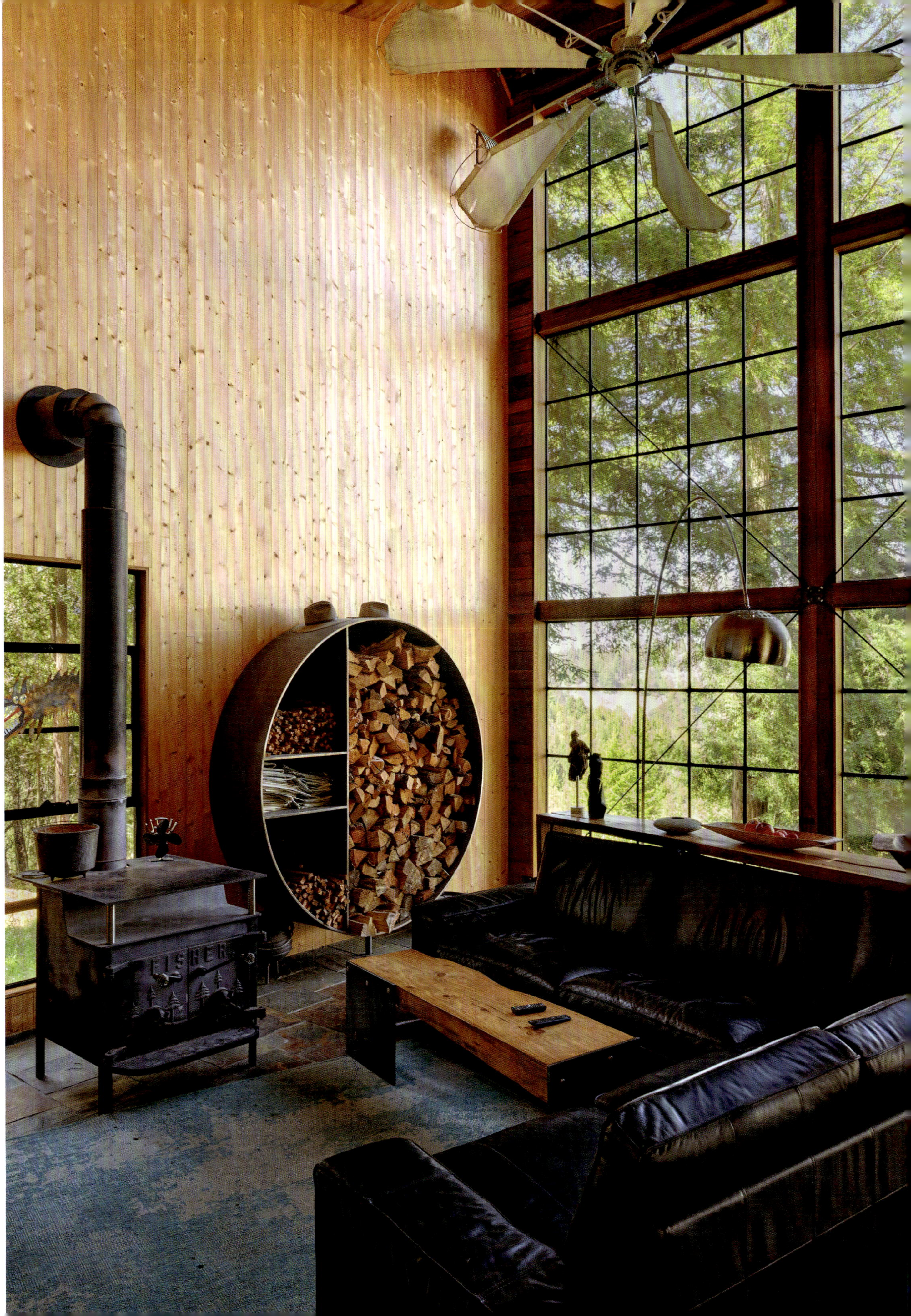
FISHER

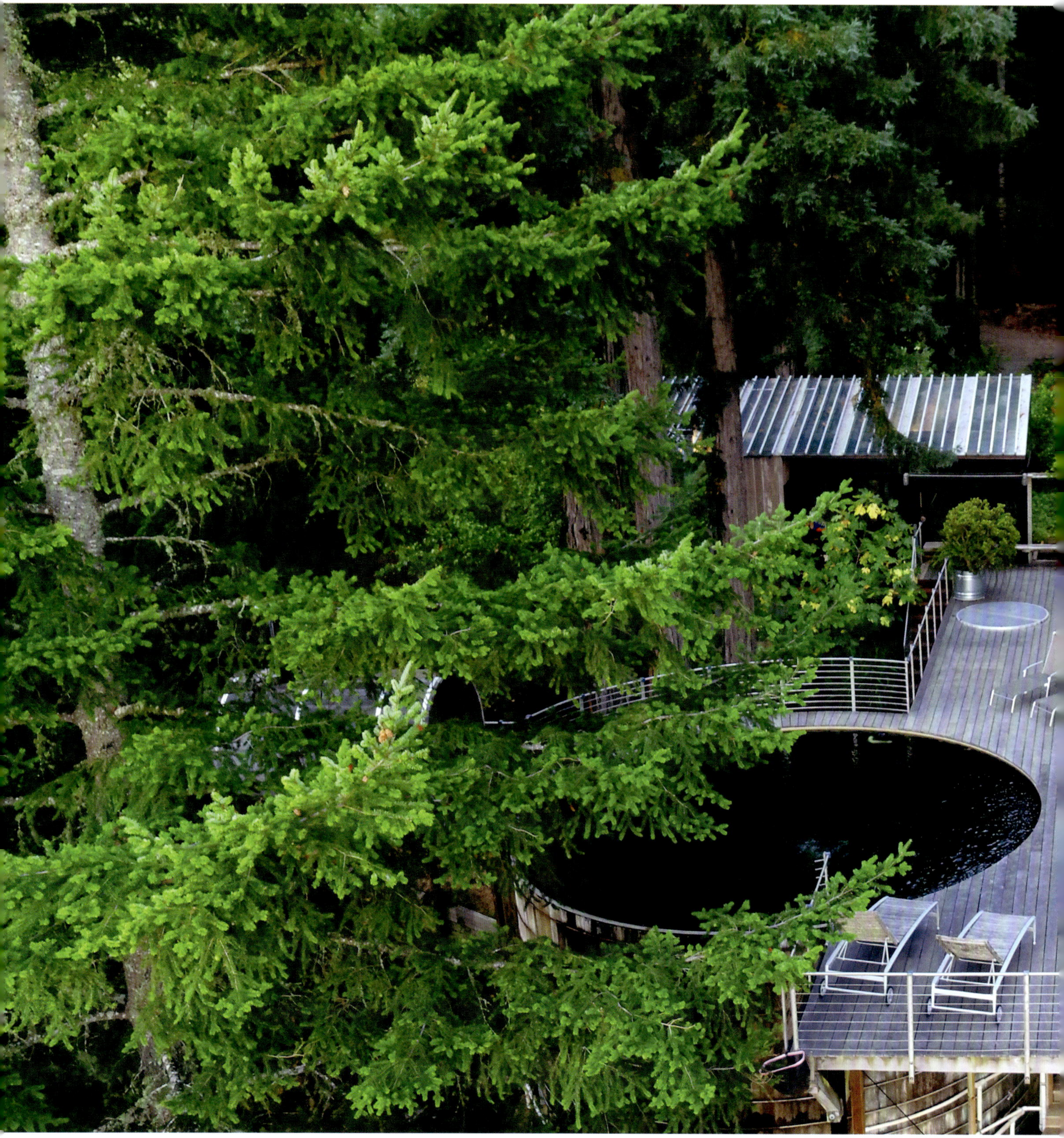

THE CABIN 243

Time will say nothing but I told you so,
Time only knows the price we have to pay;
If I could tell you I would let you know.

If we should weep when clowns put on their show,
If we should stumble when musicians play,
Time will say nothing but I told you so.

There are no fortunes to be told, although,
Because I love you more than I can say,
If I could tell you I would let you know.

The winds must come from somewhere when they blow,
There must be reasons why the leaves decay;
Time will say nothing but I told you so.

Perhaps the roses really want to grow,
The vision seriously intends to stay;
If I could tell you I would let you know.

Suppose all the lions get up and go,
And all the brooks and soldiers run away;
Will Time say nothing but I told you so?
If I could tell you I would let you know.

—W. H. Auden, "If I Could Tell You," 1940

Torsten, memorial for Olle's grandfather

THOUGHTS ON DESIGN

As a designer, what are my sources of inspiration? The first thing is the project itself: What is the functional problem to be solved? Architects are problem solvers by training, and the project program, and finding a clever way to solve it, to me is an exciting opportunity. It is one of the reasons I enjoy building things. How do I make something? What is the best, most logical way to achieve the desired end result? Even for a piece of sculpture, which we occasionally do, this becomes the functional challenge. Understanding the material you choose, both its potential and its limitations, is then part of that inspiration.

Just as important is the site. Where does the building, the piece, the sculpture, sit? What does the site offer, and how do I respond? I think of everything we design as very site specific because often my first idea, my gut reaction, comes from my initial experience of the context. I believe this is true of our furniture pieces, our sculptures, and our buildings, but allow me to focus for the moment on the building design process. What does the site offer? What is the opportunity (for there is always just one reveal that is paramount). Once you know that, then you understand the big idea, which is: How does the building express that opportunity? Solving the myriad functional requirements of a building can be extraordinarily complex, but all great architecture also needs to be very simple—the elegant execution of a singular gesture. Sometimes it is as easy as realizing that all you need to do is frame a view.

Too many options can be the death of a good idea. First of all, there is rarely a single best solution. Many solutions may solve the program's demands. So how do you choose? For me, it has always been about trusting my instinctive reaction, about the power of that first spark of inspiration. No other idea I have will have the immediacy, the gut conviction, of that first visualization. It is the moment where I see the solution, when I imagine the building and how it occupies the site. That is the form I want to build because I believe in it more than any other solution I might subsequently imagine (except when I change my mind).

I think of design as a response to nature. The forms I create are not a part of Nature—while they may reference natural form, they exist outside the natural realm, and I find it important to emphasize the difference. A human-made object is not the same as a stone. The stone exists as it is found—unaltered by human attention. An object I have designed is built from materials, which may be close or far from their natural origin. Yet no matter the natural "purity" of the material, it is my incorporation of it into my design that now makes it human-made. To me, this changes the embodied energy in a piece, and I need to understand, and in the end explain, this change through my design if I am to respect the gift that the material represents.

A weathered stone lying in a streambed, covered in moss and eroded by the elements, has an energy and a beauty that exists outside the human realm. It is a random collision of form and light, yet I perceive it as perfect—why? My reaction is instinctive. Although my life has trained me to see this moment, the awakening seems primal, as though sprung from a consciousness I do not completely understand. It is that feeling, that moment of effortless beauty, that I try to recapture in my work. I seldom succeed, yet in trying to understand the search, I feel myself getting closer.

As architects, we are trained to move the stone. Sometimes, if we are lucky, we get to work around it, or even better, with it. But usually we just alter it—we use it to solve a problem. Say I am designing a kitchen, and I know that granite makes a wonderful, practical countertop. It is durable, highly resistant to staining and heat, and has a beautiful granular structure that is revealed as one cuts it and polishes it. Yet in doing so, I feel like I have killed the stone because it is no longer recognizable as the boulder lying in the forest. The link to Nature is gone—I have managed to turn it into something completely human-made. I have robbed it of its integrity as a material. I want to find a way to not do that in my work. I think the way to that realization is through the act of making, through the hand of the craftsperson.

The challenge lies in combining the skill of the craftsperson with the eye of the designer. I wish I could do all the making. I wish I was a stonemason, a welder, or a woodworker, and at times I've tried them all. From tactile experience comes an understanding of a material's inherent properties and its potential—it is when I begin to emotionally bond with the material. I can't do what master craftspeople can do, but I can understand what it is that they look for, what they feel. It helps to work with them, at times just watching, sometimes asking questions, sometimes guiding the effort from my perspective. They of course understand their mediums, but I seek to understand the fundamental nature of the respect that they express, an expression that is found only in the actual physical work.

One of my earliest childhood memories is of walking in the forest with my grandfather. I can still hear the wind in the pine trees and the gurgling of the brook we followed. Grampie loved the forest. He would gather chanterelles in season, and I remember his happiness at finding such a gift. I don't think we talked much. Mostly he just wanted me to see and feel. This was his church, where he felt most connected to the beauty of life. I inherited that love of the forest. It is where I feel relaxed, and where I am often inspired. Every Friday morning, Mary and I and the dogs leave San Francisco and head to our cabin in the Sonoma redwoods. It is my favorite place for so many reasons—the gatherings with friends, the projects we have built, the meals we have eaten, the dogs we have buried there. Over the years there have been many cycles to the life we live at the cabin—food and cooking, foraging (mostly mushrooms), the garden, the forest, and of course our dogs.

I think most Swedes have a cultural affinity for wood. I feel like it has always been a part of me, in my DNA. But it is of course more than that; it is symbolic of a connection to nature. What is that connection? How do I understand it? How does my work express that? I describe my design approach as "nature-inspired modernism," but what does that truly mean? Modernism, as expressed by Lundberg Design, is a set of aesthetic principles that seek to define the present rather than the past. Here is what we believe:

Form follows function. Design is not decorative; it expresses a need.

Honesty. Materials matter, so express them. Honor the source, the mother. Never fake it. This is why we focus on the present, even as we honor the past.

Simplicity. Get to the fundamental idea, and do not complicate it unnecessarily. Composition is revealed through the act of editing.

Delight. We are designing for human beings, and as humans, we relate to our surroundings through our senses—sight, sound, touch, smell, taste. Remember to engage them. This is why originality matters, for only in truly original work can we surprise, and hopefully delight.

The first three statements are principles found in nature. The last is a gift in life. So I think "nature-inspired modernism" is right, as it does describe what we aspire to create.

In my youth, any shelter, whether a cave or a hollowed-out tree, was always fascinating. Then I started building things—forts and rafts and tree houses. I loved the making, the immersion in the project. When you build something, the accomplishment is so tangible, and the forest was an endless arena of possibilities. I got good at wielding a saw, a hatchet, and a knife. I still love cutting and splitting firewood. I have always been around tools and building, but my introduction came from the forest, from living in and with it. This is why the shop has always been so important to me, why I felt like I needed that kind of studio/workshop environment to be able to design. I learn from the making. From touching the materials. From engaging the senses, not just the mind. And it is why wood, of all the materials we use, is special: it is our most direct connection to nature. Because it was living. Because it reminds me of my grandfather.

Redwood "cathedral" at the cabin

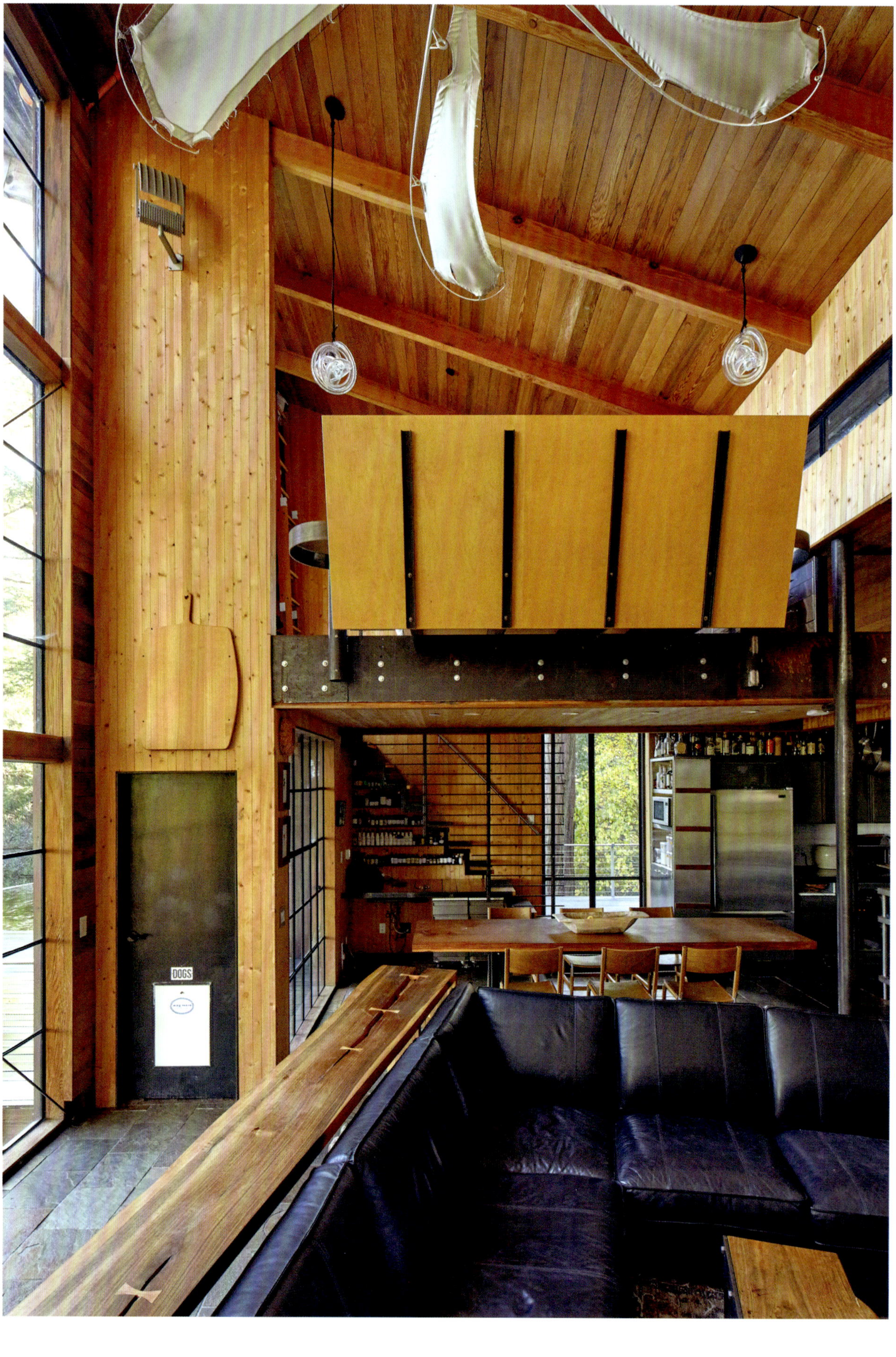
DOGS

AFTERWORD: INSIDE/OUT
DUNG NGO

Some architects, famously, live in homes they design. Le Corbusier and Alvar Aalto are two good examples, in which their own homes exemplified their particular philosophy of architecture. Other architects, somewhat less famously, did not live in homes they designed. Notably, Mies van der Rohe lived in an early twentieth-century neo-Georgian apartment building in Chicago, within eyeshot of his famous apartment towers. Olle Lundberg does neither; he lives above the shop.

Olle's work-week residence is a loft he carved out at the back end of an industrial building in the Dogpatch area of San Francisco to house his architectural office, apartment, and—most important—a shop that produces metal, wood, glass, and whatnot components and furniture pieces that are used in his best buildings. Double-height and lit with clerestory windows (not unlike an early Christian cathedral), the shop is clearly the pride of place of Lundberg Design—and Olle's heart.

But it's not as if the loft were some cold-water, unfurnished bachelor space. Elegantly finished, it has a highly sculptural steel staircase leading up to a bedroom (albeit a staircase designed and produced to test a much larger one that went into a client's house) and an open, semiprofessional kitchen—if the shop is the heart, then the kitchen is the stomach, another vital organ. (And I say "semiprofessional" because Olle is a serious cook, with chefs for clients, and neither he nor his chef clients would ever call this a "restaurant grade" kitchen.) But at the end of the day, the loft overlooks the shop, with its early-morning start and often late-night work rush to meet a deadline. And that's how Olle likes it—at least from Monday to Thursday. On most Thursday afternoons Olle and his wife, Mary, along with their dog, Ruly, make the three-hour drive to their cabin in Sonoma County, north of the Bay.

At this point the name "cabin" is a little misleading; besides the main house there is a separate structure in steel and channel glass for Mary to write in. But the star structure is a simple, single-pitched-roof building facing out to vast tracts of forested land. Built on a ridge of the Inner Coast Range, the cabin has few neighbors, none of whom are visible. If the Dogpatch building is all about looking inward—office and private life looking into the central shop—then the cabin is all about looking outward (through recycled windows from past renovations). But improbably, the double space of the main cabin echoes the San Francisco structure. In a compact footprint, Olle has skillfully fit in a sleeping loft above the kitchen and dining table, with a tilting headboard that provides a degree of privacy (and safety) from the open living space below. This sectional sleight-of-hand proves to visitors that this ain't no ordinary redneck Sonoma shack. More feats of architecture abound when you step out to the vast deck, which contains a small, circular hot tub and much larger circular pool repurposed from a fifty-thousand-gallon cattle-ranch redwood water tank. The oversized pool is fed with rainwater that has been treated with a natural biofilter, without any chemicals.

In Dogpatch, the center is the shop; at the cabin, it's an outdoor kitchen/wood-fire pizza oven/tandoori oven/rotisserie/smoker that's larger than some New York studio apartments. Olle has hosted legendary meals here, often with his many chef clients/friends. They all have their specialties and need their specific equipment, and Olle makes sure—as with the shop—that everyone has the tools they need. Both spaces are for gathering and group activities, for constructing either a 50-foot table or a meal for fifty, and both are designed to *get the job done*. And this is at the heart of Olle's architecture.

opposite
Headboard cantilevered over the living/dining area

VIKING HOT SAUCE RECIPE

Ingredients

20 lb [9 kg] hatch green chiles (extra hot, which is not very hot), peeled and diced

2 cups canola oil for sauté

3 lb [1.4 kg] onions, coarsely chopped

5 heads (not cloves, heads!) of garlic, peeled and chopped

1 ½ lb [680 g] carrots, coarsely chopped

Kosher salt to taste (about 2 cups [320 g])

3 gal [11.4 l] Bragg organic apple cider vinegar

50 dried ghost pepper pods

1 cup [200 g] cane sugar

½ cup [45 g] black pepper

1 qt [960 ml] lime juice

3 lb [1.4 kg] peaches (you can substitute any sweet fruit; mangoes are great, but remove skins)

1 lb [455 g] pineapple

½ cup [62 g] cumin

2 gal [7.6 l] leftover condiments (hot sauces, barbecue sauces, etc.) or more to taste (see note opposite)

Makes about 20 quarts

Instructions

Gather at least two gallons of leftover condiments from your pantry or refrigerator. Anything with a vinegar or brine base. Mediocre hot sauces, barbecue sauces, chili crunch, Asian sauces, Worcestershire sauce, mustards, ketchup, hot jams and jellies, fish sauce (I always make sure to add this), salsas—anything you think will add to the blend. I usually find I have about fifty different bottles of condiments that go in. Repurposed-Condiment Hot Sauce!

Place the hatch chiles in a large stainless steel (or enameled, not aluminum) stock pot. Sauté the onions and garlic in a large frying pan (you will have to do this in batches) over medium heat until soft, then add to pot. Sauté carrots until soft; add to pot. Add salt and cover with cheesecloth. Leave at room temperature for twenty-four hours, then add vinegar and ghost chiles (use disposable food-grade gloves for this step, and be really careful, ghost chiles are incredibly hot). Stir and cover again with cheesecloth (use string around the perimeter of the pot to hold tight). Let it ferment at room temperature for seven days.

After the fermentation, add the sugar, black pepper, lime juice, fruit, cumin, and repurposed condiments. Then blend in batches to a smooth consistency. If you want a more liquidy sauce, add more vinegar. Taste for salt and sugar. There should be a salty heat with a back note of sweetness.

Then bring to a boil over a low heat (ideally outside, as the chili vapors can be bothersome), stirring often to prevent burning on the bottom of the pot. Sterilize enough jars or bottles for about 5 gallons of sauce, then can per typical canning procedure. Given the vinegar, salt, and hot peppers, this sauce should be fine stored in a dark, cool place for at least a year, but I advise refrigerating after opening.

I like the pantry-cleanup part of this recipe. It ensures that every year the sauce will be different, although the heat level is pretty consistent (hot but not deadly). Over the years you'll learn what condiments add the flavors you like. I'll admit to liking Vietnamese fish sauce, mustards, and hot-pepper jellies. I try a lot of hot sauces every year, and the ones that bore me all end up in my hot sauce. When you make this, the end result will be unique to you. Your leftovers will give it a unique flavor, never to be replicated. Good cooking is like good architecture—make it personal.

PROJECT CREDITS

ROLLING WALL MUSEUM
Location: San Francisco Bay Area
Project Team: Olle Lundberg, principal; David Battenfield, project architect; Lev Bereznycky; Omer Caparti
Consultants: Strandberg Engineering, structural; Lea & Braze Engineering, civil; Meline Engineering, mechanical; HRA Engineering & Energy Services, electrical; Banks Landl, lighting; EinwillerKuehl Landscape Architecture, landscape
Craftspeople: LD—Conner Wishard, Jack Cram, Michael Esteban
General Contractor: Redhorse Constructors—David Warner, Scott Vreeland, Majid Ghafary

LAVA HOUSE
Location: Hawai'i
Project Team: Olle Lundberg, principal; Michelle Kriebel, project architect; Lev Bereznycky
Consultants: GFDS Engineers, structural; Imata & Associates; civil; CB Engineers, MEP; Banks | Ramos, lighting; David Y. Tamura Associates, landscape
Craftspeople: LD—Greg Kice, Aimee Kinder, Pat Clark
General Contractor: Ryan Associates—Paul Ryan, Mark Klinzman, Hoke Stewart, Lynn Hankins

CURLY'S COVE
Mary Breuer / Olle Lundberg
Location: Bodega Bay, California
Project Team: Olle Lundberg, principal
Craftspeople: Pat Clark; LD—Conner Wishard, Jack Cram, Michael Esteban

DOGLEG HOUSE
Location: Carmel, California
Project Team: Olle Lundberg, principal; Emily Pearl, project architect; Lev Bereznycky, Lauren Taylor
Consultants: Strandberg Engineering, structural; Benjamini Associates, civil; Banks Landl, lighting; EinwillerKuehl Landscape Architecture, landscape; Maureen Hamb, arborist
Craftspeople: LD—Conner Wishard, Jack Cram, Michael Esteban
General Contractor: Stocker & Allaire—David Stoker, Jared Kemp, Rich Morf, Brian Dutro

THE CABIN
Mary Breuer / Olle Lundberg
Location: Sonoma Coast, California
Project Team: Olle Lundberg, principal; everyone who has ever worked at LD!
Structural Engineering: Strandberg Engineering
Craftspeople: Pat Clark, Bob Dickson, Steve Dickson, David Putallaz

IMAGE CREDITS

After Hours Creative: 42 (right middle and bottom), 60 (top)
Annemae Bahia: 85 (top)
Timothy Balon: 18
Richard Barnes: 30, 31 (all), 65 (bottom), 66–67 (all), 83, 93 (bottom), 139, 142 (top), 142 (top)
Krescent Carasso: 111 (all)
Elena Dorfman: 80 (bottom right)
Joe Fletcher: 45 (top left), 64, 86 (bottom left), 88–89 (all), 94 (left and top right),
    114 (top and bottom left)
John Lewis Glass: 92 (bottom)
©Andy Goldsworthy: 8
Art Gray: 60 (bottom), 61, 90, 98
Drew Kelly: 73 (top left, bottom left), 125 (middle right, bottom row)
Thomas Kuoh: 36 (middle and bottom rows), 76 (bottom row), 107 (middle left, bottom left),
    110 (all), 115 (all)
Yoshihiro Makino: 38, 40–41(bottom right), 43 (left), 44 (bottom), 45 (middle), 50–57, 58
    (top and bottom right), 59, 75 (bottom right), 86 (middle row), 87 (bottom), 92 (top row), 99 (left),
    102, 109 (top left), 112 (right), 119, 130, 134–38, 140–41, 143 (bottom), 147 (top), 148, 184, 188–89,
    191, 192, 194, 196–97, 198–204, 208, 210, 212–13, 214, 216–17, 221, 222–23 (all), 225, 229 (left),
    230 (all), 232–34 (all), 236 (top), 239 (all), 241, 250
Matthew Millman: 78, 86 (top row), 97 (right), 151, 153–57, 160 (bottom left), 161, 164–67,
    168 (top and bottom right), 169–71, 172–73 (top)
Tony Orantes: 72 (left bottom), 73 (top right)
Adam Rouse: 74 (all)
Cesar Rubio: 2, 33, 34, 35 (all), 82 (bottom left), 84
Dale Tan: 16 (top, middle), 96 (all), 108
Chad Ziemendorf: 107 (middle right), 113 (top row)

Dedication

To my parents—my father, Olle, and my mother, Jane, whom I always just wanted to make proud of me.

To my sister, Anne, my first client, and my brother, Peter, whose work and dedication always inspire me.

To my wife, Mary, who has traveled this journey with extraordinary grace and patience.

To my dogs, Gertrude, Puff, Chutney, Diesel, Chili, Carney, Curly, and Ruly, whom I have loved beyond measure, and who loved me back even more.

To my clients, who entrusted me with their dreams. I can think of no greater compliment.

To all the wonderful people who have worked and continue to work at Lundberg Design, with special thanks to Silvia Caporale, who was invaluable in the composition and execution of this manuscript. They made the content of this book possible, a gift I will never be able to properly repay. They made it good, and fun.

And to my teachers—Jim Tuley, Mario di Valmarana, Robin Dripps, Robert Vickery, Bob Marquis, and countless other friends and colleagues whose work has inspired me throughout my life.

Olle Lundberg, 2025